Essays in Honor of
J. Dwight Pentecost

ESSAYS IN HONOR OF J. DWIGHT PENTECOST

Edited by
Stanley D. Toussaint
& Charles H. Dyer

MOODY PRESS

CHICAGO

All Scripture quotations, except those noted otherwise, are from the *New American Standard Bible,* ©
1960, 1962, 1963, 1968, 1971, 1972, 1973, 1975, and
1977 by The Lockman Foundation, and are used by
permission.

Library of Congress Cataloging-in-Publication Data

Essays in honor of J. Dwight Pentecost.

    1. Bible. N.T. Gospels—Criticism, interpretation,
etc.   2. Spiritual life.   3. Bible—Prophecies.
4. Pentecost, J. Dwight. I. Toussaint, Stanley D.,
1928-   . II. Dyer, Charles H., 1952-   .
BS2555.2.E85   1986   225.6   86-5170
ISBN 0-8024-2381-7

1 2 3 4 5 6 7 Printing/AF/Year 91 90 89 88 87 86

Printed in the United States of America

Contents

CHAPTER   PAGE

Introduction   7
    —*Stanley D. Toussaint*
A Biographical Sketch of Dr. J. Dwight Pentecost   9
    —*Edward C. Pentecost*

Part 1

The Words and Works:
Themes from the Gospels

1. The Kingdom and Matthew's Gospel   19
    —*Stanley D. Toussaint*
2. Dispensational Approaches to the Sermon on the Mount 35
    —*John A. Martin*
3. The Purpose for the Gospel of Mark   49
    —*Charles H. Dyer*
4. Jesus' Last Supper   63
    —*Harold W. Hoehner*
5. Geographical Aspects of the Gospel   75
    —*J. Carl Laney*

Part 2

The Joy of Fellowship:
Themes from the Spiritual Life

6. Balancing the Academic and the Spiritual in Seminary 91
    —*Roy B. Zuck*
7. What Prayer Will and Will Not Change   99
    —*Thomas L. Constable*

8. The Traitor in the Gates: The Christian's Conflict   115
   with the Flesh
      —*William D. Lawrence*
9. Reach the World in One Generation   133
      —*J. Ronald Blue*

Part 3

Things to Come:
Themes from Prophecy

10. The Church in God's Prophetic Program   149
      —*Donald K. Campbell*
11. The Future for Israel in God's Plan   163
      —*Louis A. Barbieri, Jr.*
12. Paul and "The Israel of God": An Exegetical and   181
    Eschatological Case-Study
      —*S. Lewis Johnson, Jr.*
13. Apocalyptic Genre in Literal Interpretation   197
      —*Elliott E. Johnson*
14. Daniel as a Contribution to Kingdom Theology   211
      —*Eugene H. Merrill*
15. The Theological Significance of Revelation 20:1-6   227
      —*John F. Walvoord*

Introduction

Stanley D. Toussaint

This *Festschrift* is dedicated to J. Dwight Pentecost, who in the spring of 1985 was recognized for having taught for thirty years at Dallas Theological Seminary. The year 1985 also marked his seventieth birthday. During these thirty years "Dr. P.," as he is affectionately called by his students, served successively in three departments: Systematic Theology, New Testament Exegesis, and Bible Exposition. While S. Lewis Johnson, Jr., was studying in Europe, Dr. Pentecost was acting department chairman of New Testament studies. In 1962 he succeeded C. Fred Lincoln as chairman of the Department of Bible Exposition, a post he held until 1980 when he retired from the department chairmanship, though he still maintained a full-time teaching load.

Dwight Pentecost distinguished himself as a student at both Hampden-Sydney College and Dallas Theological Seminary. After graduation from Seminary he was ordained and served as pastor first of the Presbyterian Church in Cambridge Springs, Pennsylvania, and then Saint John's Presbyterian Church in Devon, Pennsylvania. He joined the faculty of Philadelphia College of Bible in 1948 and ministered there until 1955 when he was invited to become a faculty member at Dallas Seminary. In 1956 Dr. Pentecost received his Doctor of Theology degree from his alma mater. His dissertation was later published as *Things to Come*, a classic and milestone in the field of prophecy. He has written sixteen other books in addition to ministering as pastor of the Grace Bible Church of Dallas for eighteen years. Besides serving as a professor, pastor, and author, Dr. Pentecost is a world-renowned conference speaker. He is beloved by his students for his sharp wit, incisive questions, knowledge of the Scriptures, and commitment to serve Christ.

Dr. Pentecost is happily married to his wife, Dorothy. They are the proud parents of Jane and Gwen, who are both married.

When the idea of a *Festschrift* to honor Dr. Pentecost was suggested, there was immediate approval. Every one of the faculty members who were invited to participate was enthusiastic about the concept.

This volume is in three sections: themes from the gospels, aspects of the spiritual life, and essays on prophecy. Each of these has been of special interest to Dwight Pentecost. Faculty and alumni were chosen to participate on the basis of their expertise in these areas.

I am especially indebted to Dr. P., not only because of his friendship and instruction, but also because of his influence in my being on the faculty at Dallas Seminary. On two occasions he recommended me to the administration, once in 1960 and again in 1973. I owe him much.

Special gratitude must also be expressed to Charles Dyer, coeditor of this volume, who carried the majority of the burden for this undertaking. His careful editing made this celebration in writing possible. Hearty thanks is also extended to Carol Wright, who typed the entire text. Her cheerful demeanor and diligent labor were an encouragement to both editors. Thanks is also in order for each of the contributors, who so willingly gave themselves to this work.

This book is a small expression of esteem and appreciation to our beloved Dr. J. Dwight Pentecost, who continues as professor emeritus in Bible exposition.

EDWARD C. PENTECOST (A.B., Hampden-Sydney College; Th.M., Dallas Theological Seminary; M.A., University of Mexico; D.Miss., Fuller Theological School of World Missions) is assistant professor of world missions at Dallas Theological Seminary. He is also Dr. J. Dwight Pentecost's brother.

A Biographical Sketch of Dr. J. Dwight Pentecost

Edward C. Pentecost

On April 24, 1915, John Dwight Pentecost was born into the home of John and Edna Pentecost in the quiet town of State College, Pennsylvania. Dwight, as he was to be called, was the couple's first child. John and Edna were Presbyterians, successors of a long heritage of believers. As devout followers of Christ they dedicated Dwight to the Lord in baptism according to the practice of their denomination.

The Pentecost family moved to the city of Schenectady, New York, where Dwight's father took a job with the General Electric Company as an electrical engineer. There the little two-year-old Dwight was joined by his first brother, the author of this brief biography. Two and one-half years later a sister, Wilma, joined the family; and after another two years the last member, Albert, was born.

By that time the Pentecost family had moved to Chester, Pennsylvania, and our father had taken a job with the Viscose Company in Marcus Hook, Delaware. Though he worked across the state line, father preferred to have his family live in Chester, which had both a strong church and a good school system. That decision typified our father's constant concern for the spiritual and educational development of his family.

Dwight was a good student who liked his studies but not always his teachers. He had a mind of his own and definite ideas of what a good teacher should be like. But his differences with some teachers never got in the way of his studies. Dwight excelled in literature and history, but he did not express much interest in math and science.

Dwight loved to read, and he always seemed to have his head buried in a magazine or book. Once our father asked Dwight to come outside and help him work on our Model "A" Ford. Dwight's job was to hold the light so father could see to work. Before going out Dwight found a magazine to take with him so he could read while he was holding the light. Evidently more light was focused on the magazine than on the automobile because it was not long before father told him to go into the house and read and to send me out to hold the light.

Dwight grew up in a home that stressed family unity and traditional Christian values. Father planned special camping and vacation times for the children. Everyone looked forward to summer vacations spent together on an uncle's farm in northern Pennsylvania or occasionally at the seashore in New Jersey.

The church was a strong part of Dwight's family life. Our parents provided loving but strict discipline at home, and they stressed faithful adherence to the law of God. This included attendance at Sunday school and morning and evening church services. The "Sabbath day" was a day to be kept holy, and no work or play was allowed. Sunday afternoons were spent around the piano with family, singing.

The summers also played an important part in Dwight's spiritual training. Abraham L. Lathem, who pastored the church that the Pentecost family attended, established a unique Summer Bible School. Dr. Lathem developed a program that met three hours each day for five weeks during the summer. The entire program was devoted to the memorization of Scripture. Dr. Lathem's goal was to fill the minds of the children with the Word of God. The program was carefully constructed with a separate curriculum for every age from first grade through high school. Thus Dwight's mind was saturated with Scripture, and that reservoir of truth has always remained.

When Dwight was thirteen a very important movement began in our church. Dr. Lathem had a concern for the spiritual training of those boys who would eventually become elders, deacons, and pastors. He approached our father and asked him if he would design a training program for the boys of the church between the ages of twelve and eighteen. After much prayerful consideration father agreed to initiate such a program, and Dwight was one of the first twelve boys to form the Awana club of the Third Presbyterian Church of Chester, where the movement was born.

Several people were used of God to influence Dwight's life. One was his uncle, Edward J. Richards, who was a pastor in the Christian Missionary

Alliance. When he came to visit, his loving and jovial character and spiritual maturity combined to produce an excellent model of a godly pastor. It is no wonder that Dwight wanted to emulate him.

Another person who influenced Dwight's life was his pastor, Abraham L. Lathem. Dr. Lathem's desire to teach clearly the Word of God and his personal example of pastoral concern for his flock were deeply etched into Dwight's personality. Dr. Lathem personally visited every member of his congregation at least once each year in addition to making special home visits whenever necessary. His example provided a clear model to follow.

Perhaps the strongest influence on the formation of Dwight's character came from our father. Father had a deep concern for the spiritual growth of his children. However, that concern was not just limited to us. He desired to see the whole group of boys in the Awana club at Third Presbyterian Church grow to become men of God. His children were of vital importance, but he showed an equal interest and affection for the boys of the church. That concern for the spiritual welfare of others influenced his own sons.

With these models and influences it is not surprising that Dwight chose to enter the ministry. Dwight's decision to be a pastor became evident when he was in high school. There was no specific moment of decision. Rather, Dwight experienced a growing conviction that this was the Lord's will for him.

But before Dwight could become a pastor he first had to attend college and seminary. What schools would best prepare him to serve the Lord? God used the ministry of one man to help him make a decision regarding college. Each year the church held a Bible Conference, and several times J. D. Eggleston, president of Hampden-Sydney College, was invited to speak. He was a man of God who knew how to teach the Word and apply it to the lives of his audience. The personal example of Dr. Eggleston was the strongest factor in Dwight's decision to attend Hampden-Sydney College in Virginia.

Having the assurance that God had called him into the ministry and that Hampden-Sydney was the college to which the Lord had directed him, Dwight undertook his studies with motivation and determination. He was an excellent student, but he tried to balance academics with other activities such as quartet singing. Dwight associated himself with the preministerial student group on campus.

The pastor of the College Chapel, W. Twyman Williams, influenced Dwight while he was at Hampden-Sydney. Dwight appreciated Dr. Williams's ministry to the college students and valued his advice. So when Dr. Williams asked Dwight to teach a Sunday school class at Oak Grove, Virginia, in the country just a few miles from the college campus, Dwight accepted and became involved in his first formal teaching experience. It was a gathering of people who met every Sunday afternoon for study, and Dwight thoroughly enjoyed the opportunity to teach God's Word.

During Dwight's college years Sunday evenings were usually spent, along with many other students, at the Presbyterian church in the nearby town of Farmville. This was partly because there was a coeducational teacher training institution in the town, and the female students were allowed to attend the evening service of their choice. It was through this opportunity that Dwight met one of the students from that institution, Dorothy Harrison, whose family was residing in Farmville. Dorothy was a true southern belle; she came from one of the foremost families in Virginia. Throughout his residence at Hampden-Sydney Dwight dated Dorothy, soon recognizing that she was God's choice as a life companion for him. However, marriage was postponed until Dwight had completed his first year of seminary.

Another individual who influenced Dwight during this time was Everett F. Harrison. Dr. Harrison came to the church in Chester after Dr. Lathem left, and our father was very appreciative of his ministry and teaching. Our family got to know Dr. Harrison personally, and he encouraged Dwight to choose the Evangelical Theological College in Dallas, Texas, for his seminary training. Dr. Harrison joined the faculty of the seminary at about the time Dwight was making his decision. The personal influence of Dr. Harrison along with that of Lewis Sperry Chafer, the president of the seminary and also a frequent speaker at our home church, made it inevitable that Dwight would continue his studies for the ministry at Dallas.

In the fall of 1937, having graduated from college magna cum laude, Dwight began his studies at Dallas Theological Seminary in Dallas, Texas. (The name had been changed from the Evangelical Theological College the year before he arrived.) It was the thirteenth year of the seminary's existence, and the student body numbered less than a hundred students. There was one dormitory for the single men and a few apartments for the married students. America was still in the grip of the Great Depression, and though jobs were available for the married students, wages were extremely low. Had the school not provided free tuition, there probably would have been no married students enrolled.

One of Dwight's goals during his first year was to secure a job that would enable him to get married. One that seemed to have potential was a bakery delivery route. The owner promised that the job would involve a minimum number of hours early in the morning, allowing Dwight to be free most of the day to pursue his studies. However, Dwight soon found that the job required him to work not only mornings making deliveries but also Saturdays making collections. Then he discovered that he had to spend afternoons tracking down individuals who were unreachable on Saturday. And further, the bakery required Dwight to deduct from his own salary what he was unable to collect during the week, recouping this payment whenever he could find the people home. When Dwight added up all his earnings and divided the sum by the hours spent on the job, he discovered that his net income was about twenty-five cents per hour.

It was not long before Dwight took a job with the John E. Mitchell Company, where many of the seminary students found employment. Although it meant night work, it was better than trying to collect bills to put food on his own table. Dwight decided that with a permanent job at the Mitchell plant he could afford to get married. Consequently the wedding was set for September 3, 1938, in Farmville, Virginia. The honeymoon was the trip back to Dallas where Dwight began his second year at the seminary.

While in seminary Dwight had frequent opportunities to preach in many rural Texas towns. W. E. Hawkins, a well-known radio preacher, constantly sent seminary students out to preach in new churches that were growing up all around Dallas. The experience of preaching and singing in quartets increased Dwight's love for sharing God's Word.

Having been brought up as a Presbyterian, it was natural for Dwight to enter the ministry in that denomination following his graduation from seminary. He was licensed to preach by Presbytery, and his first call was to a church in Cambridge Springs, a small community in northwestern Pennsylvania. Dr. Harrison had advised Dwight to set aside sufficient time in his ministry for the study of God's Word in order to grow personally and have something fresh to deliver to his congregation every time he spoke, and Dwight followed that advice. The work prospered, and Dwight established himself as an expositor of the Word.

While at Cambridge Springs Dwight learned some practical lessons. Furnishing a parsonage on his small income was a formidable task until he learned how to recognize and restore antiques. He searched out pieces of furniture hidden away in old barns or attics that were considered to be either worthless or useless by the owners. However, under Dwight's skilled hands layers of dirt and paint were removed, revealing antique treasures.

Many of those antiques still grace Dwight and Dorothy's home today.

As a pastor Dwight sought to be a positive influence on the entire community. He joined the volunteer fire company to provide a broader avenue for service and was taken to an open field for orientation and training on the equipment. His first lesson was on the proper use of the fire hose. Handed the hose, Dwight was instructed to hold it and direct the water at a target. (Normally three men are required for this task.) The water was turned on full force. Dwight held on helplessly as he was thrown to the ground and whipped around by the force of the water shooting from it. He had learned the lesson that the other firemen were seeking to teach him: never try to hold a hose single-handedly. But Dwight, the ever observant pastor, found another application of the lesson he had learned. No one individual could do the work of the ministry, either. For the church to accomplish its God-given goal all believers would need to work together.

From Cambridge Springs Dwight was called to take the pastorate of Saint John's Presbyterian Church in Devon, Pennsylvania. It was not long before leaders of the two Bible Institutes in nearby Philadelphia approached him about teaching in their schools. Dwight found himself engaged in a full-time pastoral ministry and a part-time teaching ministry and enjoying both.

During the time at Devon, Dwight made his first trip to another country, visiting Mexico where I was ministering to university students. Encountering firsthand the ruins of Mexico's ancient civilizations, Dwight was entranced by the archaeological finds, and he reveled in letting his imagination carry him back to the times when the Aztecs, Toltecs, and Mixtecs controlled the country. His interest in archaeology and history later prompted him to travel throughout the Middle East to visit those places where the events of the Bible took place.

But the most important aspect of Dwight's Mexican visit was the opportunity it provided him to see people in desperate physical and spiritual need. He observed the results of sin in the lives of people and the suffering caused by pagan worship. He witnessed superstition and idolatry first hand, such as mothers rubbing their babies' hands on the glass covering of a coffin in hope of receiving a blessing and women kneeling on bleeding knees, weeping before the statue of the Virgin and pleading for the "blessed one" to intercede on their behalf. His heart ached as he saw the grandeur of the cathedrals through which poverty-stricken people were being led into eternal condemnation. The visit to Mexico expanded Dwight's vision for world evangelization and impressed on him the need to counteract false doctrine by teaching the whole counsel of God.

Although the ministry at Devon was a growing experience, Dwight could sense God leading him elsewhere. The opportunity came when the Philadelphia School of Bible asked him to serve full-time on the faculty. One of his first assignments was a class on eschatology. Dwight had great interest in the subject, but he felt this was one area in which he had little preparation. Ultimately it was this assignment that led him to apply to the doctoral program at Dallas Theological Seminary. He was accepted, and he and Dorothy moved back to Dallas to begin his studies in the fall of 1953. He received the Th.D. degree in 1956, and the outcome of his studies was the publication of his dissertation, *Things to Come.* It was a voluminous work, and he was required to reduce its length by one-third before it was published. Most publishers felt there would be very little demand for such a volume, and many wanted Dwight not only to condense the work but to rewrite it in a form more accessible to a general reading public. These concerns quickly proved to be unfounded, and it is interesting to note that the book has been in continuous publication since 1958 and has sold more than 150,000 copies.

Just before completing his Th.D. degree Dwight was asked by John F. Walvoord, Chafer's successor as president of the seminary, to join the faculty. The invitation to teach on the seminary level appealed to Dwight. He loved the opportunity to expound God's Word in the classroom and in the pulpit. Dwight accepted Dr. Walvoord's invitation and joined the faculty of Dallas, a position he has held for over thirty years.

Dwight's style in the classroom followed the pattern he had developed in the pulpit. Those students over the years who have had the opportunity to sit under his tutelage may still remember his striding into class carrying only the Bible. He had such a grasp of his subject matter that he could lecture in depth without using any other materials. His quick wit helps keep his lectures lively and the students alert. Even as a busy teacher Dwight has always graded his own papers and tries to return them to the students as soon as possible. That helps him keep in touch with his students and to know if there is some area that has not been made clear. In spite of a hectic schedule he always has time to stop and chat with his students, who will find a listening ear and often words of wisdom in counsel.

Dwight's hobbies have given him a wealth of experience, which he uses to illustrate his teaching and preaching. In addition to refinishing antique furniture he also collects old clocks, some with wooden works, some with fancy German or Swiss works, and all with different chimes. Every room in his home has one. The clocks are set at slightly different times and on the hour one can follow the sound of the chimes through the house. Dwight also enjoys collecting artifacts from archaeological sites and representative memorabilia from the many countries he and Dorothy have visited. He greatly appreciates art, and the walls of his home are decked with paintings gathered over the years. But the hobby that gives Dwight the greatest pleasure is photography. He loves the beauty of nature, and gorgeous photographs of various scenes adorn his study walls.

Dwight has been well received as a conference speaker both in the United States and abroad, and he is often asked to speak on prophecy. His overseas travels and speaking engagements have taken him to Argentina, Australia, Brazil, Columbia, Guatemala, India, Ireland, Japan, Mexico, New Zealand, Scotland, Spain, and several countries in Africa. He has also led various tours to Israel and portions of Europe. His visits to the Holy Land provided invaluable information for his well-known work *The Words and Works of Jesus Christ.*

In addition to carrying a full load of teaching at the seminary, Dwight also pastored Grace Bible Church in Dallas, Texas, for eighteen years and has written seventeen major books and an innumerable number of magazine and journal articles.

One cannot forget that God gave Dwight a partner who has stayed by his side throughout his ministry. Dorothy is an author in her own right, having written a book entitled *The Pastor's Wife and the Church* (Moody Press) that has been widely read. She is also a teacher, Bible study leader, and women's conference speaker. She has traveled widely with her husband and encouraged him in all his undertakings. Dwight and Dorothy have two lovely daughters, Jane and Gwen. Both are married to fine Christian husbands and actively involved in the ministry of their local churches.

Through the years of ministry Dwight and Dorothy have deepened and matured in their Christian lives. They have learned to stand by those who are suffering, to encourage those who are discouraged, and to help those who are in need. The ministry has its heartaches, and Dwight knew his share. And yet, God's grace has always been evident in Dwight's life. Those of us who have known Dwight longest have seen God use him as a vessel of honor for His glory. "Victorious in Christ" best summarizes the life and ministry of Dr. J. Dwight Pentecost.

Part 1

The Words and Works:
Themes from the Gospels

STANLEY D. TOUSSAINT (A.B., Augsburg
College; Th.M., Th.D., Dallas Theological
Seminary) is chairman and professor of
Bible exposition at Dallas Theological
Seminary.

The Kingdom and Matthew's Gospel

Stanley D. Toussaint

The themes of the kingdom and biblical covenants are inextricably
bound together. Where there is one there is the other. Both of these topics
are of special interest to J. Dwight Pentecost and form a large part of his
view of the Scriptures. Many feel the single, most unifying theme of the Bible is the kingdom. It would certainly seem from Matthew 25:34 that this
was God's original goal for man. There Christ predicts the Messiah will say
to the sheep on His right hand, "Come, you who are blessed of My Father,
inherit the kingdom prepared for you from the foundation of the world."
From the very beginning God purposed for man to be sovereign over the
world.

God created Adam and Eve and gave them authority to rule the earth
(Gen. 1:28). It is no wonder that the psalmist was overcome with awe at
the Almighty Jehovah, his Master, giving man so great an honor as to have
dominion over every living creature on this planet (Ps. 8:1-8). Every premillennialist believes that this will only be accomplished when Christ returns to establish His kingdom on this earth. This is the expectation of the
New Testament as well as the Old (Heb. 2:5-9; 1 Cor. 15:25).

It is the purpose of this paper to discuss that kingdom as it is presented
in the gospel of Matthew. More particularly, this paper will discuss the usage of the terms *kingdom, kingdom of God,* and *kingdom of heaven.* Although a brief amount of time will be invested in defending the concept of
a literal earthly kingdom as held by premillennial dispensationalists, this
will not be the burden of this essay. *The purpose of this article is to contend for a consistent meaning of the term* kingdom *in Matthew's gospel.*
Every time the term *kingdom* is used theologically in Matthew it refers to

the same thing, the kingdom yet to come on this earth inaugurated and governed by the Messiah.

Such a view of *kingdom* is certainly not new nor innovative, but it is not the normative dispensational premillennial outlook. This article is only asking for a hearing so that the millennial viewpoint may be a bit more consistent.

Following a comparatively brief defense of the concept of a literal and earthly kingdom, an analysis of the usage of the term in Matthew will be presented. It is impossible in the brief confines of this paper to discuss extensively every occurrence of the term *kingdom* in Matthew. However, every instance will be touched on in order to defend the thesis of this essay.

A DEFENSE OF AN EARTHLY AND LITERAL KINGDOM

THE JEWISH EXPECTATIONS

On this point Bible students of every theological stripe agree. Whether a man is a liberal or a conservative in his theology, he will say the Jews expected an earthly, literal kingdom. Even rigid amillennialists concede this point. They believe the average Israelite anticipated the coming of an earthly kingdom, but his expectations were wrong.

It is very significant to note that the Lord Jesus never corrected the Jews' anticipations.[1] In fact, He confirmed them. In Matthew 19:28 He said to His twelve apostles, "Truly I say to you that you who have followed Me, in the regeneration when the Son of Man will sit on His glorious throne, you also shall sit upon twelve thrones, judging the twelve tribes of Israel." The allusion to the Son of Man on His throne obviously refers back to Daniel 7:13-14, a distinctly prophetic passage that states that the peoples, nations, and tribes from every language will serve the Messiah. The promise to sit as judges over the twelve tribes probably looks at Ezekiel 48, where the land of Israel is divided among the twelve tribes.

Just before He was crucified the Lord instituted the Lord's Table. In connection with the cup He said, "But I say to you, I will not drink of this fruit of the vine from now on until that day when I drink it new with you in My Father's kingdom" (Matt. 26:29). It would be strange to make such a statement if heaven were in view. Why discuss the drinking of the cup in heaven, especially when the New Covenant was associated with the reestablish-

---

1. George N. H. Peters, *The Theocratic Kingdom of Our Lord Jesus, the Christ, as Covenanted in the Old Testament and Presented in the New Testament,* 3 vols. (New York: Funk and Wagnalls, 1884), 1:95.

ment of Israel under their Messiah (Jer. 31:23-40)? This New Covenant is referred to as a covenant of peace and an everlasting covenant in Ezekiel 37:26 (cf. Ezek. 36:16—37:28). The Father's kingdom is the one given by the Father to the Son as prophesied in Daniel 7:9-14.

It is possible that both Israel and the disciples were wrong in their anticipation of an earthly kingdom. If so, the Lord did not correct the disciples in their misconception even after His death and resurrection. They still expected the kingdom to come to earth at the time of the Lord's ascension (cf. Acts 1:6-7). They asked, "Lord, is it at this time You are restoring the kingdom to Israel?" The Lord did not rebuke them for their misconception of the kingdom. He only said it was not for them to know the *time* of its arrival. If their view of the kingdom was wrong, it would be strange for Christ not to correct it, for this was the last time they would see Him before His ascension.

But some will contend Christ did correct the Jewish perspective on the kingdom. Often John 18:36 is quoted, where Jesus answered Pilate, "My kingdom is not of this world," as though Christ Jesus were stating His kingdom will not be in this world. Of course, Christ did not mean that at all. The key to this statement is the preposition *ek,* which means the Lord is affirming, "My kingdom does not have its source in this world" (cf. John 8:23).

Another commonly used passage employed against an earthly and literal kingdom is Luke 17:20-21, "Now having been questioned by the Pharisees as to when the kingdom of God was coming, He answered them and said, 'The kingdom of God is not coming with signs to be observed; nor will they say, "Look, here it is!" or, "There it is!" For behold, the kingdom of God is in your midst.' " This rather difficult passage must be interpreted in light of the following context (Luke 17:22-37). In those verses the Lord Jesus states His coming will be sudden and judgmental as in the Flood of Noah's day and the destruction of the cities of Sodom and Gomorrah in the time of Lot. This helps to explain the meaning of the somewhat unusual noun *paratēreseōs.* The return of Christ will be so sudden and cataclysmic that it will not be seen as happening gradually. It is unfortunate that the *New American Standard Bible* renders this noun as "signs to be observed," inasmuch as it is the second coming that will be presaged by signs. The return itself will be like lightening (Luke 17:24*).* That is why Christ explains the meaning of *paratēreseōs* in Luke 17:21. Men will not say, "Here is the kingdom!" or "There it is!" For the kingdom of God suddenly will be among men universally. To say the phrase *entos humōn* means "within you" is not good exegesis.[2] First, the Lord Jesus was addressing Pharisees, His inveterate opponents. Second, Christ never spoke of the kingdom's entering the hearts of men but of humans entering the kingdom. Many have observed this phenomenon in the sayings of Jesus. The fact the present tense is used for the presence of the kingdom may be easily explained as futuristic. Thus the kingdom suddenly will be in the midst of mankind. Third, Luke 17:22-37 confirms the eschatological significance of these words of Christ. Luke 17:20-21 is no argument against the earthly and literal coming of Christ's kingdom; rather, it is a statement for it.

THE PRESENTATION OF JESUS AS MESSIAH

Very often the dispensationalist school of interpretation will refer to "the offer of the kingdom" to Israel. By this is meant the contingency of the coming of the kingdom to Israel in the first century based on Israel's acceptance of Jesus as its Messiah. This concept is clearly found in the New Testament. For instance, Peter openly states the coming of the Messiah rests on Israel's repentance (Acts 3:19-21). The Lord Himself said that John the Baptist could have been the fulfillment of the Elijah prophecy of Malachi 4:5-6 if Israel had repented (Matt. 11:14).[3] Such a doctrine is implied in the "strong man" saying of Matthew 12:29 and the lament of Matthew 23:37-39. It is taught in Matthew 22:1-14 in the parable of the marriage feast.

However, dispensationalists may want to clarify their terminology. The New Testament does teach the contingency of the coming of the kingdom premised on the response of the Jews. But every Israelite wanted the kingdom to come. To say Christ offered the kingdom to Israel is true, but it leaves the impression the Jews did not want the kingdom to come. It would be far better to say Jesus offered Himself as Israel's Messiah and the coming of the kingdom was contingent on their acceptance or rejection of Him. This essay, accordingly, will refer to the offer of Jesus as Messiah and assume with this the contingency of the kingdom's coming to that generation of Israel.

---

2. H. D. A. Major, T. W. Manson, and C. J. Wright, *The Mission and Message of Jesus* (New York: Dutton, 1938), p. 596.
3. Alva J. McClain, *The Greatness of the Kingdom* (Winona Lake, Ind.: BMH, 1959), pp. 301-2.

Usage of the Term *Kingdom* in the Gospel of Matthew

THE KINGDOM OF GOD AND THE KINGDOM OF HEAVEN

Some who hold to the contingency of the coming of Christ's kingdom to this earth maintain a distinction between the terms *kingdom of God* and *kingdom of heaven*.[4] It is said that because the kingdom of heaven is likened to the lump of dough with leaven (Matt. 13:33) it contains hypocrites as well as genuine believers in that leaven portrays evil. On the other hand, the kingdom of God is composed only of the saved because John 3:3 says only the born again enter the kingdom of God. However, Matthew 18:3 also excludes hypocrites from the kingdom of heaven. Only the genuinely converted may enter this kingdom. Therefore, this chapter will assume the kingdom of God and the kingdom of heaven are essentially synonymous and both refer to the kingdom itself.[5]

THE MEANING OF THE TERM *KINGDOM* IN MATTHEW 1-7

Matthew's gospel emphasizes the discourses of the Lord Jesus. This is seen first in the formula *kai egeneto hote etelesen ho Iēsous tous logous toutous* that occurs at the end of each of the five great discourses of the first gospel (7:28; 11:1; 13:53; 19:1; 26:1). The stress on discourse is also evidenced by Matthew's didactic emphasis (cf. Matt. 28:20). A third indicator of the accent on discourse material is found in Matthew's use of narrative. He abbreviates narrative material and uses it as a backdrop for the sayings and sermons of the Lord.[6] This means that for Matthew the most important material is the discourse. This narrative is employed to introduce and explain the setting for the words of Jesus.

Understanding Matthew's use of narrative is important because any use of the term *kingdom (basileia)* in the narrative will logically have the same concept in the discourse that follows. Thus, the first occurrence of the term in Matthew 3:2 is very significant. In chapters 1-2 Matthew carefully presents the credentials of Jesus the Messiah, especially as they relate to His being the King of Israel. The genealogy of chapter 1 confirms His royal lineage followed by the fulfillment of prophecy in His virgin birth. Chapter 2 has a twofold thrust: first, it again emphasizes the fulfillment of the Old

---

4. Charles L. Feinberg, *Premillennialism or Amillennialism?* (Altadena, Calif.: The Evangelical Fellowship, 1945), pp. 298-99; Earl Miller, *The Kingdom of God and the Kingdom of Heaven* (Meadville, Pa.: By the Author, 1950), pp. 63-64.
5. W. Graham Scroggie, *A Guide to the Gospels* (Old Tappan, N.J.: Revell, 1975), p. 300.
6. The narrative material of Matthew's gospel is briefer than that found in Mark's.

Testament in the Lord Jesus, and second, it previews the various responses to the coming of Jesus. There would be worship by Gentiles and hatred by those who oppose Him.

Suddenly in Matthew 3 John the baptizer, the Lord's forerunner, appears on the scene. His message was, "Repent, for the kingdom of heaven is at hand." What does the word *kingdom* mean here? It certainly cannot be some *spiritual* kingdom in the hearts of people. That kingdom was always present (cf. Ps. 37:31).[7] Furthermore, the fact that John never explained what the term meant when the Jews clearly expected an earthly kingdom would imply that he was expecting the same type of kingdom. John's response to his imprisonment also suggests that he expected an earthly kingdom (Matt. 11:2-3).[8] The kingdom had drawn near in the coming of the Messiah. That is why John's message has such a heavy bent of judgment. Preceding the coming of the kingdom was the bar of God, and it was imminent (Matt. 3:10). The last section of Matthew 3 presents the Lord's baptism when He is anointed and confirmed by God as Israel's Messiah.

Matthew 4 shows Jesus is morally pure and spiritually qualified to rule. It is in this testing of Jesus that the term *kingdom* next occurs. In Matthew 4:8 the term is used to describe the kingdoms of this world. Not without significance is the fact that the word refers to earthly kingdoms in a plain and literal sense. Satan's offer of these kingdoms to Christ was premised on Christ's ultimate right to rule over them as Daniel 7 predicted.[9]

In Matthew 4:17 the Lord Jesus begins His public ministry with precisely the same message as was proclaimed by John the Baptist in 3:2. There was no further clarification of the terms. "Repent" meant the same; "is at hand" took the same implications; and the noun "kingdom" had identical sense. So when Christ preached the good news of the kingdom in Matthew 4:23 He simply announced the proximity of Israel's golden age. The good news meant people only needed to repent in order to enter it. Entrance was not contingent on position, wealth, or even works. It was indeed good news for entrance into the kingdom. At any rate, the term *kingdom* refers to the coming reign of the Messiah on earth. This is how the audience understood it, and unless it can be proved otherwise, this is what the Lord Christ intended to convey.

All of these events of Matthew 1-4 form the background for the Lord's

7. McClain, *Greatness of the Kingdom,* p. 303.
8. *Ibid.,* pp. 301-2.
9. Peters, 1:700.

Sermon on the Mount (Matt. 5-7). That famed discourse sets forth His ethics for the interim until the kingdom should come and establishes the kind of righteousness God has always expected from His followers. Most agree the theme of Matthew 5-7 is genuine righteousness as God sees it.

In this discourse the term *basileia* occurs eight times. The first two of these are in the beatitudes. The well-known beatitudes are each composed of three parts: first, a pronouncement of blessing; second, a description of a particular type of virtue seen in a righteous person; and third, the reason the virtuous individual is to be congratulated and pronounced blessed. This third element is very important because in each of the beatitudes it is a description of some aspect of Israel's coming kingdom. Matthew 5:4 refers to the comfort of God that is a fulfillment of Isaiah 40:1, " 'Comfort, O comfort My people,' says your God" (cf. Isa. 40:2-8; 66:13; Luke 2:25). The cause for blessing in 5:5 is the inheritance of the earth (cf. Ps. 2:8-9). It is possible and even probable for the noun *gē* that is used in Matthew 5:5 to describe the land promises extended to the patriarchs of Israel in Genesis (cf. 12:7; 13:14-17; 15:18-21; 17:7-8; 26:3-4; 28:15; 35:12). Psalm 37 promises the faithful and humble ones an inheritance in the land (vv. 9, 11). The promise of being filled with righteousness refers back to the kingdom prophecies of Isaiah 45:8; 61:12-11; 62:1-2; Jeremiah 23:6; 33:14-16; and Daniel 9:24. The beatitude promising mercy (5:7) is also millennial in its anticipation (Isa. 49:10, 13; 54:8, 10; 60:10; Zech. 10:6). The blessing of seeing God mentioned in Matthew 5:8 refers to the prophecies of Psalm 24:3-4; Isaiah 33:17; 35:2; and 40:5. In Matthew 5:9 the heirs are called sons of God. This describes the fulfillment of the well-known prophecy of Hosea 1:10. Significantly the eight beatitudes are bracketed with the promise "Theirs is the kingdom of heaven" (vv. 3, 10). The present tense of *estin* is not to be pressed; it is proleptic.[10] In each case the third part of the beatitudes is a promise of blessing in the coming kingdom of Christ on earth.

The next use of kingdom in Matthew 5 is located in verse 19, where the Lord refers to position in His future kingdom. For consistency's sake it would be wise to say this kingdom is the same as the one described in the beatitudes and the earlier chapters of Matthew. It should be observed that even here the term has eschatological overtones, for followers will be called least or great in Christ's future kingdom.

---

10. Alan Hugh M'Neile, *The Gospel According to St. Matthew* (London: Macmillan, 1915), p. 50; C. G. Montefiore, *The Synoptic Gospels*, 2 vols. (New York: KTAV, 1968), 2:33; Eduard Thurneysen, *The Sermon on the Mount* (Richmond: John Knox, 1964), p. 32.

The word *kingdom* has the same prophetic meaning in 5:20, where the Lord lays down the stricture that only those with God's kind of righteousness will enter the future kingdom.

A most important occurrence of *basileia* is found in the Lord's Prayer in Matthew 6:10. The disciples are encouraged to pray for the coming of the kingdom. To say this refers to the spread of the gospel or the increase of God's influence in men's hearts is a crass form of eisegesis. The historical setting shouts for a literal kingdom.[11] First, the hearers would undoubtedly have taken the Lord's injunction as a command to pray for an earthly kingdom. Second, a *spiritualized* kingdom divorced from a restored Israel would eviscerate the Old Testament promises. Third, the first three requests of the Lord's Prayer are for the same thing—the coming of the kingdom. Even in the Old Testament the restoration of Israel is bound with the hallowing of God's name (Ezek. 36:16-38).[12]

In 7:21 the Lord states that professing the name "Lord, Lord" is insufficient of itself for entrance into the kingdom. Once again the term is used in an eschatological and future sense.

In summary, it must be conceded the term *basileia* in Matthew 1-7 is used consistently with the meaning of the earthly kingdom predicted in the Old Testament.

THE MEANING OF THE TERM *KINGDOM* IN MATTHEW 8-10

In this section the narrative of chapters 8-9 forms the background for the discourse of chapter 10. *Basileia* occurs only four times in these three chapters.

After hearing the great affirmation of faith by the Gentile centurion, Christ predicts, "And I say to you . . . that many shall be cast out into the outer darkness" (Matt. 8:11-12). The well-known figure of the messianic banquet[13] is here employed to describe the kingdom (cf. Isa. 25:6). Again, it is eschatological. The reference to the patriarchs underscores the promises given to Abraham, Isaac, and Jacob, and these are millennial in nature. The term "sons of the kingdom" refers to the Jews who were the legal heirs but who because of spiritual failure would not enter the predicted earthly

---

11. Millar Burrows, "Thy Kingdom Come," *Journal of Biblical Literature* 74 (January 1955):4-8.
12. Willoughby C. Allen, *A Critical and Exegetical Commentary on the Gospel According to St. Matthew,* The International Critical Commentary (Edinburgh: T. & T. Clark, 1912), p. 58.
13. William Barclay, *The Gospel of Matthew,* 2 vols. (Edinburgh: Saint Andrews, 1956), 1:309; T. Herbert Bindley, "Eschatology in the Lord's Prayer," *The Expositor* 17 (October 1919):317. Also see Enoch 62:13-16; 2 Baruch 29:3-8; 2 Esdras 6:49-52.

kingdom. It should be observed in passing that the expression "weeping and gnashing of teeth" in Matthew's gospel is always used in connection with the judgment prohibiting entrance into the earthly millennial kingdom.[14]

"The gospel of the kingdom" proclaimed by Christ in Matthew 9:35 must be the same as that preached by Him in 4:23. It was the good news of the nearness of the kingdom and freedom of access by repentance. The kingdom was proximate in two senses. First, the Messiah was here on earth, and second, the kingdom's coming was contingent on Israel's response to her Messiah.[15]

A very important use of the term *basileia* in Matthew's gospel is found in 10:7. After confirming His power by a series of merciful and mighty miracles in chapters 8-9, the Lord Jesus commissions His twelve apostles. In so doing He commands them to preach saying, "The kingdom of heaven is at hand" (10:7). This is precisely the same proclamation of John the Baptist (3:2) and Christ (4:17). Here, as in 3:2 and 4:17, there is no further explanation of the meaning. The conclusion is clear. The Lord Jesus and the disciples were preaching the proximity of the long expected earthly and literal kingdom anticipated in the Old Testament and announced by John.

THE MEANING OF THE TERM *KINGDOM* IN MATTHEW 11-13

It is in this section of Matthew that many dispensational and premillennial Bible students part company with the view espoused in this essay. All dispensationalists would agree with the meaning of the term *kingdom* presented thus far. However, chapter 13 becomes more difficult. It occurs after the growth of the antagonism and opposition described in chapters 11-12.

A rather obtuse statement is found in Matthew 11:11 where Christ declares, "Truly, I say to you, among those born of women there has not arisen anyone greater than John the Baptist; yet he who is least in the kingdom of heaven is greater than he." There was no one greater than John among all the humans who preceded the Lord Jesus; but as great as he was, the least in the coming kingdom will be greater than John was before the coming of Christ.[16] The Lord used this statement to point out the

---

14. See also 13:42, 50; 22:13; 24:51; 25:30.
15. Even M'Neile asserts, "If the Jewish nation could be brought to repentance, the new age would dawn; see Ac.iii.19f., Jo.iv.22" (M'Neile, p. 134).
16. Ibid., p. 154.

greatness of the kingdom on earth. The contrast is between two periods of time: the one before the coming of the Messiah and the one after Christ establishes His kingdom. Once again the verb *estin* is used in a proleptic sense. Certainly the kingdom could not have been present then; otherwise John would have been in it.

The statement of 11:12 is as difficult and controversial as that in verse 11: "And from the days of John the Baptist until now the kingdom of heaven suffers violence, and violent men take it by force." Here the term *kingdom* is employed of the eschatological reign of Christ. Because of the time reference to John the Baptist, the word cannot refer to some spiritual reign in the hearts of men or the message of God's forgiveness. These have always been on earth. It must be an allusion to the proclamation of the nearness of the promised rule of the Messiah on earth (cf. 3:2; 4:17; 10:7). Therefore Christ was saying the kingdom is the object of violent force. But what is meant by the clause "violent men take it by force"? The verb "to snatch" (*harpazō*) was used of something seized violently or with power. So it was; the religious authorities of Israel snatched away the coming of the kingdom. Its meaning is well illustrated by the parable of the wicked husbandmen (Matt. 21:33-43) and in particular by Matthew 23:13, "But woe to you, scribes and Pharisees, hypocrites, because you shut off the kingdom of heaven from men; for you do not enter in yourselves, nor do you allow those who are entering to go in." Though Christ presented Himself as the Messiah, the leaders of Israel rejected Him and thus snatched the promised kingdom away from that generation.[17]

The climactic indication of Christ's rejection in this section (Matt. 11-13) is found in the Beelzebul accusation of Matthew 12:22-37. Here the Lord Jesus first refers to the kingdom of this earth (12:25), then Satan's kingdom (12:26), and finally to the kingdom of God (12:28). Verse 28 says, "But if I cast out demons by the Spirit of God, then the kingdom of God has come upon you." In the person of the Messiah God's kingdom had arrived (*phthanō*) among Israel. Its fulfillment was dependent on Israel's response to its Messiah. This interpretation explains the saying about binding the strong man in the following verse (12:28). In casting out demons Christ was beginning to bind Satan as Revelation 20:1-7 predicts will be true in the Millennium. The Lord Jesus was showing His power over Satan in preparation for the time He will imprison the adversary.

---

17. Hermann Cremer, *Biblico-Theological Lexicon of New Testament Greek* (Edinburgh: T. & T. Clark, 1895), p. 143. For a fuller discussion of the passage see Stanley D. Toussaint, *Behold the King* (Portland: Multnomah, 1980), pp. 150-53.

Chapters 11-12 of Matthew are narrative to prepare the reader for the parabolic sayings of chapter 13. That these parables are set in the context of rejection is evident from their stated purpose in 13:11-17. In particular, the parables were given to conceal the truth and to reveal truth regarding the kingdom of God and His Christ (see especially vv. 11-13).

The real problem in chapter 13, as far as this essay is concerned, is the meaning of *kingdom*. When the Lord refers to "mysteries of the kingdom" (v. 11), what concept is being conveyed? It is common among premillennial dispensationalists to say a *new form* of the kingdom is being introduced, namely, Christendom. Normally, dispensationalism has taught that because Israel was in the process of rejecting its Messiah, the Lord Jesus introduced a new form of the kingdom for the time until the Tribulation and the Millennium. Commonly this is referred to as the "mystery form of the kingdom," based on Matthew 13:11.

For the sake of consistency it would be far better to maintain the same meaning in this chapter as in the preceding portions of Matthew. Christ was not presenting a new form of the kingdom; instead, He was revealing new truths about the kingdom of God. There is no need to introduce a different meaning in Matthew 13 from what it meant in the preceding chapters. If the term "mystery" found in Matthew 13:11 refers to truths previously unrevealed—and that is the meaning—then Jesus is telling His disciples they are the recipients of new revelations concerning God's kingdom program.

If this consistent meaning of kingdom is maintained, the traditional interpretation of Matthew 13 held by dispensationalists may still be taught. The only difference would be that the kingdom would still be prophetic in its ultimate coming.

The outline of Matthew 13 revolves around an introductory "non-kingdom parable," six "kingdom parables," and a parabolic application.[18] The first parable, dealing with the soils (13:3-23), explains why Christ spoke in parables. It does not have the key clause "the kingdom of heaven may be compared to" or its equivalent, and it presents a concept that has always been true. People through all the ages have responded as these soils do. The last parable (13:52) likens the disciples to householders and forms a concluding application.

The six kingdom parables—three preached to the multitudes by the sea-

---

18. Stanley D. Toussaint, "The Introductory and Concluding Parables of Matthew Thirteen," *Bibliotheca Sacra* 121 (October-December 1964):351-55.

shore (13:1) and three given to the disciples in the house (13:36)—all have the key clause "the kingdom of heaven may be compared to" or some such equivalent (13:24, 31, 33, 44, 45, 47). This expression simply means there is some truth in the story that is tangential to the kingdom. It does not mean the kingdom is like a woman, or that the eschatological rule of Christ is like the story. Rather, there is some principle relating to the kingdom revealed in the story. This is well illustrated by Matthew 18:21-35. The parable of the unforgiving servant declares a principle of forgiveness that operates among heirs of the kingdom.

If this approach is followed, the parables of Matthew 13 may be interpreted as follows: The parable of the wheat and darnel (13:24-30, 36-43) shows there will be a period of time when good and evil coexist before the kingdom comes.[19] The parable of the mustard seed (13:31-32) illustrates the rapid spread of the message and the prosperous growth of the number of heirs of the kingdom. The leaven (13:33) may illustrate the truth that before the kingdom comes apostasy will corrupt the world. The fourth parable, dealing with the hidden treasure (13:44), perhaps presents the cost of purchasing the kingdom of Christ. The same basic truth may be affirmed in the parable of the precious pearl (13:45-46). Finally, the parable of the dragnet indicates the judgment warned about by John would be at the end of this age (13:47-50).

The new truths then revealed about the kingdom relate to this interadvent age preceding the coming of the kingdom.

THE MEANING OF THE TERM *KINGDOM* IN MATTHEW 14-18

An emphasis on instruction of the disciples especially emphasizing personal relationships is found in this section. The first occurrence of *kingdom* here is located in 16:19, the famous passage dealing with the keys of the kingdom promised to Peter. Most Protestants believe these keys were used by Peter in opening the gospel to Jews (Acts 2, 3), Samaritans (Acts 8:14-24), and Gentiles (Acts 10-11). Of course this is true, but is this what Peter is promised in Matthew 16:19?

There are several problems with this view. First, "binding" and "loosing" are terms used of what was not permitted and what was permitted.[20] This is common usage in rabbinic literature. Furthermore, "whatsoever"

19. Peters, *Theocratic Kingdom*, 2:421.
20. Alfred Plummer, *An Exegetical Commentary on the Gospel According to St. Matthew* (Grand Rapids: Eerdmans, 1953), p. 231.

(*ho ean*) is neuter. It hardly refers to people. Third, a consistent meaning of "kingdom" would indicate that the Lord Jesus is promising Peter authority to rule in the coming Millennium, a promise expanded to the twelve in Matthew 19:28. Allen said it well when he wrote:

> We must . . . be careful not to identify the *ekklusia* [church] with the kingdom. There is nothing here to suggest such identification. The Church was to be built on the rock of the revealed truth that Jesus was the Messiah, the Divine Son. To S. Peter were to be given the keys of the kingdom. The kingdom is here, as elsewhere in this gospel, the kingdom to be inaugurated when the Son of Man came upon the clouds of heaven . . . . The *ekklusia*, on the other hand, was the society of Christ's disciples, who were to wait for it, and who would enter into it when it came. The Church was built upon the truth of the divine Sonship. It was to proclaim the coming kingdom. In that kingdom Peter should hold the keys that conferred authority.[21]

In 16:28 the Lord promises His disciples, "Truly I say to you, there are some of those who are standing here who shall not taste death until they see the Son of Man coming in His kingdom." That this relates to the transfiguration that follows immediately in Matthew 17:1-13 is confirmed by several factors. First, Peter, one of the three who witnessed the transfiguration, interpreted it in this fashion in 2 Peter 1:16-18. Second, all three synoptics (John omits the transfiguration) place the transfiguration immediately after this prediction. There is an obvious connection between the prediction and the transfiguration. Third, only some of the apostles saw the transfiguration. Fourth, the transfiguration was proleptic of the kingdom age. Matthew 18 has four occurrences of the expression *the kingdom of heaven*. In verses 1-4 the three times the term is found look to the coming kingdom. When Christ is asked who the greatest in the kingdom will be (*estin* is again proleptic),[22] He turns the topic first to entrance into that kingdom and then to greatness by reason of humility. Of course, the implication also given in the parables of Matthew 13 is obvious: the church is an heir of the kingdom and will enter it.

The final use of *kingdom* in chapter 18 is found in verse 23 in the introduction to the parable of the forgiving king and the unforgiving slave. A spiritual principle relating to lives of those who desire entrance into the

21. Allen, p. 177.
22. Montefiore, 2:247.

kingdom is given.[23] Those who have been forgiven much should forgive their brothers a little.

In this section the narrative of chapters 19-23 prepares the reader for the discourse of Matthew 24-25. The narrative portion is filled with the concept of the rejection in anticipation of the prophetic instruction of the disciples in the Olivet Discourse. After the famous statement about marriage and divorce, the Lord affirms, "For there are eunuchs who were born that way from their mother's womb; and there are eunuchs who were made eunuchs by men; and there are also eunuchs who made themselves eunuchs for the sake of the kingdom of heaven" (19:12). There is nothing in the immediate context to help determine the meaning of "kingdom." Consistency with the meaning elsewhere in Matthew would lead one to the conclusion it refers to the coming kingdom. For the sake of the kingdom work it is good not to marry if one has the spiritual capacity for this (cf. 1 Cor.7:7, 9, 32-35).

In 19:14 the Lord once again (cf. 18:3) refers to the necessity of becoming like children in order to enter the future kingdom of heaven. The concept of entrance into the kingdom is continued in 19:23-24, where the Lord states that it is impossible for a rich man (a person who would be considered particularly blessed of God by the Jewish hierarchy) to enter the future millennial reign of Christ. With men salvation is impossible, but with God all things are possible.

The topic of rewards in the coming kingdom is in view in Matthew 19:30-20:16. Because God is sovereign and gracious He is free to give rewards equally to Jew and Gentile in the coming kingdom (cf. 1 Cor. 6:2; Rev. 2:26). Matthew 20:21, dealing with being seated at Christ's right and left hands, is particularly significant because it so clearly portrays the idea of an eschatological and earthly kingdom. Certainly the kingdom that is anticipated is the prophesied kingdom promised in the Old Testament. It should be noted especially that the Lord Jesus said nothing to correct the Jewish notion of a literal kingdom.

In Matthew 21:31 entrance into the kingdom is granted to sinners who humbly repent and obey: The verb *proagousin* (translated "will get into") is present tense but again is prophetic. It anticipates the coming of the kingdom to this earth.

23. Allen, p. 201.

The occurrence in Matthew 21:43 is especially instructive. It concludes the parable of the wicked husbandmen where the vineyard is removed from the irresponsible and violent vinegrowers and given to faithful ones. So the kingdom was taken from Israel and the blessings of that kingdom given to Gentiles. Quite obviously this anticipates the blessings of the future kingdom.[24] It teaches the same doctrine as is set forth in Romans 11:11-27 and Ephesians 2:11-22.

The same truth found in Matthew 21 is reaffirmed in 22:1-10 in the parable of the marriage feast. Those who were brought in from the streets illustrate the Gentiles, who had not originally been invited to the feast. Once again a banquet, here a wedding banquet, portrays the millennial blessings promised to Israel.

In Matthew 23:13 the Lord rebukes the scribes and Pharisees because not only do they not enter the kingdom, but they shut out those who would enter. The two occurrences of the present tense of "enter" are a bit of a problem. They indicate it is possible to enter the kingdom *now*. That is probably looking at their position as heirs of the kingdom. Positionally those who enter the kingdom stand among those who will be a part of the kingdom on earth. In this aspect the truth would be similar to Colossians 1:12-13 and Revelation 1:5; 5:10.

The Lord's rejection of Israel described in Matthew 19-23 is followed by His well-known and difficult Olivet Discourse (Matt. 24-25). The first use of kingdom is found in 24:7, where the Lord Jesus predicts "kingdom" would rise "against kingdom," an obvious reference to earthly kingdoms.

A more pertinent reference is Matthew 24:14, "And this gospel of the kingdom shall be preached in the whole world." What is this "gospel of the kingdom?" It must be the same good news as was described in 3:2; 4:17, 23; and 9:35. Entrance into the coming kingdom was based on repentance; that was and is the gospel of the kingdom. In the context, however, it would also portray the nearness of the kingdom during the Tribulation period.[25]

In the early verses of Matthew 25 Christ compares the kingdom of heaven to ten virgins waiting for a wedding procession so they might enter the marriage feast. Once again the kingdom of the future is likened to a wedding celebration.

The final reference in the Olivet Discourse is in Matthew 25:34, in the

24. McClain, p. 439.
25. M'Neile, p. 347.

climactic judgment scene preceding the establishment of God's kingdom on earth. God's goal for man was for him to establish a utopian society on earth. This will only be accomplished by Christ's millennial reign. The saved who will be physically alive when Christ returns will enter into it along with the resurrected redeemed.

THE MEANING OF THE TERM *KINGDOM* IN MATTHEW 26-28

The conclusion of this great gospel is given in the last three chapters, and in this section there is a singular occurrence of the word *kingdom:* "But I say to you, I will not drink of this fruit of the vine from now on until that day when I drink it new with you in My Father's kingdom" (Matt. 26:29). At the institution of the Communion the Lord Jesus anticipated the day when God's kingdom would come to this earth.[26]

CONCLUSION

In a genuine sense the gospel of Matthew is the kingdom gospel. It, with the gospel of Luke, presents the concept of the gospel going to Gentiles because of Israel's rejection of Jesus as its Messiah. In the many occurrences of the term *kingdom* in Matthew it was seen that in most cases the word clearly anticipated the coming of an earthly Millennium and in the remaining instances the noun permitted this idea. It is to be hoped that dispensationalists will consider with greater seriousness this idea of a consistent meaning of *kingdom* in the gospel of Matthew.

26. Allen, p. 2.

JOHN A. MARTIN (A.B., Wheaton College; Th.M., Th.D., Dallas Theological Seminary) is assistant academic dean and assistant professor of Bible exposition at Dallas Theological Seminary.

Dispensational Approaches to the Sermon on the Mount

John A. Martin

INTRODUCTION

One area of great interest to Dr. Dwight Pentecost is the life of Christ. His work on that subject has influenced a whole generation of dispensational interpreters of the gospels. His quest for accuracy has encouraged many to approach the text carefully in the interpretive process. This article is lovingly dedicated to Dr. Pentecost with deep appreciation for his devotion to the Word of God.

A perception has grown up that there is *one* dispensational approach to the interpretation of the Sermon on the Mount. For example, D. A. Carson's very helpful book on the Sermon criticizes *the* dispensational construction,[1] and Warren S. Kissinger's classic bibliography assumes that there is only one dispensational approach.[2] In reality there is no single dispensational approach to the Sermon on the Mount. Those who have this false perception must not be blamed, however, because very little has been written by dispensationalists on this important subject. The purpose of this article is to articulate a number of current dispensational interpretations

---

1. D. A. Carson, *The Sermon on the Mount; An Evangelical Exposition of Matthew 5-7* (Grand Rapids: Baker, 1978). Carson treats the dispensational approach on pages 155-57. Of dispensationalism he states: "Moreover, this theological construction is so all-embracing that it is extremely difficult for a member of this school of thought to accept a different interpretation of any particular passage without endangering the entire system" (p. 155). It is that very misconception that this article seeks, in part, to address.
2. Warren S. Kissinger, *The Sermon on the Mount: A History of Interpretation and Bibliography* (Metuchen, N.J.: Scarecrow, 1975). Dispensationalism is treated on pages 61-66.

of the Sermon on the Mount. It is hoped such a survey will stimulate further discussion and debate on this section of Scripture.

In the Sermon on the Mount there are a number of statements extremely difficult to apply if taken literally.[3] Some have thought the Sermon contradicts other parts of Scripture. That raises the question about how the Sermon is to be interpreted, that is, what hermeneutic is to be used to understand it?

Dispensationalists have maintained that Scripture is to be interpreted in a literal, grammatical, historical, rhetorical way. When the Sermon is examined in the context of Matthew it is found that it appears in the early part of the book in which John the Baptist and Jesus were preaching the message "Repent, for the kingdom of heaven is at hand."[4] Matthew placed the Sermon prior to the religious leaders' rejection of Jesus (chaps. 11 and 12) and prior to Jesus' rejection of them, which is immediately followed by His revelation of an interim period preceding the anticipated Old Testament kingdom (chap. 13). This has driven some dispensationalists to affirm that the Sermon on the Mount refers to the kingdom age exclusively and that it has only "secondary application" to the church.

Dispensationalists have not been alone in their quandary over the Sermon on the Mount. There have been many proposals from many theological perspectives on how to interpret it.[5] Problems of consistency are not relegated to dispensationalists in an understanding of the Sermon. Any open-minded interpreter of these chapters must admit that a consistent approach, although desirable, is difficult to achieve.

This article will proceed by examining the setting of the Sermon followed by an introduction to four major dispensational approaches to its interpretation. The approaches are not new, for it is not the purpose of this article to break new ground in the interpretation of specifics in the Sermon. The purpose is to elucidate what dispensationalists are currently saying about the Sermon on the Mount and to evaluate the strengths and weaknesses of each approach.

3. Note especially 5:38-42, which over the centuries has probably been the major passage of controversy in the Sermon. Also difficult are 5:29-30, 34, 44; 6:3, 6, 14-15, 34.
4. John the Baptist preached the message in Matthew 3:2, Jesus in 4:17, and the disciples in 10:7. Most modern dispensationalists *see the kingdom of heaven* and *the kingdom of God* as synonymous terms.
5. Kissinger, *Sermon on the Mount*, pp. 1-125, lists thirty-three schools of interpretation. Also helpful in classifying interpretations are Harvey K. McArthur, *Understanding the Sermon on the Mount* (New York: Harper, 1960) and Archibald Hunter, *A Pattern for Life: An Exposition of the Sermon on the Mount* (Philadelphia: Westminster, 1953).

THE SETTING

As stated above, the setting of the Sermon on the Mount is in the context of the offer/announcement of the kingdom.[6] John, the forerunner, had been preaching the message of the kingdom.[7] Jesus, the announced king, had been preaching the same message[8] and performing messianic signs that authenticated His message.[9] Crowds were beginning to come to Jesus in anticipation of the beginning of the kingdom age.[10] A literary understanding of Matthew reveals the purpose for which the book of Matthew was written. In chapters 1-10 Matthew is revealing who Jesus claimed to be and what His purpose was in coming to earth. In chapters 11-13 Jesus is rejected by the religious establishment of the day and therefore postpones the inauguration of the kingdom age because of the unbelief of the covenant people.[11] It is in the early stage of the announcement of the kingdom that Matthew placed the Sermon on the Mount.[12] It was a time, humanly speaking, when Jesus, John, and their disciples could have expected the

6. Although most dispensationalists speak of the "offer of the kingdom" in Matthew's gospel, there are a number who do not like the term *offer*. They prefer to say that Christ presented Himself to the nation of Israel for salvation. The kingdom as presented in the Old Testament comes by divine intervention, not because of Israel's response; God sovereignly foreknew and planned the church age. Therefore, it is more accurate to say that Jesus offered *Himself* and announced that the kingdom will come through His power. To my knowledge there is nothing published to date clearly explaining the details of this view, but it seems to be a growing alternative to the common "offer of the kingdom" position.

7. The first mention of John's message is in Matthew 3:2. John was clearly the Elijah figure of whom Malachi spoke in Malachi 3:1 and 4:5-6 (cf. 3:23-24 in Hebrew text). John was preaching the same message of repentance that the prophets of old were commissioned to preach. The eschatological kingdom was not just a message of hope; it was a message designed to change the lives of the people who were listening to the prophet and waiting for the coming kingdom.

8. Matthew 4:17 is a turning point in the gospel, for it is at this point that Jesus began His ministry, that is, He began to tell people about the kingdom program. Jesus and John preached the same message of repentance. In the Old Testament repentance was the natural outgrowth of a realization of God's message communicated to the nation.

9. The text of Matthew does not delineate the miracles of Jesus to a large extent before the Sermon on the Mount, simply noting that He healed every sort of disease while He was preaching the gospel of the kingdom (Matt. 4:23). These messianic miracles later became a key in Jesus' self revelation. All of the gospels point this out, but it is clearly the focus of the gospel of John with the seven signs.

10. Why these crowds were following is not made clear in Matthew. There must have been many who truly believed that He was the Messiah. But there were many others who wanted to be fed and healed but who did not accept Him as the Messiah.

11. No matter what position is taken on the offer/announcement of the kingdom (see no. 6 above) almost all would say that the "postponement" was in the sovereign plan of God. Matthew's gospel was written in a manner designed to develop the theology of rejection. The discourse sections are a major key in interpreting the book. See H. J. Bernard Combrink, "The Structure of the Gospel of Matthew as Narrative," *Tyndale Bulletin* 34 (1983):61-90.

12. Matthew placed the Sermon in a very early position in the ministry of Jesus. Luke seems to place it later. Matthew's order clearly points out the difference between those who follow Jesus and those who do not. As the first major discourse in Matthew the Sermon carries special significance.

nation of Israel to follow Jesus as their Messiah. Placed in this setting the
Sermon can be seen to refer to the time preceding the kingdom rather
than in the kingdom period itself. That is, Jesus was giving an ethic in light
of the fact that the kingdom was going to be established but was not yet
present.

PROPOSED SOLUTIONS

At least four major interpretations of Jesus' famous sermon are present
in the evangelical dispensational community.[13] The interpretations are
mutually exclusive. It is interesting, however, that although the method of
interpretation varies widely, when it comes to specific application from the
text there is often little difference. Each of the interpretations will be examined and critiqued.

THE KINGDOM APPROACH

Many older dispensationalists have taken this approach.[14] It is the view
normally thought of by nondispensationalists when a *dispensational* interpretation is considered.[15] Lewis Sperry Chafer espoused the view in his *Systematic Theology* as did C. I. Scofield in his *Reference Bible.*[16]

The view. The approach stems from the desire to maintain a distinction
between Israel and the church.[17] For this interpretation the law/grace distinction is also extremely important. As the argument goes, the Old Testament prophets anticipated the long-promised kingdom to be ushered in by
the power of God. John the Baptist, the greatest of the prophets, was expecting the same thing. And the disciples even after the resurrection—not
yet fully comprehending the dispensational change—still expected the

13. John MacArthur, *Understanding the Sermon on the Mount,* identifies twelve types of interpreta-
    tions in the history of interpretation of the Sermon on the Mount. I know of no written source for
    dispensational interpretations. The four selected in the remainder of the article have been distilled
    from interaction on the subject over the last seven years.
14. The term, not a reflection on the age of any interpreter, is my own. Perhaps it should be called
    "historic dispensationalism," but I shy away from that term because it makes all other interpreta-
    tions seem like an abandonment of dispensationalism itself. Such is not the case.
15. Note especially Carson and Kissinger. It is somewhat surprising that Kissinger devotes so much
    space in his bibliography to a dispensationalist interpretation. This may be because the method of
    interpretation is not widely known in scholarly circles.
16. L. S. Chafer, *Systematic Theology,* 8 vols. (Dallas: Seminary Press, 1948), 4:207-25; 5:97-114.
17. This distinction is fundamental to dispensationalism, and it is a good one to maintain. However,
    one must be careful to remember that Matthew's gospel was written in the church age, even
    though the narrative material happened in the prechurch age. Making too large a distinction in
    Matthew's gospel can easily lead to hyperdispensationalism.

kingdom to come soon (Acts 1:6), confirming the pattern of their original belief. Moreover, the Sermon on the Mount is found in the gospel of Matthew in the section in which Jesus was offering/announcing the anticipated kingdom/king to Israel.[18] When Jesus preached the Sermon He was still operating in the dispensation of the law. Therefore He required His listeners to respond to the legal commands that had been promulgated throughout the Old Testament. Later, when the Messiah was rejected by the nation of Israel, those legal demands were done away as God began to deal with people in a new way in the dispensation of the church. But in the Sermon the church was not yet in view because the offer of the kingdom was a true offer. Therefore in it Jesus must have been thinking in terms of the Jewish kingdom (i.e., the Millennium) rather than the church age. This would explain why Jesus gave such demanding commands, which, of course, could never be fulfilled either in the Jewish context or in the church age, but only in the millennial kingdom.

A critique. Historically *the kingdom approach* has been widely held by dispensationalists. It is based on three main foundations: (a) a theological presupposition that the law/grace distinction was sharp in Matthew's theology, (b) a supposition that Jesus (quoted by Matthew) used the term *law* in the same sense that Paul uses the term in Romans and Galatians, and (c) the place of the Sermon on the Mount in the chronotheological development of Matthew.[19]

Matthew's law/grace distinction. One implicit assumption of this position is that Jesus was speaking in terms of the old dispensation of the law, which was superseded by the dispensation of grace. Therefore the ethic that was presented in the Sermon was "merely" an Old Testament ethic, which is not applicable to the church today. Chafer is very strong on this point, noting that the Sermon presents "the hopeless, blasting character of the law which this discourse announces and from which the Christian has been saved (Rom. 6:14; Gal. 5:1)."[20] He also observed that there are "three complete and wholly independent rules for human conduct," the one for

---

18. See above, note 6.
19. The term is my own. By *chronotheological* I mean the relationship to one another of the narrative events as presented by the author in order to make a theological point. Most interpreters of the gospels understand that the gospel writers arranged narrative and didactic material for theological reasons. A study of the synoptics shows chronological schematization for the same reason. Matthew apparently stylized his gospel more than Mark or Luke because of his theological understanding of the kingdom program. For instance, in Matthew the Sermon on the Mount follows Jesus' baptism, the wilderness experience, and His early ministry as a touchstone for defining who had and who had not followed Him.
20. Chafer, *Systematic Theology,* 5:97.

this age being found "in the Gospel of John, the Acts, and the Epistles of the New Testament."[21]

There are some serious problems with this view. They can be summarized under three categories.

1. There is a curious absence of thought about both the time of composition of the gospel of Matthew and the original readers of the book. Everyone would grant that the action of the narrative took place before the church age began. But the time of writing undoubtedly was sometime in the A. D. fifties or sixties, a generation after the events of the narrative. That is, Matthew belonged to the dispensation of the church, ministered and worked in a church, and wrote to church age people.

Inasmuch as the gospel of Matthew revolves around the five great discourses of Jesus,[22] it is very significant that the final words of Jesus focus on the command "teaching them to do all that I have commanded you." For the original readers of the text "all that I have commanded you" would have been none other than the five great discourse sections that are the highlights of that gospel. It could be argued that the second of those discourses (chap. 10—the sending out of the twelve) applies to contemporary disciples but not to future ones. But even if that premise were granted, the prohibition against going to the Gentiles and the Samaritans is explicitly counteracted in chapter 28 with the command to go to "all nations." There is never a recanting of ethical norms in the book of Matthew. It would appear then that Matthew was leading the original readers to understand that Jesus' ethical commands to His immediate followers were also requirements for prospective disciples not only in Matthew's day but on into the future.

2. The Sermon on the Mount clearly anticipates the coming of the kingdom. There is not the slightest hint that it is an ethic for the kingdom *only*. On the contrary, it looks forward to a time when people will enter the kingdom (5:20; 7:21) and speaks of future rewards (5:12, 19, 46; 6:1, 2, 4, 5, 6, 18). It teaches the disciples to pray for the coming of the kingdom (6:10) and sustenance and strength until it comes. It recognizes a time of judgment before the establishment of the kingdom (7:19-23) and, prior to that, a time of persecution and false prophets (5:11-12; 7:15-18). If the Ser-

21. Ibid., 5:98.
22. The importance of the discourses in understanding Matthew's gospel cannot be overestimated. Combrink (see n. 11) has pointed out the chiastic arrangement of the five discourses, with the emphasis being on the middle one, that is, discourse three in chapter 13. That discourse has long been held by dispensationalists as a key in understanding the structure of Matthew. Combrink comes to that view on literary and not theological grounds.

mon was anticipating the coming kingdom in these ways, then it is hard to explain it as an ethic to be put into effect only after the kingdom arrives. Clearly it was to be lived in some fashion as the life-style of the disciples prior to that.

3. The insistence that this type of life-style is impossible to maintain in the present church age and that Jesus therefore must have meant it for the future kingdom is a very weak argument for several reasons. First, even if it could be granted that Matthew is "Old Testament" literature, such an argument does not exempt the church from obeying its teaching. All are sinners, and no one is perfect, but the Old Testament does not excuse anyone for sin. Nor does it hint that because a command is difficult it is not applicable for that reason. The prophets implied just the opposite. They demanded that the Old Testament people live according to the law no matter how difficult it was. Recognizing there would be failures, they demanded obedience to the revealed Word of God nonetheless. Second, there are many other commands in the New Testament that are impossible to fulfill completely (cf. 1 Pet. 1:15; 1 John 2:1; Col. 3:13; Phil. 3:12, to name just a few). However, the New Testament authors expect their readers to seek to comply with the righteous demands of God. Just so, in the Sermon on the Mount Christ was setting forth standards that might indeed be unattainable but are still to be the mark of a believer and, further, to be attempted by disciples in dependence on God. Third, the argument is weak because it is used selectively in the Sermon. The main source of ethical contention in the Sermon is found in 5:38-42—Jesus' teaching about retaliation. It is here that most kingdom interpreters note the impossibility of its demands and opt for a fulfillment during the Millennium.[23] However, no such plea is made in relation to the sections on murder/hatred and adultery/lust. Yet all of these ethical considerations are found in the same section of the Sermon (5:17-45, which deals with a proper understanding of the law). If the retaliation section is set aside because of the difficulty in living up to it in the present age, then the hatred and lusting sections should also be set aside for the same reason. The selectivity of the argument shows its weakness.

In conclusion, it is not as easy to make a law/grace distinction in the

---

23. The idea is that in the millennial kingdom righteous living will be esteemed and the King of Righteousness will be ruling. Therefore a person who stands up for righteousness will be taken care of by governmental authorities. How different this is from the picture presented in the Sermon that such righteous activity should be carried out even though persecution will come as a result (5:10-12).

gospel of Matthew as some of the kingdom interpreters would maintain. Chafer's statement about the "blasting character of the Law" misrepresents the function of the law, which was given for the sanctification of a redeemed people.[24] Commands of God have been given in various dispensations—not to blast people but to guide them in proper behavior. God's ethical norms do not change, though the forms they take sometimes do. Matthew appears to be quoting Jesus in an attempt to impress on his readers the importance of living a righteous life in the present age while waiting for the promised kingdom.

The law in Matthew's Sermon account. One of the major misconceptions of *the kingdom approach* is the idea that *law* is a technical term in the Sermon referring to the Mosaic legal code. And since, as Paul so ably noted in several places in the New Testament, the believer is no longer under the law, logically the New Testament believer is not commanded to live according to the Sermon on the Mount.[25] Unfortunately for the view *law* has a wider meaning than simply the legal code. The Hebrew Bible was made up of three sections: The Law, (i.e., the Pentateuch), the Prophets (the former—Joshua, Judges, Samuel, Kings; the latter—Isaiah, Jeremiah, Ezekiel, and the twelve), and the Writings (the rest of the Old Testament). Fundamental to the whole Old Testament was the Mosaic covenant. This covenant was seen by the prophets as being made up not of religious formalism but of true inner worship.[26] Sometimes the Old Testament was called "the Law, the Prophets, and the Writings," sometimes it was called "the Law and the Prophets," and sometimes it was merely called "the Law." In the Sermon on the Mount *law* is clearly "the Law and the Prophets." The expression occurs on two occasions (5:17; 7:12) and forms an *inclusio* for Jesus' teaching on ethics. To fulfill the demands of the Old Testa-

---

24. This is one of the areas in which Dr. Pentecost has been very influential over the last generation at Dallas Theological Seminary. He has constantly stressed that the law was designed to sanctify a people previously redeemed from slavery in Egypt. It was designed to get them to realize how to have fellowship with a holy God.

25. One area of discussion in which many dispensationalists are currently engaged is the relationship between the Testaments. This is true not only on the textual and theological levels but also on the application level. There is a great need for further work in the area of application from all genres of literature in the Old Testament. Very few would be as dogmatic about the lack of applicability from the Old Testament as was Chafer.

26. One example is found in Isaiah 1, which is an indictment of the nation for its lack of faithfulness to the covenant. It was not the formalism of the sacrifices, offerings, festivals, and prayers that God desired (Isa. 1:10-15); it was righteous and holy deeds that were needed (Isa. 1:16-17). This message is reiterated throughout the prophets. Likewise John, the greatest of the prophets, and Jesus preached the same message—not religious formalism, but a righteous and holy life-style based on the revealed word of God.

ment (which Jesus noted that He was doing) would mean to live in the way He was teaching (7:24-27). To say that the Sermon on the Mount is not applicable for Matthew's readers would be to say that the whole Old Testament is not applicable for Matthew's readers.

The place of the Sermon in Matthew's gospel. The fact that the Sermon appears in the first half of the gospel leads some kingdom interpreters to dismiss it as if it only applied to Jews in Jesus' day. Such argumentation will not hold up for several reasons. First, as was pointed out above, Matthew noted his purpose was to fulfill Jesus' command to teach the world "all that I have commanded you" (28:20). Nowhere in the gospel does Jesus negate any of the ethical commands given in the Sermon. Second, the Sermon recorded in Luke 6 (generally considered to be a further condensation of the same message) is not tied to the same chronotheological development. Luke apparently expected his readers (Theophilus and other Gentiles) to accept and practice the things spoken by Jesus. Similar difficult ethical demands were recorded by Luke. Third, the Sermon was of great influence on later New Testament thought. Paul, James, and Peter all reflect teachings from the Sermon on the Mount.[27]

THE PENITENTIAL APPROACH

The view. A second common interpretation of the Sermon on the Mount is *the penitential, or repentance, view.*[28] Those who take this view see the purpose of the Sermon as being designed to bring people to a place where they will realize that they need to depend on Jesus alone for their salvation. This view draws heavily on Matthew 5:17-20 in which Jesus noted that He had not come "to abolish the Law or the Prophets" but "to fulfill" them. If Jesus was speaking in a legal setting, the effect of the Sermon would be the same as the effect of the law—no one can be justified by the law and therefore there has to be some other means of salvation. People of faith in the Old Testament realized that they needed to depend on the mercy of God for their salvation.[29] This view also stresses that Jesus told His audience that they had to surpass the scribes and Pharisees in their righteousness (5:20). Since the scribes and the Pharisees were the "most righteous" peo-

---

27. Some examples are James 1:22-27; 2:8, 12-13; 5:12; 1 Peter 2:12; 4:14.
28. This is mentioned but not spelled out completely by Dr. Pentecost in *Design for Living: The Sermon on the Mount* (Chicago: Moody, 1975). It has also been referred to as *the Lutheran view.*
29. This is clear not only from the book of Hebrews but also from the fact that the Day of Atonement was necessary. It is reflected in a number of great prayers in the Old Testament, including Isaiah's (Is. 6), Ezra's (Ezra 9), and the Levites' in Nehemiah's day (Neh. 9).

ple of their day (outwardly), the effect would be to force the hearers into a position to realize that they could not save themselves and therefore that they could only trust in Jesus for their eventual entry into the kingdom. Coupled with the difficult demands that follow in the Sermon, the comparison should be enough to bring anyone who is spiritually sensitive to a realization that it would take a power outside of himself to make him right with God. This position is related to *the kingdom view* in seeing the Sermon on the Mount as being "Old Testament law." As the law showed that no one could live up to the righteous demands of a holy God, so the Sermon on the Mount showed the same thing in Jesus' day.[30]

A critique. One problem inherent in this view, the law/grace distinction, has already been dealt with in the critique of *the kingdom approach.* A further problem with the position is that Matthew's gospel does not picture the scribes and the Pharisees as being the most righteous people of their day. Just the opposite, the Pharisees were pictured as being hypocritical in their religiosity. It is doubtful that Jesus was the only one who noticed that the outward religion of the Pharisees did not match the inward attitude of their hearts (Matt. 23). Indeed, John the Baptist apparently noticed the same thing (Matt. 3:7-12), instructing the religious classes to change their behavior to conform to their creed. John was merely echoing the denunciation of the prophets.

Another problem is that Jesus did not identify His coming simply with the Mosaic law but with the whole Old Testament ("the Law and the Prophets"). His coming fulfilled the Old Testament. Jesus' teaching echoed what the prophets before Him had demanded of the Israelites—that they dedicate themselves to live according to the covenant. Further, the Old Testament proclamation had not clearly revealed what Jesus' ultimate purpose would be in coming to earth. That purpose—His death and resurrection—would not be entirely manifest until after the confession by His disciples.[31]

---

30. Many have noted Matthew's arrangement of the material in chapters 1-4. Jesus' experience paralleled the experience of the nation of Israel in conception, birth, experience in Egypt, deliverance, and time in the wilderness. It is possible that Jesus' giving of the "Law" on the mountain parallels the experience of Israel in receiving the law from God through Moses on Mt. Sinai.
31. Matthew 16:13-28; Mark 8:27-38; and Luke 9:18-27.

THE INTERIM ETHIC APPROACH

The view. *The interim ethic view* was proposed by Albert Schweitzer.[32] Schweitzer understood the kingdom to be completely eschatological. It was to be brought about by the catastrophic irruption of God into history, bringing the day of judgment and an end to the world as it is known. In this respect Schweitzer understood the gospel of Matthew in much the same way as a modern dispensationalist. Because Jesus' preaching was concerned with the kingdom, his ethic was an ethic for the interim period until the arrival of the kingdom. Just as special laws go into effect during a time of war, so Jesus taught that a new, strict ethic was necessary for the interim period of time until the kingdom would come. The disciples were to be the soldiers during the time of waiting for the kingdom. They were to conduct themselves in a special way during this time. They would have to be more strict with themselves than the people of the Old Testament times. This is why Jesus made the ethical demands of the Old Testament "more difficult."

For Schweitzer, because the kingdom did not come at the time of Jesus there is little applicability of the Sermon to Christians of the twentieth century. But Schweitzer's interim idea has been seen as an attractive alternative to the *kingdom* and *penitential* views by some dispensationalists. At first sight this interpretation seems to be of help to the dispensationalist who rejects the idea that the ethic is for the kingdom age only, that it is only an "Old Testament" ethic, or that it was designed to bring people to faith in Jesus. *The interim ethic approach* makes a break between the Old Testament law and this new "Law" that Jesus was laying down for the interim period. It frees one from the constricting interpretation that the Sermon was intended for the kingdom period and therefore is not applicable to the church age. It also acknowledges that the Sermon is addressed not primarily to nonbelievers who need to come to faith but to believers who need to be encouraged to live holy lives because of their faith.

A critique. Unfortunately for the view there are two main difficulties that arise when the interim ethic is held up to close scrutiny.

1. When does the interim period end? Seemingly it would have its beginning either at the time Jesus offered the kingdom or at the time He spoke the Sermon. But does the interim period end when Jesus is rejected by the religious leaders? Or does it end when the kingdom arrives? If it

---

32. Albert Schweitzer, *The Mystery of the Kingdom of God,* trans. Walter Lowrie (New York: Dodd and Mead, 1914).

ends at the rejection of Jesus, then one is forced to the position that the ethic has no bearing on the church except in a "secondary way" (like *the kingdom view*). One is also forced to conclude that the ethic was only in effect for about three years. If, however, one takes the second position, that the interim period ends when the kingdom arrives, then the church would be directly under the teaching of the Sermon on the Mount.[33]

2. Why would Jesus "change the Law?" This is a more difficult question. It not only asks *when* the interim ethic began but *why*. For if Jesus was giving a "new ethic," it appears that He was changing the law rather than affirming it as He says (Matt. 5:17-20). But if Jesus was affirming the law, He could not be giving an interim ethic. That is, if Jesus was giving a "true understanding of the Law," then it could not be termed an interim ethic, for His ethic would really be the same ethic as that of the Old Testament.

As pointed out above, *law* has been much misunderstood in this passage. The term is parallel to "the Prophets" and should be taken with it to be an abbreviation for the whole Old Testament. Matthew has given an abundance of hints enabling his readers to understand that Jesus was explaining the true significance of the law (which a person of faith in the Old Testament would have clearly understood[34]). Therefore, Jesus was not making the law more strict. He was affirming and explaining what the Old Testament already taught—righteousness is internal as well as external.

THE BELIEVER'S ETHIC

The view. The believer's ethic approach is so named because it takes the Sermon as applicable to believers of any age (dispensation) in God's dealings with mankind. It is dispensational because it recognizes the progressive nature of Scripture. The view is widely held by nondispensational evangelical interpreters.[35]

Jesus affirmed that He was within the bounds of the Law and the Prophets (Matt. 5:17-20). He was not giving a new, more radical ethic but rather

---

33. Stanley Toussaint, *Behold the King* (Portland: Multnomah, 1980), also calls his view of the Sermon the interim ethic. However, he does not state clearly when the interim period ends. It appears from what he says elsewhere that his view of the interim ethic is really more like *the believer's ethic* mentioned as the next view.
34. The general tone of the Sermon is set by Jesus' posture. Sitting down to instruct disciples was the normal posture of a rabbi. He also constantly drew from the Old Testament throughout the discourse.
35. This is the view taken by D. A. Carson and many others.

the *true interpretation* of the Old Testament ethic.[36] It is significant that Matthew did not record Jesus' words on ceremonial or dietary laws in his record of the Sermon. He used laws of basic morality, which transcend the Mosaic covenant and are applicable to all men of all time. This ethic, therefore, applies to all ages. Because it fulfills the Law and the Prophets, it will endure into the kingdom age.

It has been seen that *the kingdom approach* sees only a "secondary" application of the Sermon on the Mount for the church today. Some who take *the interim approach* would also say that the Sermon has only secondary application for today. *The believer's ethic approach* affirms that the Sermon is applicable to the church age. It is recognized, of course, that applicable does not mean that a person should cut off his hand or pluck out his eye. Hermeneutical considerations are still necessary to interpret various aspects of the Sermon.

A critique. Several points of evidence will be introduced to support the idea of the Sermon's applicability for today.

1. The book of Matthew is divided into sections with a discourse closing out each major section. The discourses have long been seen as Matthew's main purpose in writing the book. As the gospel draws to a close the resurrected Jesus appears, speaking to His disciples and telling them what to do with their lives. In Matthew 28:20 the disciples are instructed to teach new converts to observe all that He had commanded them. Given Matthew's theology, what teachings could Jesus have been referring to other than the discourse sections that highlight the book?

2. When Jesus delivered the Sermon He was still in the time frame of the law, that is, the kingdom was being offered, but the people were still under the law. However, Matthew recorded the Sermon during the age of the church. Matthew was a churchman presumably firmly entrenched in a local church. Therefore his gospel was written not only as an evangelistic tool but also as a teaching tool for church people.

3. Whereas it is true that in the present day some of the situations of the law no longer exist (for instance, Matt. 5:23-24 and the offering at the altar is no longer practiced), yet the change of culture and even dispensation in

---

36. For example, Jesus noted that the "pure in heart will see God," reflecting the psalmist's understanding of the law in Psalm 24:3: "Who may ascend into the hill of the Lord? And who may stand in His holy place? He who has clean hands and a pure heart, who has not lifted up his soul to falsehood, and has not sworn deceitfully." Keeping the righteous demands of the law showed that one was ceremonially clean to stand before the Lord. It was not the acts of religiosity that purified a person; it was attitude and action under the covenant.

no way invalidates the principles that Jesus taught and Matthew recorded during the church age. It would have been nonsense for Jesus to address the Sermon to the church, for it did not exist at this stage in the development of God's plan recorded in Matthew.

4. A major objection to the view that the Sermon is applicable today is that it is impossible to live the way Jesus instructed unless one is inhabiting the kingdom when righteousness will be esteemed. Jesus noted both the difficulty of living by His ethical commands and the persecution it would bring (Matt. 5:10-12). However, there are many examples from the epistles that set forth unattainable standards for Christian conduct. None would say that they should not be attempted because they are difficult. Similarly, the Sermon sets forth the life that is to be the mark of the believer. It is unattainable, but nevertheless it is to be attempted by disciples in dependence on God.

5. Many have noted the congruity between the Sermon, James's epistle, and 1 Peter. In the latter books many of the same concepts found in the Sermon are developed and applied to church-age believers. For James good works are an evidence of genuine faith (James 2:18). In the Sermon good works are a result of true repentance (Matt. 5:17-20; 7:16-23).

6. In Galatians Paul noted that if a person is truly a believer righteousness will follow. Galatians is one of the strongest books in the New Testament in stressing that salvation is by faith and that God's grace does not come by works of the law.

7. It has been said that the Sermon is inapplicable before the Millennium because it is impossible to know how far to take commands like the law against retribution. No doubt the disciples had similar questions—just how far does one go in following this teaching? However, such questions do not invalidate the applicability of the demands.

CONCLUSION

There is a misconception that all dispensationalists hold to *the kingdom view* in the interpretation of the Sermon on the Mount. Actually, *the kingdom view* is probably a minority position among modern dispensationalists. It is hoped that this article will spawn further discussion and debate on this important aspect of Jesus' teaching and gospel studies, especially among those who do recognize dispensational distinctives in the interpretive process.

CHARLES H. DYER (A.B., Washington Bible College; Th.M., Dallas Theological
Seminary; candidate for Th.D., Dallas
Theological Seminary) is vice-president
and associate professor at Washington Bible College and Capital Bible Seminary.

The Purpose for the Gospel of Mark

Charles H. Dyer

INTRODUCTION

Throughout his years of ministry J. Dwight Pentecost has been stressing
the unity and purposeful arrangement of the four gospels as well as their
historical accuracy and inspired nature. When other scholars were dividing
the gospels up into various "sources," Dr. Pentecost was arguing that each
gospel (and every other book of the Bible) had to be examined as a complete unit with its own theme, purpose, and structure. He further argued
that each book, because it was inspired by God, was an accurate account of
the events that occurred and could be "harmonized" to reconstruct the
events of Christ's ministry on earth.

Today the pendulum of gospel studies is again swinging back toward examining each gospel as a complete literary unit. Unfortunately many of
these efforts stress literary design at the expense of historical accuracy.[1]
Whereas these scholars are recognizing that each gospel writer arranged
his material to present a unique message, they still deny the historical accuracy of the details that the writers included. Redaction criticism and literary criticism are helpful in their stress on the purposeful arrangement of
the individual gospels, but to the extent that they deny the historical accuracy of the details they must be rejected by conservative evangelicals.

Dr. Pentecost's contributions to gospel studies have stood the test of

---

1. The most recent study to stress literary design at the expense of historical accuracy is Robert H.
   Gundry, *Matthew: A Commentary on His Literary and Theological Art* (Grand Rapids: Eerdmans,
   1982). One could also add that earlier work of Willi Marxsen, *Mark the Evangelist: Studies on the
   Redaction History of the Gospel* (New York: Abingdon, 1969), who pioneered redaction criticism.

time. His stress on the individual "argument" of a book has been most helpful in the studies that have been done on the book of Matthew. His stress on the historicity of the gospels has produced *The Words and Works of Jesus Christ*—a book that has helped produce a historical study of the life of Christ.

This article is written with deep appreciation to a man who has influenced countless students at Dallas Theological Seminary to "handle accurately the Word of Truth" (2 Tim. 2:15). This brief study will apply principles to the gospel of Mark stressed by Dr. Pentecost. The goal is to develop the theme, purpose, and structure of this gospel.

BACKGROUND STUDIES

To understand the purpose of a book one should first try to gain as much information as possible on the author, audience, date of writing, and circumstances for writing. This information is not always available, but whatever can be determined is helpful.

THE AUTHOR

The testimony of the early church is unanimous in ascribing the gospel of Mark to John Mark. Papias, Clement of Alexandria, Origen, Irenaeus, Tertullian, and Jerome all refer to John Mark as the author of the book.[2] But who is John Mark? He is referred to at least ten times in the New Testament, being called Mark, Marcus, John Mark, or John who was called Mark (cf. Acts 12:12, 25; 13:5, 13; 15:37, 39; Col. 4:10; 2 Tim. 4:11; Philem. 24; 1 Pet. 5:13).

Evidently Mark was from Jerusalem and grew up in a house that served as a gathering place for the early church (Acts 12:12). It is possible that the story of the young man who fled naked at the arrest of Christ (which is preserved only in Mark) is an autobiographical reference to John Mark and his early association with Christ (Mark 14:51-52).[3] His mother's name was Mary, and evidently the family was wealthy enough to have servants and a house of a size to serve as a primary meeting place for the church (cf. Acts 12:12-13). Mark's two names also seem to imply that he was from a well-

---

2. Papias's statement was recorded by Eusebius *(Ecclesiastical History* 3. 39. 15) as were the statements of Clement of Alexandria *(Ecclesiastical History* 2. 15. 1-2; 6. 14. 6) and Origen *(Ecclesiastical History* 6. 25. 5). For others see Irenaeus *Against Heresies* 3. 1-2; Tertullian *Against Marcion* 4. 5; and Jerome *Lives of Illustrious Men* 8.
3. John D. Grassmick, "Mark," in *The Bible Knowledge Commentary* (Wheaton, Ill.: Victor, 1983), pp. 181-82.

to-do family. John was his Jewish name, but he had also been given the Roman name Mark.[4] This could indicate that his family maintained some ties (possibly commercial or political) with Roman society that would require the use of dual names. However, one cannot be dogmatic on this point.

John Mark again surfaces in connection with the expanding ministry of Barnabas and Paul. When Barnabas and Paul returned to Antioch after visiting Jerusalem to minister to the church, they took John Mark along with them (Acts 12:25). Mark was Barnabas's cousin (Col. 4:10), and it is possible that Paul and Barnabas took him along to Antioch to serve them in their ministry. As the first missionary journey began, he was accompanying the duo on their trip and serving as their helper or servant-assistant (Acts 13:5).[5] However, when the expedition reached Asia Minor, John Mark deserted the group and returned home to Jerusalem (Acts 13:13). This was so upsetting to Paul that he refused to take Mark (who evidently expressed a change of heart) on the second missionary journey. Paul felt so strongly about this that he and Barnabas parted ways over the issue (Acts 15:36-40).

Barnabas was able to work with John Mark and mold him into an effective minister for Christ. Later in Paul's life Paul freely admitted that he was a trusted and valued companion in the ministry (2 Tim. 4:11). John Mark also was associated with the apostle Peter (1 Pet. 5:13). Peter's reference to Mark as his "son" has led many to conclude that the apostle was his spiritual father. The tradition of the early church was that John Mark wrote his gospel because of his association with Peter and that the gospel of Mark bears the stamp of Peter's authority. This does seem possible, and the close parallels between Peter's messages in the book of Acts and the gospel of Mark are quite remarkable.[6]

THE DATE OF WRITING

There is no clear evidence in the book that allows one to establish a definite date for the gospel. However, some general parameters can be determined. First, the association between Mark and Peter preserved in the writings of church Fathers clearly implies that the gospel was written near the time of Peter's martyrdom about A.D. 67-68. According to Irenaeus,

4. George G. Parker, "The Argument of the Gospel of Mark" (Th.D. dissertation, Dallas Theological Seminary, 1967), p. 20.
5. William L. Lane, *The Gospel of Mark*, The New International Commentary on the New Testament (Grand Rapids: Eerdmans, 1974), pp. 22-23.
6. Ibid., pp. 10-11.

Mark wrote his gospel after the death of Peter.[7] However, Clement of Alexandria stated that Mark wrote his gospel while Peter was still alive.[8] In either case the date seems to correspond to the later years of Peter's ministry. Second, the tradition that the book was written in Rome seems to limit the possible date to two periods of time when John Mark was definitely in the city. The first period when John Mark was in Rome would be about A.D. 61 when he was there with the apostle Paul during Paul's first imprisonment (cf. Col. 4:10). The second period when John Mark was in Rome would be about A.D. 66-67 when Timothy was summoned to Rome by the Apostle Paul. The apostle directed Timothy to "pick up Mark and bring him with you, for he is useful to me for service" (2 Tim. 4:11). This period seems more likely as the time when John Mark wrote his gospel because tradition also places Peter in Rome at this time.

THE AUDIENCE

For whom did Mark write his gospel? Although some have suggested that it was a Jewish gospel written in Palestine,[9] most have concluded that it was primarily a Gentile gospel written in Rome.[10] Several reasons point to this conclusion. First, with the sole exception of John Chrysostom the unanimous testimony of the early church Fathers is that Mark's gospel was written in Rome for Gentile Roman Christians.[11]

Second, the internal evidence supports the view that the gospel was written for Gentiles. Mark translated several Aramaic expressions into Greek (cf. 3:17; 5:41; 7:11, 34; 9:43; 10:46; 14:36; 15:22, 34), implying that his readers did not understand these Jewish expressions. Mark also explained several Jewish customs that would be unfamiliar to a Gentile audience (cf. 7:3-4; 14:12; 15:42), and he gave additional geographical markers

---

7. "And after the death of these [i.e., Peter and Paul] Mark, the disciple and interpreter of Peter, also transmitted to us in writing the things preached by Peter" (Irenaeus *Against Heresies* 3. 1. 2).

8. "The Gospel according to Mark had this occasion. As Peter had preached the Word publicly at Rome, and declared the Gospel by the Spirit, many who were present declared that Mark, who had followed him for a long time and remembered his sayings, should write them out. After having composed the Gospel he gave it to those who had requested it. When Peter learned of this, he neither directly forbade nor encouraged it" (Clement of Alexandria as quoted by Eusebius *Ecclesiastical History* 6. 14. 6).

9. Marxsen, pp. 66, 106-9, 210. For an analysis of Willi Marxsen's work see D. Trent Hyatt, "An Examination of Willi Marxsen's Redaction-Critical Study of Mark" (Th.M. thesis, Dallas Theological Seminary, 1973).

10. For a detailed study of Mark's audience see Kenneth Martin Nordby, "Did Mark Write for Gentiles?" (Th.M. thesis, Dallas Theological Seminary, 1984).

11. John Chrysostom held that Mark wrote his gospel in Egypt *(Homily 1 on Matthew)*. For a listing of the early church Fathers who supported the Roman origin of the gospel see the list in footnote 2.

to help an audience that would not be familiar with specific locations in Israel (cf. 11:1; 13:3).

Third, the internal evidence supports the view that the gospel was written for Romans. Mark used several Latin terms instead of their Greek counterparts (cf. 5:9, where Mark uses the Roman military term "Legion"; 6:27, where Mark uses *spekoulatora,* a transliteration of the Latin word for "guardsman"; 12:42, where Mark states the value of the widow's contribution in terms of Roman coinage; and 15:16, where Mark describes the palace by using the Latin loanword "Praetorium"). Mark also stopped to identify Simon of Cyrene (the one forced to carry Christ's cross) as "the father of Alexander and Rufus" (Mark 15:21). This addition seems odd unless Mark was identifying some individuals who would be known to his readers. Rufus is identified in Romans 16:13 as a prominent member of the church in Rome.

All of this evidence when joined together points to a Roman, Gentile audience for Mark's gospel. Very likely John Mark wrote his gospel for the believers in the church at Rome. Most of these believers were Gentiles, though some Jewish believers were also in the congregation. Thus Mark's gospel was more for the edification of believers than for the evangelization of unbelievers.[12]

THE PURPOSE STATED

The purpose of Mark is more difficult to determine. Many have thought that Mark's purpose was to present Jesus Christ as the Servant of God.[13] These individuals point to Mark 10:45 as the key verse of the book: "For even the Son of Man did not come to be served, but to serve, and to give His life a ransom for many." However, there are some problems in seeing this one idea as the dominant theme of the book. First, Mark does not cite the Old Testament passages that refer to Christ as the Servant of Yahweh (cf. Isa. 42:1-4).[14] In fact, in places where Matthew does make this connec-

---

12. Kenneth Roger Will, "The Pericope of Mark 10:46-52 as It Relates to Mark's Gospel" (Th.M. thesis, Dallas Theological Seminary, 1984), pp. 35-36.
13. Some of those who take the purpose of Mark to be a presentation of Christ as the Servant of the Lord include J. H. Farmer in *International Standard Bible Encyclopedia,* 1939 ed., s.v. "Mark, The Gospel According to," 3:1993-94; Arthur W. Pink, *Why Four Gospels?* (Swengel, Pa.: Bible Truth Depot, 1921), p. 61; E. Schuyler English, *Studies in the Gospel According to Mark* (New York: Our Hope, 1943), p. 1; and W. Graham Scroggie, *A Guide to the Gospels* (London: Pickering & Inglis, 1948), p. 129.
14. For a study of Mark's use of Isaiah see John W. Minnema, "The Use of the Direct Quotations of Isaiah in Mark" (Th.M. thesis, Dallas Theological Seminary, 1982).

tion, Mark does not (cf. Matt. 12:10-21 with Mark 3:1-12). One must explain Mark's absence of references to the Old Testament Servant of Yahweh if, indeed, this was the theme that he was trying to develop.

Second, the names that Mark used of Christ do not seem to place a great deal of emphasis on Christ as the Servant. Christ is referred to as "Jesus" (83 times), "Lord" (10), "Son of Man" (14), "Teacher" (12), "Christ" (7), "Rabbi/Rabboni" (4), "Son of David" (4), "Bridegroom" (3), "Prophet" (2), and "My Beloved Son" (2). The following titles are each used once: "the Carpenter," "the Coming One," "His well-beloved Son," "the Holy One of God," "King of Israel," "Shepherd," "the Son," and "the Son of Mary." Mark's emphasis in these references seems to be on the human and divine relationships of Christ rather than on His servanthood.

Third, it is possible that Mark 10:45 is not the theme of the book. The verse is in a section on discipleship, and it is very likely that the verse should be applied only to that particular section. Mark certainly does not use the title "Servant" as a direct title of Christ.

It is this writer's belief that the main theme of the book can be found in the opening verse. There Mark indicated that he was presenting the good news of "Jesus Christ, the Son of God." Mark wanted his audience to realize that Jesus (the name he used most often) was both the Christ (the Messiah whom the Jews long awaited) and the divine Son of God. As Vincent Taylor has noted, "The words, moreover, point far beyond the story of the Fore-runner and admirably sum up the substance of the Gospel."[15] Several structural markers were used by Mark to present his message. First, Mark used two major confessions in the book to prove his point. The first is the confession of Peter in 8:27-33. Peter's response of faith to Christ's inquiry was to announce that "Thou art the Christ." The second confession is that of the centurion who stood at the base of the cross during the crucifixion (15:33-39). After observing all the events that happened, the centurion declared, "Truly this man was the Son of God!" It is no accident that this final confession is made by a representative of the people to whom Mark was addressing his gospel.

Second, Mark used two miracles of restoring sight to show the progression of faith in Christ. The first miracle (8:22-26) preceded Peter's confession of faith (8:27-33) and is unique to the gospel of Mark.[16] That miracle, at first glance, seems to have Christ performing an incomplete healing that

15. Vincent Taylor, The Gospel According to St. Mark (London: Macmillan, 1959), p. 152.
16. Mark Allen Anderson, "The Miracles Unique to the Gospel of Mark" (Th.M. thesis, Dallas Theological Seminary, 1980).

He must then redo. And yet, the omnipotence of Christ makes such an assertion ridiculous. Why, then, did Christ perform the miracle in two stages? The answer seems to be that He was trying to show that the faith and understanding of the disciples (represented by the restoration of sight) developed in stages. John D. Grassmick notes that "sight was a widely used metaphor for understanding. This miracle depicts the correct but incomplete understanding of the disciples."[17] This miracle then foreshadows the story of Peter's confession. Peter's confession represented "partial sight" in that he believed Jesus was the Christ but rebuked Christ when He foretold His crucifixion. Peter needed further instruction to understand fully the true mission of Israel's Messiah and the requirements placed on those who would follow the Messiah. Perhaps it was the realization of this truth that later prompted Peter to write about the twofold ministry of the Messiah (1 Pet. 1:10-12) and the response expected of those who have placed their trust in Him (1:13—2:10).

The second miracle of healing (10:46-52) ends the second section of Mark's gospel (8:34—10:52). This section focuses on Christ's teaching to His disciples. Christ was attempting to open fully their eyes of faith. The healing of Bartimaeus (10:46-52) represented the disciples' response of faith to the Messiah. Bartimaeus recognized the messianic character of Jesus ("Jesus, Son of David, have mercy on me"), and he refused to be silenced by the multitudes. In response to this confession, Christ performed an instantaneous healing. Kenneth Roger Will sees the significance of Mark's inclusion of this miracle:

> Mark focused upon one of the blind men in order to tie the incident to both discipleship and the revelation of Jesus. . . . Thus Mark intends Bartimaeus to model proper discipleship so that even amid opposition his readers might humbly turn to Jesus for help in understanding. Therefore, the significance (application) of the Bartimaeus pericope is this: the kind of disciples Jesus wants are those who not only know who He is, but "see" the implications of that revelation, that is, that following *the* Christ demands a life of self-denying, humble service.[18]

Taking all of these elements into consideration, it is this writer's belief that the purpose of the gospel of Mark involved primarily edification. Mark was writing to believers in Rome to help them grow in their faith by intro-

17. Grassmick, p. 138.
18. Will, p. 53.

ducing them to Christ's way of discipleship for His followers. The Messiah of the world was the Son of Man and the Son of God. As the Son of Man He had come to suffer, and as the Son of God He had the power to save. The Romans could look to Christ for salvation and strength, but Mark also forced them to evaluate the implications for their service to Christ. "They needed to understand the nature of discipleship—what it means to follow Jesus—in light of who Jesus is and what He had done and would keep doing for them."[19]

THE PURPOSE DEVELOPED

MARK 1:1-20

Mark began his gospel by stating the broad theme that he would develop (1:1). His message announced the good news of Jesus, who was both the Messiah and the Son of God. This good news had been announced earlier by Isaiah the prophet (1:2-3). Isaiah had predicted that one would come to prepare the way for the Lord in the wilderness. That prophecy was fulfilled historically in John the Baptist (1:4-8). John's ministry was one of calling Israel to repentance because of her coming Messiah. The final announcement of Jesus as the Messiah came from heaven itself (1:9-11). As Christ was being baptized by John, the Holy Spirit descended on Him to single Him out as the one chosen by God. A voice from heaven identified Christ as God's beloved Son who enjoyed the favor of God.

The announcement of Jesus as the Messiah was followed by Mark's discussion of the preparation of Jesus as the Messiah (1:12-20). Christ's temptation in the wilderness (1:12-13), His proclamation of the gospel of the kingdom (1:14-15), and His call of His disciples (1:16-20) prepared the way for His ministry to the Jews. The temptation by Satan verified the right of Christ to claim His titles of Messiah and Son of God. He was tried by Satan and found to be without sin. This allowed Him to make His other necessary preparations that would establish His claim to Israel's throne.

MARK 1:21—3:19

The Messiah was presenting Himself to Israel, but what authority did He have to back up His claims? Mark presents the authority of Christ in 1:21—3:19. This section has been called Christ's "Early Galilean Minis-

19. Grassmick, p. 101.

try."[20] Through a series of miracles Mark showed that Christ had authority over demons (1:21-28), disease (1:29—2:12), tradition (2:13-22), and the Sabbath (2:23—3:6). Throughout this section the religious leaders confronted Christ and questioned His authority. At the same time the claims of Christ were obvious. He was the "Holy One of God" (1:24), who had the authority of God to forgive sin (2:7) and who was Lord of the Sabbath (2:28).

Christ had authority over these areas, and He exercised dominion over them as Israel's Messiah (3:7-19). Mark showed Christ's dominion over the multitudes as He taught the vast crowds that flocked to see and hear Him (3:7-10). His dominion also existed over the demons, who correctly identified Christ as "the Son of God" (3:11-12). Finally, Christ's dominion extended over His disciples (3:13-19). Christ appointed the twelve and sent them out in His authority to preach and to cast out demons.

MARK 3:20—6:29

If Christ was the Messiah, why was He rejected by Israel? Mark had already indicated some opposition to Christ (cf. 3:6), but in 3:20—6:29 he pictures the growing opposition to Christ's claims. Christ was opposed by the people of His hometown, who believed that He had lost His senses (3:20-21). The scribes also rejected Christ. They could not deny that He was performing miracles, so they claimed instead that His power to perform those miracles came from Satan rather than from God (3:22). Christ responded by using parables and direct warnings to show these leaders that in rejecting Him they were rejecting God (3:23-30). Even Christ's family did not accept His claims (3:31-35). This rejection of Christ caused Him to change His ministry.

First, He began to speak in parables (4:1-34). The parables of the sower and the soils, the lamp, the growing seed, and the mustard seed were designed to hide the truth from the unbelieving and to reveal it to the true disciples. Second, Christ began to reveal Himself in more detail to His disciples (4:35—5:43). Again He performed miracles to show His power over nature (4:35—5:43), demons (5:1-20), and disease and death (5:21-43).

The opposition to Christ continued with the people of Nazareth's rejection of Him (6:1-6). They heard His message, but they refused to accept His authority because He was a "hometown boy." Their lack of faith aston-

20. Ibid.

ished even Christ. The twelve had already been appointed and given authority (3:13-21), but Christ now sent them out into Israel to announce His message (6:7-13). Yet even in His commissioning of the twelve, Christ implied that their message would not be accepted (6:14-29). Still, the twelve did carry the name of Christ throughout Israel, and word eventually reached King Herod (6:14-29). Mark ended this section on opposition by focusing on Herod to show that Herod also was opposed to Christ. Herod's opposition was sparked by his earlier murder of John the Baptist. Herod mistakenly thought that Jesus was John the Baptist restored to life.

MARK 6:30—8:33

Jesus had claimed the authority of the Messiah and the Son of God, but His claims had been rejected. He then began to reveal Himself in a special way (primarily to His disciples) as the Messiah (6:30—8:33). He did this first through His provision for the five thousand (6:30-44), revealing His sufficiency to the disciples. Second, Christ revealed His character to the disciples by the miracle of walking on the water (6:45-52). He had power and control over nature, but Mark records that the disciples still did not grasp the meaning of Christ's object lesson.[21] Several other incidents were designed to reveal the authority and character of Christ. His healing of the multitudes in Gennesaret (6:53-56) showed that many non-Jews were responding to His message. These individuals contrasted sharply with the Pharisees, who accused Christ of breaking their traditions (7:1-23). Christ finally took His disciples to the Gentiles, who again responded to His message (7:24—8:10). The healing of the Syrophoenician woman's daughter, the healing of a deaf and dumb man from Decapolis, and the feeding of the four thousand taught the disciples that Christ's ministry extended beyond Israel and incorporated the Gentiles as well. Christ instructed the disciples on the hypocrisy of the Pharisees and on His sufficiency for their needs (8:11-21), but Mark again notes that the disciples failed to grasp Christ's message.

Mark ended his section on the presentation of Christ as the Messiah (1:1—8:33) by combining two related stories. The first was Jesus' restoration of sight to the blind man (8:22-26). This blind man symbolized the disciples. They had responded in faith to Christ, but their sight was still

---

21. For a discussion of the three boat scenes in the gospel of Mark (4:35-41; 6:45-52; 8:14-21) and their relationship to the argument of the book see Raymond E. Good, "The Significance of the Boat Scenes in Mark's Gospel" (Th.M. thesis, Dallas Theological Seminary, 1983).

dim. Their spiritual sight had been partially restored, but it still had to be restored further. Christ's miracle showed the gradual progression of faith and understanding on the part of His disciples. This miracle was followed by the story of Peter's confession (8:27-33). Peter displayed his (and the disciples') partial sight by confession that Jesus was the *Messiah*.

Some scholars wrongly argue that Mark's account alone preserves the original statement of Peter and that the accounts in Matthew and Luke have added words that were not actually spoken.[22] It is better to allow the texts to be harmonized and to conclude with Carrington that "we need not suppose that Mark intended that the four words, 'Thou art the Christ,' were all that Peter said on this occasion."[23] Mark did not include "the Son of the living God" (cf. Matt. 16:16) in Peter's confession because Mark's purpose through this first section was to focus on Christ's messiahship. (Though the phrase "Son of God" was also used as a messianic title [cf. Matt. 26:63], it seemed to emphasize the divine origin of Jesus more than His claim to be Israel's king). That is what Peter's confession was to highlight. And yet, Peter's sight was only partial, because as Christ began to explain His coming death, Peter rebuked Him (Mark 8:31-33). The disciples were in need of instruction from their Messiah on what His messiahship entailed and on how they were to live in light of His claims as Messiah.

MARK 8:34—10:52

The second section of Mark's gospel focuses on the instruction given by the Messiah to His disciples (8:34—10:52). Geographically this section has been entitled the "Journey to Jerusalem."[24] It includes much of Christ's teaching on the life of a disciple. Mark opened the section by revealing Christ's explanation of the cost of discipleship (8:34-38). Christ's followers were to take up their cross and follow Him.[25] And yet, there is a hope given to these disciples. The transfiguration was designed to give them a foretaste of the glory of the kingdom (9:1-13). It was a demonstration to the disciples of the power and glory of their Messiah that would one day be revealed (cf. 2 Pet. 1:16-18).

The key to discipleship was a life of faith. Mark recorded the incident of

22. Cf. Taylor, p. 376.
23. Philip Carrington, *The Gospel According to Mark: A Running Commentary on the Oldest Gospel* (Cambridge: At the U. Press, 1960), p. 176.
24. Grassmick, p. 102.
25. Michael P. Green, "The Meaning of Cross-Bearing," *Bibliotheca Sacra* 140 (April-June 1983):117-33.

the demon-possessed son (9:14-29) to show the importance of faith in accomplishing Christ's will. Christ again reminded the disciples of the certainty of His death (9:30-32), but they still failed to grasp the true meaning of His statement.

The middle section of the gospel of Mark ends with Christ's instruction on the life of a disciple (9:33—10:45).[26] Christ explained to His followers the true attitude that they should have toward service (9:33-37), and He warned them to avoid causing stumbling (9:42-50) and to remain faithful in marriage (10:1-12). Christ also went on to teach His disciples the importance of childlike faith (10:13-16) and of maintaining a proper attitude toward wealth (10:17-31). For a third time He explained His coming death (10:32-34), but again the disciples failed to understand as they sought for positions of honor in the coming kingdom (10:35-37). Christ was forced to explain the need for the disciples to follow His example of sacrificial service (10:38-45). This section ends with the second story of a blind man (10:46-52). Mark used the story of Bartimaeus as an illustration of the faith of a true disciple.[27] Bartimaeus recognized Jesus as the Messiah (the "Son of David"), and he refused to let the unbelieving multitudes silence his public confession of faith. He received full physical sight because of his spiritual sight. He had grasped the teaching of the Messiah that the disciples did not yet understand.

MARK 11:1—16:20

The final section of the book of Mark records the sacrificial death of the Son of God (11:1—16:20). Geographically this section has been entitled the "Ministry in and Around Jerusalem."[28] This is the fulfillment of what Christ had already predicted to His disciples three times (8:31; 9:31-32; 10:32-34). Mark began this final section by recording the presentation of the Son of God to Israel (11:1-26). Christ rode into Jerusalem as Israel's Messiah to claim His throne. And yet, by including the story of the barren fig tree in this account (11:12-26), Mark indicated what Israel's response would be. Israel's faith was barren profession, and therefore it would be judged.

---

26. Rage Anderaos, "Lordship of Christ: God's Pattern for the Christian Life as Seen in the Gospel of Mark" (Th.M. thesis, Dallas Theological Seminary, 1984), pp. 62-67.
27. Will, p. 39-45, shows that Mark's use of structure, symbolism (i.e., 'blindness"), and terms that denote discipleship such as "way" (*hodos*, 10:52) and "follow" (*akoloutheō*, 10:52) all point to Mark's use of the story as a fitting conclusion to his section on discipleship.
28. Grassmick, p. 102.

The purpose in the illustration of the fig tree is borne out by the response of the leaders of the nation. Instead of accepting their Messiah, the leaders opposed Him and tried to discredit Him (11:27—12:44). Christ answered all of their objections, and then He posed a question for them (12:35-44). His question is important because it was designed to show that the Messiah was also the Lord. When the leaders refused to answer Christ, He rebuked them for their false pride and sinful actions. The rejection of these leaders sealed Israel's judgment. Christ therefore described to the disciples the judgment and persecution that would prevail until the time of His second coming (13:1-13). Christ's emphasis was again on faithfulness amidst opposition.

The story of Christ's passion is given in 14:1—15:47. Mark recorded the Passover Supper/Lord's Supper and the plot by Judas to betray Christ. The time of prayer in Gethsemane and arrest of Christ are followed by the accounts of the trials and crucifixion. Perhaps the highlight that Mark recorded was the response of the Roman centurion at the cross. After observing all the events of the crucifixion, this representative of Roman society confessed, "Truly this man was the Son of God!" (15:39). This was the purpose toward which Mark was moving throughout his book. As Lane has noted, "the centurion's words constitute an appropriate complement to the affirmation of Peter that Jesus is the Messiah in Chapter 8:29 and the triumphant climax to the gospel in terms of the pragmatic confession of Jesus in Chapter 1:1."[29] What the Jews had failed to grasp was understood by the Gentiles. Jesus the Messiah was also the Son of God, who had died for the sins of the world.

Mark closed his gospel by recording the resurrection of the Son of God. He does not spend a great deal of time on this section because it was not the main point of his story. However, he did record that Christ arose from the dead (16:1-8), that He appeared to many individuals (16:9-18), and that He ascended into heaven after commanding the disciples to carry His message into all the world (16:19-20).[30] That is why the gospel message had been brought to Rome. The gospel of Mark contained a call to commitment and discipleship from the divine Messiah, Jesus.

29. Lane, p. 576.
30. It is beyond the scope of this article to examine the problem of the ending of Mark's gospel. The entire question is much in doubt, but this writer believes there is some evidence for holding to the longer ending.

CONCLUSION

The gospel of Mark is more than a condensed version of Matthew or Luke. It is more than just a biography of Christ. It is more than a compilation of the key events in Jesus' ministry. The gospel of Mark is a carefully constructed work with a specific purpose for a specific audience. Those who hold dear the doctrine of verbal plenary inspiration must follow the trail blazed by J. Dwight Pentecost in stressing the purposeful arrangement and unique message of each part of God's Word. Only then will each believer be able to present himself to God as an approved workman "who correctly handles the word of truth" (2 Tim. 2:15).

HAROLD W. HOEHNER (A.B., Barrington
College; Th.M., Th.D., Dallas Theological
Seminary; Ph.D., Cambridge University)
is director of Th.D. studies and chairman
and professor of New Testament literature and exegesis at Dallas Theological
Seminary.

Jesus' Last Supper

Harold W. Hoehner

INTRODUCTION

There is some debate among scholars whether Jesus' Last Supper was a
Passover celebration. Several arguments given by scholars[1] seem to provide overwhelming evidence that it was a Passover meal. First, the Synoptic gospels explicitly assert that it was a Passover (Matt. 26:2, 17, 18, 19;
Mark 14:1, 12, 14, 16; Luke 22:1, 7, 8, 13, 15). Second, the meal was eaten
as required by the law (Deut. 16:7) within the gates of Jerusalem, even
though the city was crowded with pilgrims. Prior to this Jesus and His disciples had been staying outside of Jerusalem at Bethany. Third, there was
no difficulty in obtaining the upper room, in keeping with the Passover
custom. Fourth, the meal was eaten at night (Matt. 26:20; Mark 14:17;
John 13:30; 1 Cor. 11:23). Whereas normally the mealtimes were in the
morning and afternoon, the Passover could not be eaten earlier than the
evening. Fifth, although many times Jesus ate with a large number of followers, He limited Himself to the twelve for this meal, which corresponds
to requirement of the Passover's being celebrated with a small group of
around ten persons. Sixth, the reclining position of the guests at the meal
(Mark 14:18; John 13:23, 28) was for special festive meals only. Seventh,
the guests ate the Passover meal in the required Levitical purity (John

---

1. For further details see Joachim Jeremias, *The Eucharistic Words of Jesus,* trans. Norman Perrin
(London: SCM, 1966), pp. 41-56; Gustaf Dalman, *Jesus-Jeshua,* trans. Paul P. Levertoff (London:
SPCK, 1929), pp. 106-32; Leon Morris, *The Gospel According to John* (Grand Rapids: Eerdmans,
1971), pp. 774-75. I. Howard Marshall, *Last Supper and Lord's Supper* (Grand Rapids: Eerdmans,
1981), pp. 58-62; E. Robinson, "The Alleged Discrepancy Between John and the Other Evangelists
Respecting Our Lord's Last Passover," *Bibliotheca Sacra* 2 (August 1845):406-26.

13:10). Eighth, the bread was broken, distributed, and eaten in the middle of the meal (Matt. 26:26; Mark 14:22) rather than at the beginning of the meal as was normally done. Ninth, they drank red wine, which was used only for special occasions. Tenth, some of the disciples surmised that Judas left to purchase items for the feast (John 13:29). This would have been unnecessary if the Last Supper was a day before Passover, because he would have had the whole next day available to make the purchases. Eleventh, some of the disciples speculated that Judas left to give money to the poor (John 13:29). This was customary on Passover night. Twelfth, the Last Supper ended with singing, which would correspond to the last half of the Passover *hallel*. Thirteenth, Jesus and the disciples did not return to Bethany, which was outside of Jerusalem's limit, but spent the night on the Mount of Olives, which was within the expanded city limits, for the purpose of the Passover feast. Fourteenth, Jesus' interpreting the significance of the bread and wine to the disciples is in line with the normal practice of the Passover ritual. These arguments are forceful and make good sense.

There are some scholars who do not think that the Last Supper was a Passover.[2] However, their arguments do not seem to be persuasive and are beyond the scope of this study.[3] It seems most reasonable that Jesus celebrated the Passover at His Last Supper.

The Passover was an important feast and is mentioned about fifty times in the Old Testament (cf. Ex.12:1-13, 21-27, 43-49; Lev. 9:1-5; 23:5; Num. 28:16-25; Deut. 16:1-8). In connection with Jesus' ministry it is mentioned frequently (Matt. 26:2, 17, 18, 19; Mark 14:1, 12 [twice], 14, 16; Luke 2:41; 22:1, 7, 8, 11, 13, 15; John 2:13, 23; 6:4, 55 [twice]; 12:1; 13:1; 18:28, 39; 19:14; 1 Cor. 5:7). John mentions the three Passovers of Jesus' life (2:13; 6:4; 11:55). The most important Passover is, of course, the final Passover, that is, the one celebrated by Jesus and His disciples in His Last Supper.

---

2. For a discussion of this view see A. J. B. Higgins, *The Lord's Supper in the New Testament* (London: SCM, 1952), pp. 20-23; J. B. Segal, *The Hebrew Passover from the Earliest Times to A.D. 70* (London: Oxford U., 1963), pp. 242-47; Maurice Goguel, *The Primitive Church*, trans. H. C. Snape (London: Allen & Unwin, 1964), pp. 330-31; William Frederick, "Did Jesus Eat the Passover?" *Bibliotheca Sacra* 68 (July 1911):503-9. Stauffer believes that since Jesus was regarded as a preacher of apostasy, He would not have been allowed by the Temple officials to have a paschal lamb slain (Ethelbert Stauffer, *Jesus and His Story*, trans. Dorothea M. Barton [London, SCM, 1960], pp. 94-95).

3. For a discussion of their objections to the Last Supper's being a Passover see Jeremias, pp. 62-84; Higgins, pp. 16-20; George Ogg, "The Chronology of the Last Supper," *Historicity and Chronology in the New Testament* (London: SPCK, 1965), pp. 76-77; Harold W. Hoehner, *Chronological Aspects of the Life of Christ* (Grand Rapids: Zondervan, 1977), pp. 77-80; Marshall, pp. 62-66.

THE INSTITUTION OF THE PASSOVER

DEFINITION

The New Testament term for "Passover" is *pascha*, which has a technical connotation, referring to the Passover feast. The background of this term is the Hebrew term *pesah*, which denotes the celebration of the Passover feast and probably is derived from the verb having the idea "to leap over, to pass over, to spare" (cf. Ex. 12:13, 23, 27), although there is some dispute about this.[4]

CELEBRATION

The biblical picture (Ex. 12) is that the unblemished year-old lamb or goat that was selected on Nisan (March/April) 10 was to be killed at twilight of Nisan 14. Its blood was to be sprinkled on the two doorposts and the lintel, and later that night the people were to eat it with unleavened bread and bitter herbs. That very night the Lord brought forth the tenth plague wherein He struck the firstborn of the Egyptian people and cattle but did "passover" the houses of those who sprinkled blood on doorposts and lintels. This was to be followed by the Feast of Unleavened Bread on Nisan 15-21 (Ex. 12). However, by New Testament times these two feasts were looked on as one feast (Matt. 26:17; Mark 14:12; Luke 22:1, 7), and, in fact, Josephus described it as a feast of eight days.[5]

PREPARATION FOR PASSOVER IN THE TIME OF CHRIST

MORNING

Work ceased. On the day that the Passover lamb was to be slain the Galileans did not work at all, and the Judeans ceased their work by midday.[6] The reason for the difference between the two groups may point to a difference in their reckoning of a day, namely, the Galileans reckoned the day from sunrise and the Judeans from sunset.[7] Regardless, the cessation from work was for their preparation of the celebration of the Passover festival.

Leavened bread removed. The eating of leavened bread ceased between

4. *The New International Dictionary of New Testament Theology*, s.v. "Feast, Passover, *pascha*," by Bernd Schaller, 1 (1975):632; *Theological Dictionary of the New Testament*, s.v. "*pascha*," by Joachim Jeremias, 5 (1967):896-99.
5. Josephus *Jewish Antiquities* 2. 15. 17; 317; however, see 3. 10. 5 249.
6. Mishnah: Pesachim 4:1, 5-6; Tosefta: Pesachim 3:18.
7. It is beyond the scope of this article to discuss this problem; see Hoehner, pp. 81-90.

10:00 and 11:00 A.M., and all leavened bread had to be destroyed by noon. The leftover bread was disposed of by burning it, scattering it to the wind, or throwing it into the sea.[8]

Early afternoon. Necessary preparations were made for the eating of the paschal lamb. Jesus instructed Peter and John to go into Jerusalem and make preparations (Matt. 26:17-19; Mark 14:12-16; Luke 22:7-13). Although part of the preparations could have been made in the morning, the final preparations probably were done in the early afternoon. They included the setting out of the unleavened bread, wine, bitter herbs, fruit puree sauce, the arranging of couches or carpets for reclining at the meal, and the preparation of the lamps. The reason that the preparation took place in Jerusalem is because the Passover was to be celebrated there (Deut. 16:7), and according to Jewish tradition all of the houses in Jerusalem were considered as common property during the feasts. Thus, they could not be let for money. However, it was a custom of the pilgrims to give the host the hide of the sacrificed animal.[9]

The offering of the daily evening sacrifice normally was slain at 2:30 P.M. and offered at 3:30. However, at the time of the Passover the evening offering was moved up one hour, and if the Passover was on the eve of the Sabbath, then it was moved up two hours.[10] The reason for moving the time of the evening offering was so the Temple would be free at the designated time for offering the paschal lamb.

Late afternoon. The final preparation Peter and John would have made was the sacrifice of the paschal lamb. According to the Scripture the selection of an unblemished paschal lamb was to be done on Nisan 10 (Ex. 12:3-5). One lamb was to be killed for no less than ten but no more than twenty people.[11] The reason for this was that the whole animal was to be consumed before midnight (Ex. 12:8; 34:15; Num. 9:12). Whatever was not eaten must be burned on Nisan 16 unless it was a Sabbath, and then it would be burned on Nisan 17.[12]

8. Mishnah: Pesachim 1:4-5; 2:1; Tosefta: Pesachim 1:8.
9. Babylonian Talmud: Megillah 26a; Yoma 12a. Cf. Jeremias, p. 44. See also Joachim Jeremias, *Jerusalem in the Time of Jesus,* trans. F. H. and C. H. Cave (Philadelphia: Fortress, 1969), pp. 60-62.
10. Mishnah: Pesachim 5:1.
11. Josephus *War* 6. 9. 3 423, 425. In Exodus 12:4 it is commanded that if one's household is too small, then he and his neighbor are to have one lamb between, so they can consume it. This is certainly implied in the Mishnah: Pesachim 7:13; 8:1, 4, 7; 9:10. Cf. also Mishnah: Zebahim 5:8.
12. Mishnah: Pesachim 7:10; cf. Babylonian Talmud: Shabbath 24b.

The Israelites were to take their paschal lamb to the Temple. The people were divided into three groups. The first group was admitted with their lambs into the court of the priests. The massive gates were closed, and the priests gave a threefold blast from their silver trumpets while the people slew their lambs.[13] They were to slay them at twilight or, literally, "between the two evenings" (Ex.12:6; Lev. 23:5; Num. 9:3, 5), which according to Josephus was between the ninth and eleventh hours,[14] that is, from 3:00 to 5:00 P.M. The priests stood in two rows, one row holding golden bowls, the other silver bowls. When the individual Israelite slaughtered his offering, the priest would catch the blood in the bowl and pass it down his respective row and receive back an empty bowl. The priest nearest the altar would toss the blood at the base of the altar. While this was going on, they would sing the *hallel* that was composed of Psalms 113-18. If they finished the *hallel* before completing the ceremony, they simply sang it again.[15] Next, the carcasses were hung with hooks along the court or laid on staves held by two worshipers. The priests then flayed the lambs, removed the sacrificial portions (cf. Lev. 3:3-4), and placed those portions on the altar of burnt offering.[16] In this case it is in all likelihood that Peter and John were the two men who held up the carcass of the paschal lamb. This completed the sacrifice. In the same fashion the second group was admitted and then after them the third group.

After the three groups had finished, the priests washed the Temple court because so much blood had been spilled.[17]

CELEBRATION OF PASSOVER IN THE TIME OF CHRIST

The paschal lamb was then taken home and roasted on a spit (Ex. 12:8).[18] None of the bones were to be broken (Ex. 12:46; Num.9:12).[19] The Passover meal was to be eaten at night, after sunset (Ex. 12:8; 34:25; Num. 9:12).[20] That would give enough time to roast it after it was sacrificed at the Temple. The New Testament explicitly states that Jesus celebrated the Passover with His disciples at night (Matt. 26:20, 34; Mark 14:17, 30; John 13:30; 1 Cor. 11:23), whereas the last meal of the day was normally in the

13. Mishnah: Pesachim 5:5; Tosefta: Pesachim 4:10.
14. Josephus *War* 6. 9. 3 423.
15. Mishnah: Pesachim 5:5-7; Tosefta: Pesachim 4:11.
16. Mishnah: Pesachim 5:9; 7:10.
17. Tosefta: Pesachim 4:12. This reference speaks of blood up to the priest's ankle.
18. Mishnah: Pesachim 7:1-3; Tosefta: Pesachim 5:8.
19. Cf. Mishnah: Pesachim 7:11-12; Tosefta: Pesachim 6:8.
20. Jubilees 49:1, 12; Mishnah: Pesachim 10:1; Tosefta: Pesachim 10:1; Mekilta: Ex 12:6.

afternoon or before nightfall.[21] Rather than sitting,[22] Jesus and His disciples reclined at the table (Greek, *anakeimai*—Matt. 26:20; Mark 14:18; John 13:23, 28; *anapiptō*—Luke 22:14; John 13:12, 25), that being the normal posture at the Passover meal.[23] The meal can be divided either into three parts: the preliminary course, the main course, and the conclusion; or it can be divided into four parts, revolving around the four cups of wine that were the minimum even for the poorest person.[24] The tradition of the four cups of wine is based on the four-fold promise of redemption or liberty expressed in Exodus 6:6-7:[25] "Say, therefore, to the sons of Israel, 'I am the Lord, and I will bring you out from under the burdens of the Egyptians [=first cup], and I will deliver you from their bondage [=second cup]. I will also redeem you with an outstretched arm and with great judgments [=third cup]. Then I will take you for my people, and I will be your God; and you shall know that I am the Lord your God, who brought you out from under the burdens of the Egyptians [=fourth cup]." In this study the Passover meal will be divided into the three parts but with the understanding that the four cups of wine were an integral part of the Passover celebration.

PRELIMINARY COURSE

Benediction over first cup of wine. With the arrival of guests the wine was brought in and mixed with warm water.[26] The father or host pronounced a blessing upon the festival day (Hebrew, *kiddush)* and over the first cup of wine (*kiddush* cup).[27] In this case it was Jesus who pronounced the blessing. This fits well with the tradition of the first cup of wine in connection with Exodus 6:6*a* where God says, "I am the Lord, and I will bring

21. Jeremias, *Eucharistic Words,* pp. 44-46; a good discussion of the Passover meal is given by Gordon J. Bahr, "The Seder of Passover and the Eucharistic Words," *Novum Testamentum* 12 (April 1970):181-202; here 190.
22. Jeremias, *Eucharistic Words,* p. 48; Bahr, p. 190.
23. Tosefta: Pesachim 10:1; Babylonian Talmud: Berakhoth 43a; Pesachim 108a.
24. Mishnah: Pesachim 10:1; Tosefta: Pesachim 10:1; Babylonian Talmud: Pesachim 109b-110a.
25. Midrash: Ex. Rabbah 6:4 (6:6); Jerusalem Talmud: Pesachim 10:1; Babylonian Talmud: Pesachim 109b-110a.
26. Mishnah: Pesachim 7:13; Bahr, pp. 191-92. It is thought that there would be one part wine to three parts of water, cf. Hermann L. Strack und Paul Billerbeck, *Kommentar zum Neuen Testament aus Talmud und Midrasch* 4.1 (Munchen: C. H. Bech'sche Verlagsbuchhandlung, 1928):72.
27. Mishnah: Pesachim 10:2; Tosefta: Pesachim 10:2. There was a debate between the two schools. The order outlined above was according to the school of Shammai. The school of Hillel reversed the order so that the father pronounced the blessing over the cup of wine and then the blessing over the day (cf. also, Mishnah: Cerakoth 8.1).

you out from under the burdens of the Egyptians." This promise was a blessing to the enslaved people.

Hors d'oeuvres. Hors d'oeuvres consisting of lettuce, bitter herbs, and a fruit puree (Hebrew, *charoseth*—a mixture of squeezed and grated figs, dates, raisins, apples, and almonds with spices and vinegar) was served as an appetizer.[28] The bitter herbs were to remind Israel of the bitter experience they had during the Egyptian exile.

MAIN COURSE

This is the main part of the feast. It began with the second cup of wine called the *haggadah* cup and ended with the third cup of wine called the cup of blessing. There were seven parts to this course.

Meal served and second cup mixed. The Passover meal was served but not yet eaten, and the second cup of wine was mixed and placed on the table though not yet drunk.[29] Not eating the paschal lamb or drinking the wine that was prepared aroused curiosity and led naturally into the Passover liturgy.

Passover narrative given. The Passover narrative, or *haggadah,* was recited by the father. It was a review of the first Passover in Egypt, which Israel was instructed to rehearse at every Passover (Ex. 12:24-27). The Mishnah presents it in Pesachim 10:4-5 as follows:

> 4. They then mix him the second cup. And here the son asks his father (and if the son has not enough understanding his father instructs him [how to ask]), "Why is this night different from other nights? For on other nights we eat seasoned food once, but this night twice; on other nights we eat leavened or unleavened bread, but this night all is unleavened; on other nights we eat flesh roast, stewed, or cooked, but this night all is roast." And according to the understanding of the son his father instructs him. He begins with the disgrace and ends with the glory; and he expounds from *A Wandering Aramean was my father* . . . until he finishes the whole section.
> 5. Rabban Gamaliel used to say: Whosoever has not said [the verses concerning] these three things at Passover has not fulfilled his obligation. And these are they: Passover, unleavened bread, and bitter herbs: 'Passover'—because God passed over the houses of our fathers in Egypt; 'bitter herbs'—because the Egyptians embittered the lives of our fathers

28. Mishnah: Pesachim 10:3.
29. Mishnah: Pesachim 10:4.

in Egypt. In every generation a man must so regard himself as if he came forth himself out of Egypt, for it is written, *And thou shalt tell* thy son in that day saying, it is because of what the Lord did *for me when I came forth out of Egypt.* Therefore are we bound to give thanks, to praise, to glorify, to honor, to exalt, to extol, and to bless him who wrought all these wonders for our fathers and for us. He brought us out from bondage to freedom, from sorrow to gladness, and from mourning to Festival-day, and from darkness to great light, and from servitude to redemption; so let us say before him the *Hallelujah.*[30]

First part of hallel sung. The last word of the above paragraph, *Hallelujah,* refers to the *hallel* (Ps. 113-18) that was to be sung right after the Passover *Haggadah.* However, only part of the *hallel* was sung at this point. There was a great debate about how much of it was to be sung at this juncture. The school of Shammai sang only Psalm 113, whereas the school of Hillel sang both Psalms 113 and 114[31] because Psalm 114 mentions God's deliverance of Israel from Egypt.[32]

Second cup drunk. This second cup of wine is called the *haggadah* cup. After singing the *hallel* the family drank this second cup of wine. This fits well with the tradition of the second cup of wine in connection with Exodus 6:6b, where God promised to deliver Israel from Egyptian bondage. The eating of the bitter herbs reminded them of their bondage and their wonderful deliverance by God Himself.

Grace over the unleavened bread spoken. The father spoke grace over the unleavened bread, broke it, and distributed it. This fits well with the passion narrative of Christ. Matthew 26:26; Mark 14:22; and Luke 22:19 stated that, while Christ and the disciples were eating, Jesus took the bread, blessed (God) or gave thanks,[33] broke it, and distributed it to His disciples. Jeremias pointedly shows that it is significant that the breaking of

30. All the brackets, parenthetical marks, italics, and punctuation marks are not mine but are cited from *The Mishnah,* trans. Herbert Danby (Oxford: Oxford U., 1933), pp. 150-51.
31. Mishnah: Pesachim 10:6; Tosefta: Pesachim 10:9.
32. Modern scholars debate this. Jeremias (*Eucharistic Words,* p. 51, n. 1) and Marshall (*Last Supper,* p. 179) think that only Psalm 113 was sung in Jesus' day, whereas Theodor Herzl Gaster (*Passover: Its History and Traditions* [New York: Henry Schuman, 1949], p. 64) and Joseph Tabory ("The Passover Eve Ceremony—An Historical Outline," *Immanuel* 12 [Spring 1981]:42) think both psalms were sung.
33. Matthew 26:26 and Mark 14:22 use *eulogeō,* "to bless," with the object being God and not the bread. This is substantiated by the parallel passage where in Luke 22:19 the word *eucharisteō,* "to give thanks," is used, and certainly one does not give thanks to the bread but to God who provides the bread. Furthermore, the benedictions of the Jews show that God is the object of blessing when they praise Him for the bread by saying, "Blessed art Thou who causes the bread to come forth from the earth" (Mishnah: Berakoth 6.1).

bread was during the course of the meal. This was true only at the Passover meal, whereas ordinarily meals began with the breaking of bread. In addition, at the Last Supper the disciples had already dipped their hands (without bread) into a dish (Matt. 26:23; Mark 14:20)[34] before the breaking of bread (Matt. 26:26; Mark 14:22). This is further substantiated by the fact that the children asked their father (in the *haggadah*) why it was that every other evening they dipped bread into the dish, but on Passover night they simply dipped (without bread) into the dish.[35] Thus, first there was the preliminary course and then the unleavened bread (see the *haggadah* quoted above). Jesus applied the breaking of bread to His own body's being broken.

Passover meal eaten. This consisted of the paschal lamb, unleavened bread, bitter herbs (Ex. 12:8) with fruit puree, and wine. Normally, this was a joyous meal among the Jews[36] in commemoration of God's deliverance of the nation from the Egyptian bondage. In sharp contrast, this must have been a bewildering experience for the twelve who looked upon it as the farewell meal with their Master. He had predicted His ignominious death (Matt. 16:21; 17:22-23; 20:18-19; Mark 8:31; 9:31; 10:33-34; Luke 9:22, 44; 18:32-33), and He had announced that one of the disciples would betray Him (Matt. 26:21-24; Mark 14:18-21). No doubt the disciples were wondering how all this fit together with the celebration of the Passover. The twelve looked back to God's wondrous deliverance in the Exodus and pondered how God would bring forth a new deliverance for Jesus and them in the next few hours.

Grace over the third cup spoken. The third cup of wine was mixed after the main course had been eaten (cf. 1 Cor. 11:25), and it was called the cup of blessing (cf. 1 Cor. 10:16) or the cup of redemption.[37] The host would give thanks[38] over the meal and its significance. Likewise in this context Je-

---

34. It is unfortunate that both the RSV and the NIV in Mark 14:20 translate *embaptō* "to dip bread," whereas the KJV, ASV, and NASB translate it "to dip." This later translation is better because the only other time it is used is in Matthew 26:23 where it is used in connection with *ten cheira* ("the hand"), that is, "to dip the hand in the dish." There is no bread served in the preliminary course.
35. Jerusalem Talmud: Pesachim 10:3; cf. Jeremias, *Eucharistic Words,* pp. 49-50.
36. Mishnah: Pesachim 10:5. In fact, they were warned not to let the joy of the Passover meal degenerate into revelry (10:9).
37. Very little is said about this cup. In the Mishnah (Pesachim 10:7) only the cup's being mixed is mentioned, and this followed by grace over the meal just eaten. It is normally referred to as the "cup of blessing." However, since in the immediately preceding context there is a discussion of the Exodus and an offering of praise to God for His redemption of Israel (10:6) that the Tosefta (Pesachim 10:9) calls the "prayer of redemption," it could also be thought of as the "cup of redemption."
38. For a discussion of the thanksgiving or praise, see Strack und Billerbeck, 4.2:628, 630.

sus took the cup, gave thanks, and then instructed the disciples to drink it. Jesus then explained the significance of the cup of wine with regard to His own sacrificial death for the forgiveness of sins (Matt. 26:27-28; Mark 14:23-24; Luke 22:17, 20[39]). As the cup of blessing in the Passover pointed back to the blood of the sacrificial lamb sprinkled on the door posts and lintels so that God's wrath would pass over the children of Israel, so Jesus spoke of this cup as the cup of His sacrificial death. The Israelites were redeemed from Egyptian bondage, and Jesus used the cup to point to the forgiveness of sins by His death.[40] As the Old Covenant was ratified by the sprinkling of blood (Ex. 24:6-8), so the New Covenant that was promised in Jeremiah 31:31 was inaugurated by Jesus' sacrificial death. The third cup was a cup of blessing, expressing thanksgiving for the Passover meal that commemorated Israel's redemption. Jesus used the grace over the third cup as an opportunity to point to His death as a redemption from sin.

This also fits well with the traditional third cup of wine in connection with Exodus 6:6c where God said, "I will also redeem you with an outstretched arm and with great judgments." The cup of blessing is the cup of redemption.

CONCLUSION

Second part of hallel sung. Because of God's great deliverance of Israel from Egypt commemorated in the Passover, the Jews sang praises to God in the second part of the *hallel.* The school of Shammai sang Psalms 114-18, and the school of Hillel sang Psalms 115-18. Jesus and His disciples sang before they left for the Mount of Olives (Matt. 26:30; Mark 14:26). Although the English versions give the impression that they sang only one hymn, the Greek states it in a verbal form, namely, that when they finished *singing*, they went to the Mount of Olives. Most likely this has reference to their singing the second part of the *hallel.* Normally these psalms were sung antiphonally, where the leader would sing the lines and the followers would respond with "Hallelujah." This part of the *hallel* must have had

39. There is debate whether the longer version of Luke 22 (vv. 17-20) or the shorter version (vv. 17-19a) should be accepted. The longer version has far better manuscript support and geographical distribution and therefore should be accepted. For further discussion of this, see Bruce M. Metzger, *A Textual Commentary on the Greek New Testament* (New York: United Bible Societies, 1971), pp. 173-77; I. Howard Marshall, *The Gospel of Luke* (Grand Rapids: Eerdmans, 1978), pp. 799-801.
40. The various views regarding the Lord's Supper have been debated over the centuries. It is beyond the purview of this study for such a long and involved discussion. For a good starting point, see Marshall, *Last Supper,* pp. 106-57.

great significance to Jesus and His disciples because it speaks of God's deliverance and saving goodness.

Grace over the fourth cup spoken. This final cup of wine[41] is called the *hallel* cup. However, Jesus did not drink this cup of wine, for He told His disciples that henceforth He would not drink the fruit of the vine until the kingdom of God is ushered in (Matt. 26:29; Mark 14:25; Luke 22:18).[42]

This fits well with the tradition of the fourth cup of wine in connection with Exodus 6:7, where God says, "Then I will take you for My people, and I will be your God; and you shall know that I am the Lord your God, who brought you out from under the burdens of the Egyptians." Jesus did not drink this cup because the nation Israel did not claim Him as their God nor had He claimed them as His people. However, when Christ returns, Israel will mourn for Him whom they pierced (Zech. 12:10), and "they will call on My name, and I will answer them; I will say, 'They are My people,' and they will say, 'The Lord is my God' "(Zech. 13:9). In Romans 11:25-27 one sees that Israel's hardening will continue until the "fullness of the Gentiles," and then Messiah will come from Jerusalem and remove Israel's ungodliness and take away their sins as He has covenanted with them. Jesus, then, will drink that fourth cup of wine in the millennial kingdom when they recognize Him as their God and He recognizes them as His people. It is thus very fitting for Jesus not to have drunk the fourth cup of wine.

Although some have argued that Jesus refused to drink the third cup,

---

41. Some mention a fifth cup of wine, but as Tabory (12:42) points out this tradition began sometime between the seventh and tenth centuries A.D.

42. Luke's order of this saying is different from the other two gospels. For a discussion and bibliography of the problem, see Marshall, *Luke,* pp. 792-99. It has been suggested that the cup in Luke 22:17 refers to the first cup (*kiddush cup*), and this would imply that Jesus did not partake of the cup of blessing or redemption mentioned in verse 20 (Jacob Mann, "Rabbinic Studies in the Synoptic Gospels," *Hebrew Union College Annual* 1 [1924]:342). Jeremias thinks that Jesus abstained from eating the Passover meal (*Eucharistic Words,* pp. 207-18). This is untenable, for the whole tenor of the passage points to Jesus eating the Passover with His disciples. Luke specifically mentions that Jesus commissioned Peter and John to make preparations so that He could participate in the Passover with His disciples (Luke 22:8, 11). The other two gospels state the same thing, except they each mention it only once (Matt. 26:18; Mark 14:14). Petzer offers a valid suggestion, that is, that Luke arranged his narration in a parallel structure so that the first part (vv. 15-18) emphasizes the eschatological meaning of the Passover, and the second part (vv. 19-20) deals with the historical institution of the Lord's Supper in connection with His death, paralleling the other two gospels (J. H. Petzer, "Luke 22:19b-20 and the Structure of the Passage," *Novum Testamentum* 26 [July 1984]:249-52). Certainly the first part emphasizes Jesus' last Passover meal with His disciples, and the second part deals with the institution of the Lord's Supper. Thus, Luke is not contradicting the other two gospels but just structuring the account differently. For further discussion and bibliography on this problem, see Marshall, *Luke,* pp. 792-94; Walter L. Leifeld, "Luke," in The Expositor's Bible Commentary 8 (Grand Rapids: Zondervan, 1984):1026-27; Bahr, pp. 200-202.

his refusal fits best with the fourth cup. The third cup is the cup of blessing in connection with redemption, and He drank it showing that His death was for the forgiveness of sins. Furthermore, as mentioned above, the breaking of bread occurred in the midst of the main course and the cup of blessing was taken right after the supper; likewise, this is what Jesus did when He inaugurated the two elements of the Lord's Supper (Matt. 26:26-28; Mark 14:22-24; Luke 22:19-20; 1 Cor. 11:23-25). The refusal to drink does not fit with the third cup but with the fourth cup. Finally, David Daube shows how Jesus' and His disciples' departure to the Mount of Olives right after they sang makes better sense. "The implication is that they go out directly after the 'hymn,' without drinking the fourth cup and probably also without reciting the 'blessing of the song.' This portion of the liturgy is postponed till the arrival of the actual, final kingdom."[43] Therefore Jesus' refusal to drink until the coming of His kingdom best fits with the fourth cup of wine that signifies Israel's recognition of His being God and His recognition of them being His people.

CONCLUSION

On Thursday night, April 2, A.D. 33,[44] Jesus ate the Passover with His disciples. Looking backward, the disciples commemorated God's deliverance of Israel from the Egyptian bondage. Looking forward, there was nothing but sadness and confusion. They were told that their Master would suffer death and that one of them was going to betray Him. However, their joint participation in the Passover was a rehearsal of God's redemption of Israel from the Egyptian bondage that served as a basis for God's future redemption through His Son, Jesus. His sacrificial death became the center of the New Testament preaching.

---

43. David Daube, *The New Testament and Rabbinic Judaism* (London: U. of London, Athlone, 1956), p. 331.
44. For a discussion of the problem of the day of the crucifixion, see Hoehner, pp. 65-93.

J. CARL LANEY (B.S., University of Oregon; M.Div., Th.M., Western Conservative Baptist Seminary; Th.D., Dallas Theological Seminary) is associate professor of biblical literature at Western Conservative Baptist Seminary in Portland, Oregon.

Geographical Aspects of the Gospel

J. Carl Laney

Geography, history, and divine revelation are thoroughly interwoven in the presentation of the Bible's message. For that reason, the study of biblical geography is essential to a proper understanding and clear exposition of God's Word. There is no place where this is more evident than the gospels. The four gospels contain 428 geographical references and employ 55 different place-names.[1] The most frequently used place-name is "Jerusalem" (68 occurrences) with "Galilee" taking a close second (58 occurrences). It is quite obvious that the gospel writers had a geographical interest and perspective. They employed the geography of Bible lands to elucidate the life and ministry of Jesus.

The purpose of this essay, in honor of my esteemed teacher Dr. J. Dwight Pentecost, is to identify and clarify the major interpretive issues of gospel geography.

TERRITORIES

The ministry of Jesus extended to the territories of Galilee, Samaria, Judea, Perea, and Decapolis (Matt. 4:25; John 4:5). A brief consideration of each of these territories will serve to introduce the geography of the gospels.

---

1. Excluding "Cananaean" (Matt. 10:4; Mark 3:18), better translated "Zealot," and "Perea," a variant in Luke 6:17.

GALILEE

Galilee is the name applied to the northern district of Israel that was surrounded on three sides by foreign nations. The term literally means "circle" or "district," the fuller expression of which is "district of the Gentiles" (Isa. 9:1). According to Josephus's description of Galilee, the territory was divided into upper and lower regions.[2] Upper Galilee, being mountainous and isolated, does not enter much into biblical history. Lower Galilee served as the location for most of Christ's ministry as recorded in the synoptic gospels. The region is divided into a series of east-west valleys and basins. Galilee's fertility is highly praised by Josephus, who states that no part of the land was left uncultivated.[3]

JUDEA

Judea is the name used to refer to the southern region of Palestine. Since most of the exiles returning from the Babylonian captivity were of the tribe of Judah, they came to be called Jews and their land, Yehud. The name "Judea" (the Graeco-Latin form of Judah) was used in the Hellenistic period to describe the area where the Jews of the land of Israel lived. Judea is made up of a massive upwarp of Cenomanian limestone rising from the coastal plain on the west and bending down towards the wilderness and Dead Sea on the east. The region also encompasses the Negev ("desertland") to the south, the Shephelah ("lowland"), and a transitional region between the coastal plain and the hill country. Judea provides the geographical background for the greater part of John's gospel.

SAMARIA

Samaria was the name of the capital of the Northern Kingdom of Israel that Omri built on a hill purchased from Shemer (1 Kings 16:24). Samaria eventually became synonymous with the Northern Kingdom (1 Kings 13:32) and in Roman times was applied to the administrative region situated between Galilee and Judea. Samaria is more open and accessible than the hill country to the south. According to Josephus, "Its character differs in no wise from that of Judea."[4] Both regions have fertile soil and are well watered. Josephus writes that these areas are "well wooded and abound in

2. Josephus *The Jewish War* 3.35-40.
3. Ibid., 3.42-43.
4. Ibid., 3.48-50.

fruits, both wild and cultivated." Jesus' travels between Galilee and Judea sometimes took Him through Samaria (John 4:4-5; cf. Luke 9:52-53; 17:11).

PEREA

Perea, a term used regularly by Josephus to refer to Transjordan, is not found in the Bible except in a variant of Luke 6:17. The term is used to describe both the political district administered by Herod Antipas and the land beyond the Jordan in general. Perea was a long, narrow territory (about thirteen miles wide) encompassing the area between the Rift Valley and the Syrian Desert. The territory extends from the River Arnon in the south to the borders of Pella in the north. Perea was less densely populated in the first century than Galilee or Judea and figures less in the life of Christ than these regions (cf. Matt. 19:1). Though he admits to exceptions, Josephus regards Perea as generally "rugged and too wild to bring tender fruits to maturity."[5]

DECAPOLIS

Decapolis (lit., "ten city") refers to the region in southern Syria and northeastern Palestine composed of territories of certain Hellenistic cities. The traditional view that Decapolis was a federation of cities has been recently challenged. A study of the ancient sources reveals no evidence of any political, military, or commercial arrangements among the members.[6] As indicated by the name, the number of cities was originally ten, but the number and members varied from time to time. These cities were all Greco-Roman and shared a common religious and cultural identity. Jesus attracted followers from Decapolis and ministered in this region (Matt. 4:25; Mark 5:1-20; 7:31).

TRAVEL ROUTES

The broken landscape of Palestine provided natural limitations on the travel of the ancient Israelites. Geographers recognize four main routes that were open for north-south travel: the coastal plain, the crest of the hill country, the Jordan rift, and the Transjordan plateau. These principal

---

5. Ibid., 3.44-45.
6. S. Thomas Parker, "The Decapolis Reviewed," *Journal of Biblical Literature* 94 (September 1975):440.

north-south roads were linked by east-west roads of local importance to major centers of population. Because of the topography, these patterns remained rather fixed through the various historical periods.

Perhaps the most important highway of the ancient Near Eastern world was the "Way of the Sea" (Isa. 9:1), or *Via Maris* as it was called in Crusader times. This route traversed Palestine, linking two greater centers of oriental culture, Mesopotamia and Egypt. It runs along Palestine's coastal plain, passes through Mount Carmel, traverses the Plain of Esdraelon, passing between Mount Tabor and the Nazareth hills, and brushes the northwest shores of the Sea of Galilee before crossing the Jordan and ascending the Golan to Damascus.

Second in importance to the *Via Maris* was the "King's Highway" (Num. 20:17; 21:22) of Transjordan. This route followed the fringe of the Syrian Desert and extended from Elath in the south to Damascus in the north.

A third highway extended through the middle of Judea and Samaria. It has been called the Hill Road, the Ridge Route, and the Way of the Patriarchs. Known as the "water-parting route," this route followed the crest of the hill country along the relatively flat land between the valleys and steep slopes to the east and west. The route began at Beersheba and continued north through Hebron, Bethlehem, Jerusalem, Ramah, Bethel, and Shechem to the Plain of Esdraelon.

The fourth major north-south route through Israel was the Valley Road. This highway followed the Jordan Valley from Jericho to Scythopolis. It then continued on north to link the settlements along the western shore of the Sea of Galilee.

Although the routes used by Jesus are not always described in detail by the gospel writers, the roads of New Testament Palestine were part of a network of routes that had developed and endured through the centuries.[7] Given His point of departure and destination, the routes of Jesus may be adequately reconstructed.

One problem regarding the gospel references to Jesus' travels demands more attention. According to Josephus, the Hill Road through Samaria was usually taken by the Galilean pilgrims enroute to Jerusalem. He writes, "It was the custom of the Galileans at the time of a festival to pass through the Samaritan territory on their way to the Holy City."[8] This route was more dangerous than other alternatives, but it did permit travel from

---

7. M. Avi-Yonah, "The Development of the Roman Road System in Palestine," *Israel Exploration Journal* 1 (1950-51):54-60.
8. Josephus *Antiquities* 20.118.

Galilee to Jerusalem in just three days.[9] The gospels, however, present Jesus and the disciples traveling to Jerusalem along the circuitous route through Perea (Matt. 19:1; 20:17, 29; Mark 10:1, 32; Luke 18:31, 35; John 12:1).

Did Jesus customarily travel the Hill Road through Samaria on His journeys from Galilee to Jerusalem? If so, was His last journey to Jerusalem a unique exception? It is a popular notion that the Perean travel route was normative for Galilean pilgrims. Historical records indicate that Galilean Jews en route to Jerusalem did use the Hill Road leading through Samaria. Yet there were incidents (Luke 9:51-53) and sometimes bloody encounters. Josephus mentions that he provided an armed escort of 500 men to ensure the safe passage of a group of travelers through Samaria to Jerusalem.[10] In addition, because of their idolatrous background and polluted ethnic heritage (1 Kings 17), the Samaritans were considered highly contaminated.[11]

Undoubtedly the more scrupulous Jews, like the Pharisees, avoided Samaritan territory as much as possible. They would have gladly added several days travel to their itinerary to avoid the possibility of contamination by the "unclean" Samaritans. Such prejudices, of course, would not have influenced the conduct of Jesus. He was willing to drink from a Samaritan vessel and minister to the Samaritan people (John 4:4-42).

Jesus' choice of the Perean route on His last journey to Jerusalem may have been motivated by a desire to avoid being part of a disturbance that could have led to a premature arrest and ministry crisis. This also gave Jesus many teaching opportunities with the pilgrim travelers (cf. Matt. 19:1—20:34; Mark 10:1-52; Luke 10:31—19:28).

SITE IDENTIFICATION

The geographical accuracy of the gospels has been undermined by those who discount many of the place-names as misinformation or unauthentic accretions from a later period. The comment by F. C. Grant is representative of many critics, "He [Mark] was certainly unfamiliar with the geogra-

---

9. Josephus *Life* 269.
10. Ibid., 266-70.
11. Joachim Jeremias, *Jerusalem in the Time of Jesus,* trans. F. H. and C. H. Cave (Philadelphia: Fortress, 1969), p. 353; Wayne A. Brindle, "The Origin and History of the Samaritans, *Grace Journal* 5 (Spring 1984):47-75. The apostle's comment, "For Jews have no dealings with Samaritans" (John 4:9), is the classic understatement of John's gospel.

phy and topography of Northern Palestine."[12]

Much of the criticism of gospel geography arises from an inability to identify some of the significant sites where Jesus ministered. Great progress, however, has been made in recent years, demonstrating that the gospel writers were not unfamiliar with Palestinian geography but, in fact, described it accurately.

Before giving attention to the identification of some of the significant sites of Jesus' ministry, a basic approach must be established. W. F. Albright suggests that the geographer must consider five aspects of any topographical problem: (1) criticism of the written sources in which ancient place-names occur, (2) the approximate location of sites from documentary indications, (3) toponymy, or the analysis of place-names and their linguistic transmission, (4) archaeological indications, and (5) the evidence of tradition.[13] These factors serve as the basis for site identification in the following discussion.

BETHANY BEYOND THE JORDON

Jesus was baptized by John at Bethany beyond the Jordan and later ministered with His disciples at this site (John 1:28; 10:40-41). By the third century A.D. there was confusion regarding the identification of the site. On the basis of his allegorical interpretation of Scripture, Origen suggested that the proper reading was Bethabara ("house of preparation") and that the site was to be located west of the Jordan. Yet the reading "Bethany" is attested by overwhelming documentary evidence. And the phrase "beyond the Jordan" clearly distinguishes it from the Bethany near Jerusalem (Matt. 21:17; Mark 11:1), placing the site east, not west, of the Jordan River.[14]

It has been suggested that the name Bethany is derived from *bet anivvah,* meaning "house of the boat/ship."[15] This would be an appropriate name for a ford community on the Jordan. Two such fords are represented on the Madeba mosaic map (ca. A.D. 560). An archaeological survey of these sites is not possible because of the Jordan's flooding and because of

12. F. C. Grant, "The Gospel According to St. Mark," in *The Interpreter's Bible,* ed. G. A. Buttrick, 12 vols. (New York: Abingdon, 1951-57), 7 (1951):631.
13. W. F. Albright, "The Rediscovery of the Biblical World," in *The Westminster Historical Atlas to the Bible,* rev. ed., ed. G. E. Wright and F. V. Filson (Philadelphia: Westminster, 1956), p. 14.
14. For a thorough discussion of the textual issue, see C. K. Barrett, *The Gospel According to St. John,* 2d ed. (London: SPCK, 1978), p. 175.
15. Clemens Kopp, *The Holy Places of the Gospels,* trans. Ronald Walls (New York: Herder and Herder, 1963), p. 114.

changes in the river channel. Remains from ford communities would have long since washed away. Yet there is a strong tradition from the earliest times that links Jesus' ministry with Hajlah ford in the vicinity of the Wadi el-Kharrar about seven miles southeast of Jericho.[16] If archaeological data were available, the site of Bethany beyond the Jordan could be expected to be found in this area.

BETHSAIDA OF GALILEE

Bethsaida was the home of Philip and the city of Andrew and Peter (John 1:44; 12:21). It was at a "lonely place" (Mark 6:31) near Bethsaida that Jesus fed the five thousand (Luke 9:10-17). Where was Bethsaida located?

Many Bible atlases and maps have indicated that there were two Bethsaidas—one in Galilee and the other east of the Jordan in Gaulanitis. Josephus tells how Philip the Tetrarch advanced the village of Bethsaida, near the northeast shore of the Sea of Galilee, to the status of a "city" (polis) by strengthening its fortifications, increasing its population, and naming it "Julias" after the emperor's daughter. This site has been identified as et-Tell, situated about a mile and a half north of where the Jordan River empties into the Sea of Galilee.

The principal argument for the existence of a second Bethsaida west of the Jordan is based on a misinterpretation of a brief phrase in Mark 6:45. After the feeding of the five thousand the disciples departed "to [pros] Bethsaida," and yet they ended up at Gennesaret (Mark 6:53), a site clearly west of the Jordan. However, the Greek preposition pros may indicate direction towards rather than arrival at.[17] In that case, Mark 6:45 can be interpreted to mean that the disciples merely started off in the direction of Bethsaida, their ultimate destination being the Plain of Gennesaret. Early pilgrim tradition knows of only one Bethsaida, Julias, and no evidence for a western Bethsaida appears until the time of the Crusades, when sites were moved in wholesale fashion to suit the convenience of the pilgrims.

The two most probable sites for Bethsaida-Julias are el-'Araj and et-Tell, just a mile and a half to the north of the Sea of Galilee. The location of et-Tell hardly qualifies it as a fishing village (cf. Matt. 14:22; Mark 6:45; Luke 9:10); and el-'Araj, on the marshy floodplain of the Jordan, is an unlikely site for a fortress city named after the emperor's daughter. A solution has been found with the discovery of an aqueduct and Roman road joining the

---

16. Ibid., pp. 113-29.
17. Vincent Taylor, *The Gospel According to St. Mark,* 2d ed. (London: Macmillan, 1966), pp. 327-28.

two sites.[18] Bethsaida-Julias, it appears, was a double site with a fishing village suburb on the Galilean lakeshore within reasonable proximity of the fortified city et-Tell.

CANA OF GALILEE

At Cana of Galilee, the home of Nathanael (John 21:2), Jesus began His miraculous signs by turning water into wine (John 2:1-11). From the same village He assured the nobleman of Capernaum that his son had been healed (John 4:46-54). The exact location of Cana has been disputed, and two major sites compete for the honor. Kefr Kenna ("the village of Kenna") makes a fairly convincing claim to be Cana of Galilee. The Franciscan church in the heart of the village is reportedly built on the actual remains of the house in which the miracle took place. Tourists may view an old water jar that is said to have held wine after the miracle.

The earliest pilgrim tradition, however, points to a site about nine miles north of Nazareth called Khirbet Kana ("ruin of Cana"). Josephus refers to Cana as his military quarters and then later describes his quarters as being in the Plain of Asochis (the Bet Netofa Valley).[19] The analysis of the name *Cana* ("place of reeds") would also suggest Khirbet Kana, located on a hill overlooking the marshy stretches of the Bet Netofa Valley. Although the site has not been excavated, surface exploration has led to the discovery of ruins from the Roman period, including ancient tombs, wall foundations, and thirty-one cisterns.[20] There is no evidence that ruins at the competing site, Kefr Kenna, date from the Roman period. Future excavation may confirm (or refute) the identification; but the evidence, including early pilgrim itineraries, definitely points to Khirbet Kana as the site of Jesus' first Galilean miracle.[21]

SYCHAR, A CITY OF SAMARIA

After His ministry in Judea following the Passover of A.D. 30, Jesus proceeded north to Galilee by way of Samaria (John 4:3-4). He came to a city

18. *Interpreters Dictionary of the Bible,* s.v. "Bethsaida," by Michael Avi-Yonah, 1:397; James F. Strange, "Survey of Lower Galilee, 1982," *Israel Exploration Journal* 32 (1982):255.
19. Josephus *Life* 86.207.
20. Aapeli Saarisalo, "Topographical Researches in Galilee," *The Journal of the Palestine Oriental Society* 9 (1929):27-40. Strange reports that occupation of the site was confined to the first through sixth centuries C.E., although 4 percent of the sherds were from the Iron Age, "Survey of Lower Galilee, 1982," pp. 254-55.
21. Richard M. Mackowski, "Scholars' qanah": A Re-examination of the Evidence in Favor of Khirbet-qanah," *Biblische Zeitschrift* 2 (1979):278-84.

of Samaria called Sychar (John 4:5) and met a Samaritan woman at Jacob's well. There is no problem in identifying the well. Few sites in the Holy Land have a better claim to antiquity and authenticity. The location of the site of biblical Sychar, however, is debated.

Many have sought to identify Sychar with the Old Testament site of Shechem located at Tell Balatah. It is asserted that "Sychar" is a corruption of "Shechem." However, there is no textual evidence for this suggested emendation. Neither is there certain evidence of Roman occupation at Tell Balatah during the time of Christ.

A more likely site for Sychar was first changed to the Samaritan Iskar (with the initial *'Ain*) and then to the Arabic 'Askar.[22] The name 'Askar in Arabic means "collection," hence "army," indicating that the village may have once been a military camp. Perhaps the original name was slightly altered in keeping with this historical development.

Although 'Askar, an inhabited village, has not been excavated, the recent discovery of Roman tombs in the vicinity of the village suggest that it was inhabited in the time of Christ.[23] The Madeba mosaic map, which marks the site by a church just north of Jacob's well, and early pilgrim itineraries confirm beyond reasonable doubt that 'Askar may be identified as biblical Sychar.

GERASA OR GADARA

Somewhere along the southeastern shore of the Sea of Galilee Jesus healed two men who were demon possessed. The geographical problem is that the gospels record different place-names for the location of the miracle. According to Matthew 8:28 the miracle took place in "the country of the Gadarenes," though Mark 5:1 and Luke 8:26, 37 record "the country of the Garasenes."[24] How can the miracle be represented as having taken place in two different territories? The solution is found in a historical understanding of Decapolis and its two city-states, Gadara and Gerasa.

Decapolis was not a definitely bounded political unit. It was made up of the territories of a number of independent cities. Each city controlled the territory and villages of its immediate vicinity, and some even controlled separate enclaves of land. Ancient coins portraying a ship and bearing the

22. C. R. Conder, "Samaritan Topography," *Palestine Exploration Fund, Quarterly Statement* 8 (1976):182-97.
23. E. Damati, " 'Askar," *Israel Exploration Journal* 22 (1972):174.
24. The name "Gergesenes" was introduced into the text by Origen, who had geographical objections to the other readings and preferred the allegorical significance he found in the name.

name *Gadara*, along with references from Josephus,[25] indicate that Gadara possessed territory on the shores of the Sea of Galilee. Being the closest city of Decapolis to the site of the miracle (five miles southeast of the lake shore) and possessing a sizable Jewish population, it is reasonable that Matthew would describe the miracle as taking place in the territory of Gadara. Certainly this place would have been familiar to his Jewish readers.

Mark and Luke, on the other hand, wrote to Roman and Greek readers respectively. Undoubtedly these readers would have heard of the splendor of Gerasa with its temples, theaters, hippodrome, and public buildings. It is likely that Mark and Luke identified the vicinity of the miracle in relationship to this famous city, which would be more well known among the readers unfamiliar with Palestine. Although Gerasa (Jerash) is thirty-five miles southeast of the Sea of Galilee, there is evidence that the city controlled a large territory. The geographical boundaries of the cities of Decapolis may have overlapped even as the boundaries of Damascus overlapped with Syria.[26] The biblical and historical data suggests that Gerasa shared the jurisdiction over the southeast lake shore with Gadara.

In recording the location of the miracle, Matthew gives a more specific reference, identifying the incident in relationship to the nearby city of Gadara. Mark and Luke provided a more general description of the location, placing the miracle in the extended territory of the well-known city of Gerasa. The geography and history allowed for either name. The authors chose the one that would communicate most effectively to their respective readers.

MAGADAN, MAGDALA, OR DALMANUTHA

After the miraculous feeding of the four thousand, Jesus dismissed the multitudes and traveled with His disciples by boat to the western shore of the Sea of Galilee where they were confronted by a group of Jewish leaders. According to Matthew the incident took place in "the region of Magadan," or according to a variant, "Magdala" (Matt. 15:39). However, Mark 8:10 names "the district of Dalmanutha" as the scene of the confrontation.

The textual evidence for Matthew's "Magadan" is strong.[27] Yet many geographers opt for the reading "Magdala" because of the village by that

---

25. Josephus *Life* 42; *War* 3.37.
26. *Zondervan Pictorial Encyclopedia of the Bible*, s.v. "Gadara, Gadarenes," by J. C. DeYoung, 2:622.
27. Bruce M. Metzger, *A Textual Commentary on the Greek New Testament* (London: United Bible Societies, 1971), p. 41.

name that suits the location admirably. Magadan and Magdala may both be traced to an original Hebrew name, Magdal. In all probability, Magadan is the correct text in Matthew, whereas the authentic site may be found at Magdala.

But what about "Dalmanutha" in Mark 8:10? The manuscript evidence overwhelmingly supports the reading as original. It has been suggested that "Dalmanutha" is the transliteration of the emphatic form of a Syriac (an eastern dialect of Aramaic) word *dalmynyth'*, meaning "of the harbor."[28] In other words Matthew recorded the arrival of Christ in the neighborhood of Magadan (Magdala), whereas Mark, who was dependent on the preaching of Peter,[29] recorded that Jesus had reached the site of the harbor. This is not to suggest an Aramaic original for Mark's gospel. Rather, the word *Dalmanutha* may be an Aramaized form of the word for "harbor" that was then transliterated into the Greek text, as in the case of Golgotha ("skull," Mark 16:22). Matthew and Mark are both right. Once again, the gospel records are seen to be complimentary rather than contradictory.

INTERPRETIVE ISSUES

Many interpretive issues can be clarified as a result of giving careful attention to geographical details. An excellent example is found in the travel narrative in Luke 9:51—19:18. Luke clearly indicates that Jesus was traveling to Jerusalem (9:51; 13:22; 17:11). The difficulty arises in trying to trace the course of His journey. Jesus began by going through Samaria (9:52), but later He was at Bethany (10:38-42). Luke then placed Him "between Samaria and Galilee" (17:11), and still later Luke said He was at Jericho (19:1). The apparent disarray of the topographical notices has led many to question the geographical accuracy of Luke.

Following the lead of C. C. McCown, many scholars have concluded that Luke's account does not record a literal journey but is, rather, a collection of detached episodes arranged around a travel motif.[30] H. Conzelmann refers to this section as "a piece of deliberate editorial work."[31] He adds, "Luke develops the idea of a journey, for which there is little support in the

---

28. N. Herz, "Dalmanutha," *The Expository Times* 8 (1896-97):563; (1897-98):95.
29. Eusebius, *Historia Ecclesiastica* 2.15.
30. C. C. McCown, "The Geography of Luke's Central Section," *Journal of Biblical Literature* 57 (1938):51-66.
31. Hans Conzelmann, *The Theology of St. Luke,* trans. Geoffrey Busell (Philadelphia: Fortress, 1982), p. 62.

material available to him."[32] The sequence of movement in this narrative, according to these scholars, is only a literary device that Luke employed to focus on the theological significance of Jesus' ministry. There is a great deal of dispute, however, over just what significance is intended.[33] The diversity of viewpoint suggests that any supposed theological significance is not clearly marked.

There is a geographically defensible alternative to the "journey motif" approach advocated by McCown. It has been noted that Luke's three references to Jesus making His way to Jerusalem (Luke 9:51; 13:22; 17:11) correspond closely to John's mention of three journeys to Jerusalem during the last six months of His ministry (John 7:2, 10; 10:22; 12:1).[34] This would suggest that Luke's central section is substantially more geographically and chronologically accurate than has been supposed.

Harold W. Hoehner notes that Jesus' return to Bethany to raise Lazarus (John 11) would actually constitute a fourth visit to Jerusalem during this period. He therefore links the three journeys of Luke's gospel with the Jerusalem visits recorded in John 10:22; 11:1-54; and 11:55—12:1.[35] Although this reconstruction is plausible, there is no mention in John 11:1-54 of Jesus's actually visiting Jerusalem. Bethany was His destination (John 11:1, 7, 30). Threats on His life at this time (John 11:47-53) would have probably deterred His going into the city of Jerusalem. It may be best to link the three Lukan travel notices with John 7:2, 10; 10:22; and 12:1. Either way, the geography of Luke's gospel is seen to be clearly discernible and in keeping with his purposes as an accurate historian (Luke 1:1-4).

ACCURACY AND INERRANCY

The integrity of Scripture has been undermined in recent years by those who would limit its infallibility. Inerrancy is deemed not relevant to the issue of biblical authority. Infallibility is limited to matters of "faith and practice," allowing for errors in the areas of history, science, and geogra-

---

32. Ibid.
33. J. Carl Laney, "Selective Geographical Problems in the Life of Christ" (Th.D. dissertation, Dallas Theological Seminary, 1978):286-89.
34. Alfred Edersheim, *The Life and Times of Jesus the Messiah,* 2 vols. (New York: Longmans, Green, and Co., 1899), 2:126-27; H. E. Gilleband, "The Travel Narrative in St. Luke (IX:51-XVIII:14)," *Bibliotheca Sacra* 80 (1923):237-45. It is surprising that I. H. Marshall's fine *Commentary On Luke,* NIGTC (Grand Rapids: Eerdmans, 1978), does not even consider this possibility. He writes, "Luke cannot have been consciously providing a geographical progress from Galilee to Jerusalem," p. 401.
35. Harold Hoehner, "Chronological Aspects of the Life of Christ, Part III, The Duration of Christ's Ministry," *Bibliotheca Sacra* 131 (April-June 1974):161-62.

phy. The critics point out seemingly insoluble discrepancies as the basis for their argument that the Bible is not completely accurate. In many cases solutions are available, but all too often the study done by the critics has not been sufficiently thorough. It is easier to say, "That's an error," than to invest in the time and research required to uncover other reasonable and defensible alternatives.

The possibilities for satisfactory solutions to geographical "discrepancies" have been illustrated in the discussion regarding Gadara/Geresa and Magadan/Magdala/Dalmanutha. Similarly, a solution may be found for Luke's "geographical inaccuracy" in his reference to Emmaus being 60, rather than 120, stadia from Jerusalem (Luke 24:13). It is assumed that the traditional location of Emmaus at 'Imwas is right and that Luke's distance must therefore be wrong. However, both internal and external textual evidence supports the reading of 60 stadia.[36] This disqualifies 'Imwas as a possible site for biblical Emmaus.

The traditional identification, dating from Eusebius, must be set aside in favor of a site more in keeping with the biblical data. A more likely possibility would be el-Qubeibeh, known as Castellum Emmaus in the Crusader period, situated just 63 stadia from Jerusalem. Excavation has confirmed the existence of occupation at the site during the Roman period. Thorough investigation continues to confirm the geographical accuracy of the gospels.[37]

SUMMARY AND CONCLUSION

From a study of the geography of the gospels, one gains several strong impressions:

1. The gospel writers had a definite geographical perspective and emphasis, but they were not obsessed by this interest. They were not writing a geography of the life of Christ, but they used selective geographical notices to elucidate His life and ministry.

2. The general framework of the life of Christ is clear. The places of His birth, childhood, and death are known. The major portion of His ministry was in Galilee, and the center of His Galilean ministry was at Capernaum.

3. Relatively few of the places where Jesus ministered are definitely named and identified by the gospel writers. The writers were more interested in Christ's message than the place He delivered it. They used geogra-

---

36. Antonine DeGuglielmo, "Emmaus," *Catholic Biblical Quarterly* 3 (1941):295.
37. For further study, see Laney, pp. 326-66.

phy only where it furthered that objective.

4. Jesus' ministry was confined almost entirely to Jewish centers free from Gentile influence. His ministry was primarily to the Jews. He had little to do with the Hellenistic centers such as Sepphoris, Scythopolis, and Tiberias.

5. The gospels reflect not only a geographical perspective and emphasis, they are topographically accurate. Satisfactory explanations are available that refute the arguments of the critics and vindicate the accuracy of the gospels.

Part 2

The Joy of Fellowship:
Themes from the Spiritual Life

Roy B. Zuck (A.B., Biola University; Th.M., Th.D., Dallas Theological Seminary) is academic dean and professor of Bible exposition at Dallas Theological Seminary.

Balancing the Academic and the Spiritual in Seminary

Roy B. Zuck

When I was a student at Dallas Theological Seminary from 1953 to 1959, Dr. Dwight Pentecost was beginning his teaching career at the Seminary. As I sat in several of his Bible courses, I, along with others, sensed his love for the Savior and his commitment to and knowledge of the Scriptures. In addition I sensed his concern that his students acquire more than an intellectual knowledge of the Bible, that they live the truth and love the Lord. As a teacher his desire has always been that students blend their academic studies with spiritual growth. He exemplifies the balance suggested in this essay.

Students repeatedly affirm that the academic atmosphere of a seminary program somehow relates to their growing cold spiritually. A recent graduate of Dallas Seminary told me that when he came to seminary four years earlier he was spiritually "hot," but when he graduated he was "cold."

Why does this drop in spiritual temperature occur? Why are some students less turned on about the Scriptures when they leave than when they come? Should it not be the other way around? Inasmuch as students are in contact with the Scriptures daily, should they not be warmer rather than colder spiritually? After all, should not the study of the Word deepen people's spiritual lives?

Of course students are maturing and becoming more knowledgeable, but why should that put them in the spiritual doldrums? Should not students be more "fired-up" when they are graduating than when they are matriculating? Why do they digress in the spiritual life, going from the oven to the deep freeze?

The problem is not the frequency of one's contact with the Word. Instead the problem involves a fallacy in that. Believers often approach the Scriptures with the head only rather than with the head and the heart. Unfortunately many people know the Scriptures but fail to obey them. Jesus said that the person who does or obeys what He taught is blessed (John 13:17). Twenty-seven times in Deuteronomy Moses said to that generation ready to move into the Promised Land, "Obey the Word, obey God's decrees, obey God's commands." James put it this way, "Do not merely listen to the Word. . . . Do what it says" (James 1:22, NIV). Ezra said that he "devoted himself" to studying, obeying, and teaching the Scriptures (Ezra 7:10).

Yet many students omit that middle step and move from studying to teaching without bothering to obey the Scriptures. Many become interested only in the perception of the truth and neglect the reception of it. They approach the Bible like a human book to be grasped intellectually rather than like a divine book to be grasped intellectually and experientially. They have control of the Bible, but the Bible may not have control of them.

How can seminary students continue to be spiritually sensitive and avoid growing cold and callous? Basically the answer is to realize that a seminary education is an academic *and* a spiritual pursuit. To have the academic without the spiritual is like having a car without gasoline or like having wood on a cold day with no match for a fire. A seminary is an educational institution, but it is *more* than that. One writer somewhat facetiously stated that "the function of the seminary is to turn [the students] up (recruiting), sort them out (admissions), shape them up (teaching), shake them down (examinations), and pass them on (graduation and placement)."[1] However, that is not the full picture.

If a person approaches the Scriptures only to learn what they say and stops with that, then spiritual warmth will not be there. The fire will die down. Of course a seminary should be concerned about quality, about excellence in the curriculum and the classroom. But it is to be concerned about the spiritual *as well* as the academic.

But why? Why should studying in a seminary be considered an educational *and* a spiritual endeavor? Several reasons may be suggested.

---

1. James D. Glasse, "Seminaries and Professional Education," *Theological Education* 8 (Autumn 1971):3-4.

THE RELATIONSHIP OF THE WORD OF GOD AND THE SPIRIT OF GOD

The Word of God and the Holy Spirit are to function together. The Word generates faith (Ps. 19:7; Rom.10:17; James 1:18; 1 Pet.1:23); so does the Holy Spirit (John 3:5-7; Titus 3:5). The Word sanctifies (John 17:17-19); so does the Holy Spirit (2 Thess. 2:13; 1 Pet. 1:2). The Word enlightens (Ps. 119:105, 130; 2 Tim. 3:16); the Holy Spirit does the same (John 14:26; 16:13; 1 Cor. 2:10-15). They go together, and both are needed.[2] So if we leave out the ministry of the Holy Spirit, then all we have is the knowledge of a book.

John Calvin taught that the Bible has "no efficacy unless at the same time the Holy Spirit works in the hearts of the hearers, creating faith and making men's minds open to receive the Word."[3] The work of the Holy Spirit accompanies the ministry of the Word. Without His work the Word is not efficacious.

THE NATURE OF THE SPIRITUAL LIFE

Another reason a seminary education is a spiritual as well as an academic endeavor is the nature of the spiritual life. Spiritual growth comes not just from hearing but from hearing and doing. Repeatedly the New Testament states that the Christian life is a walk (e.g., Rom. 13:13; Eph. 4:1; 5:2, 8; Phil. 3:16; Col. 1:10; 2:6; 4:5; 1 Thess. 2:12; 1 John 1:7; 2:6; 2 John 6; 3 John 4) and that one's conduct is to be affected by God's truth. In attitude and action believers are to bear the fruit of the Holy Spirit (Gal. 5:22-23). Martin Luther wrote that the Bible "is not merely to be repeated or known, but to be lived and felt."[4]

THE NATURE OF THE MINISTRY

In 1925 Lewis Sperry Chafer wrote this statement: "In view of the fact that Christian service is effective solely as it is wrought in the power of the Holy Spirit and that power is realized only through the Scriptural provisions for personal adjustment to the Spirit, the theological curriculum is

---

2. Roy B. Zuck, *The Holy Spirit in Your Teaching*, rev. ed. (Wheaton, Ill.: Victor Books, 1984), pp. 17-18.
3. John Calvin, cited in Ronald S. Wallace, *Calvin's Doctrine of the Word and Scripture* (Grand Rapids: Eerdmans, 1957), pp. 128-29.
4. Martin Luther, cited by A. Skevington Wood, *The Principles of Biblical Interpretation* (Grand Rapids: Zondervan, 1967), p. 80.

fundamentally lacking which does not provide the student with the training, power and personal victory in Jesus Christ."[5]

People are hurting. They have all kinds of problems. They have deep
needs. Therefore they need knowledge, the knowledge of the Word of God,
but they need knowledge *and* application of that truth to their problems. If
a child is sick, the parents want the doctor to do more than *describe* the
medicine. They want him to *prescribe* it to help the child overcome the
problem. Our task is that of "fitting [people] to live in perfect harmony
with the will of God."[6] Paul expressed it this way: his and Timothy's task
was that of "admonishing and teaching everyone with all wisdom so that
we may present everyone perfect [mature] in Christ" (Col. 1:28).

A primary concern of those in the ministry should be that lives are
transformed, not just that curiosity is satisfied; that people are growing
spiritually as well as intellectually; that people know the God of the Word
and not just the Word of God; that people are deepened in their walk with
God and not just in their knowledge about Him.

For example, Christian leaders want to see people's marriages improve.
But how is this accomplished? By telling them what the Bible says? Yes,
that is the starting point, pointing out to them God's standards, God's values, God's commands. People need the facts, but they also need to have
commitment and obedience to those standards and those facts to appropriate God's truth to their needs.

On September 20, 1903, Benjamin Breckenridge Warfield spoke in the
opening chapel to the student body of Princeton Theological Seminary. In
that message he said, "Intellectual training alone will never make a true
minister." He added, "It behoves us above everything else to remember
that the ministry is a spiritual office."[7]

WAYS TO BALANCE THE SPIRITUAL WITH THE ACADEMIC

How then can the Bible be approached in this dual way with the heart as
well as the mind? Four things may be suggested.

---

5. Lewis Sperry Chafer, "Effective Ministerial Training" (Dallas: Dallas Theological Seminary, May
   1925), pp. 10-11.
6. James De Forest Murch, *Christian Education and the Local Church*, rev. ed. (Cincinnati; Standard, 1943), p. 100.
7. Benjamin Breckenridge Warfield, "Spiritual Culture in the Theological Seminary, " *Princeton
   Theological Review* 2 (January 1904):65. (Reprinted in *Selected Shorter Writings of Benjamin B.
   Warfield* 2, ed. John E. Meeter [Nutley, NJ: Presbyterian and Reformed, 1973], pp. 488-96.)

RECOGNIZE THE SUPERNATURAL ELEMENT IN ALL TEACHING AND LEARNING

Faculty and students at Dallas Seminary are in a unique position. They are not merely in a human enterprise; teaching God's Word is a divine-human enterprise. Believers are to cooperate with the Holy Spirit in their teaching and learning. One Christian educator said that "teaching the Word in the wisdom and power of the Spirit becomes a great adventure with the Master Teacher Himself."[8] John F. Walvoord has often referred to a statement made by Chafer that Dallas Seminary has a faculty of One, that is, ultimately the Holy Spirit is our Teacher. According to the Seminary's current catalog,

> To be properly qualified for seminary instruction the student must be walking in fellowship with God so that he can be taught by the Holy Spirit. While recognizing the importance of high standards of research and technical skill implicit in all true biblical scholarship the fact remains that scholarship is not enough. In addition, the teaching ministry of the Holy Spirit is necessary for it adds a unique spiritual dynamic to the teaching and learning process. The cultivation of the spiritual life is inseparably fused with the scholarly study of biblically related subjects thus providing an unusual classroom climate and a distinct theological education.[9]

The need is for reverent scholarship—not just scholarship, but scholarship that is characterized by devotion to Jesus Christ. One way of recognizing the supernatural is by living the truth, by embodying biblical principles in one's life. Paul wrote along this line in 1 Thessalonians 1:5, "Our gospel" —what he communicated to them—"came to you not simply with words." It was not mere talk. It was communicated "also with power, with the Holy Spirit and with deep conviction. You know how we lived among you for your sake." Here was content *and* conduct, communication *and* conviction. Paul wrote to the Philippians, "Join with others in following my example, brothers, and take note of those who live according to the pattern we gave you" (Phil. 3:17). "Whatever you have learned or received or heard from me, or seen in me—put it into practice" (Phil. 4:9). Faculty and students alike are to be examples of Christian character and conduct, to live out the truth. In the classroom faculty members are to relate the truth to life, to apply it, to help students see the relevance of the content of Scrip-

8. Lois E. LeBar, *Focus on People in Christian Education* (Westwood, N.J.: Revell, 1968), p. 24.
9. *Dallas Seminary Catalog* 1985-86, p. 9.

ture to living. Kenneth O. Gangel in his W. H. Griffith Thomas lectureship to the Dallas Seminary student body in 1978 said, "Learning unrelated to life is as dead as faith without works."[10]

Recognizing the supernatural element in the seminary classroom means that the faculty are to model the truth and point up its relevance. It also means that they are interested in what they are teaching, that they are enthusiastic about it.

RELATE THE WORD OF GOD TO ONE'S NEEDS

To the Thessalonians Paul wrote, "You became imitators of us and of the Lord; in spite of severe suffering you welcomed the message with the joy given by the Holy Spirit" (1 Thess. 1:6). He expanded on that in 2:13: "We also thank God continually because when you received the Word of God, which you heard from us, you accepted [lit., welcomed] it not as the word of men, but as it actually is, the Word of God, which is at work in you who believe." Faculty and students can "welcome" the Word by relating it to areas of their need. They can list areas of need—pride, laziness, procrastination, disorganization, temptation to lust, lack of control of the tongue or temper, jealousy, poor attitude toward one's spouse—and then ask God to make them sensitive to parts of the Bible they are studying that relate to those areas of need. That is one way believers keep their spiritual temperature from dropping. Also believers can ask the Lord to expose them through His Word to other areas they may need to work on. Teachers can ask and answer the applicational question "So what?" What does this Bible passage or theological truth mean to us? What is its significance for life? And students can ask the same question of themselves or the study: "So what? What is God saying to me from this passage or 'doctrinal issue?' "

REMOVE OBSTACLES TO THE MINISTRY OF THE HOLY SPIRIT

Spiritual coldness often comes because sin is blocking the ministry of the Holy Spirit. One reason spiritual doldrums set in after a few semesters of seminary study is lack of obedience to God. Sin leads to spiritual slumps. Spiritual growth, on the other hand, comes from being yielded to the Holy Spirit, being filled with the Spirit (Eph. 5:22), walking by means of the Spirit (Gal. 5:16), confessing and forsaking sin (1 John 1:9).

10. Kenneth O. Gangel, "Integrating Faith and Learning: Principles and Process," *Bibliotheca Sacra* 135 (April-June 1978):108.

Readiness is an important principle of learning. If a student is ready for class both academically and intellectually, he learns more. But the study of the Scriptures involves spiritual readiness as well. Failure to be spiritually receptive to the truth explains why students do not experience the full benefits of an academic-spiritual education. "Illumination is possible only as a believer is open to the Spirit's sanctifying and cleansing work."[11] As students walk to a class, they should pray. As they enter the classroom, they should ask God for an openness to His truth, for a readiness for the Word, and an eagerness to live out what He has for them. And as they leave the class, they should pray about those truths. That prayerful attitude, walking into and out of a classroom in a spirit of prayer, makes a profound difference in students' attitudes.

RESPOND TO THE TRUTH IN SPECIFIC WAYS

The Thessalonian believers put the truth into action. They "became a model to all the believers in Macedonia and Achaia. The Lord's message rang out from [them]." As a result their "faith in God [was] known everywhere" (1 Thess. 1:7-8). Warfield urged his students to "assimilate the Bible, to make it [their] own."[12] Francis A. Schaeffer wrote,

> Does inerrancy really make a difference—in the way we live our lives...? Sadly we must say that we evangelicals who truly hold to the full authority of Scriptures have not always done well in this respect. I have said that inerrancy is the watershed of the evangelical world. But it is not just a theological debating point. *It is the obeying of the Scripture which is the watershed. It is believing and applying to our lives* which demonstrate whether we in fact believe it."[13]

Christian living involves cooperation between the Holy Spirit and the believer. The more specific a person is in opening his heart to areas of need and the more specific teachers are in helping others see how they can apply the truth, the more effective the Holy Spirit can be.

CONCLUSION

A seminary is to be an academic *and* a spiritual institution. This is be-

11. Zuck, p. 64.
12. Warfield, p. 79.
13. Francis A. Schaeffer, *The Great Evangelical Disaster* (Westchester, Ill.: Crossway, 1984), p. 61 (italics his).

cause of the nature of the Word, because of the nature of the spiritual life, and because of the nature of the ministry. Therefore the problem of spiritual coldness comes when students or faculty approach their studies only from an intellectual standpoint. Studying the truth without desiring to let it penetrate and permeate one's life results in spiritual coldness. If a person knows the Word of God but does not let it change him, he becomes spiritually weak and ineffective. Without the spiritual dimension, academics in a seminary are anemic. To quote Warfield again, "Knowledge [of the Word] is a powerful thing. . . . And so is a locomotive a powerful thing—provided it has steam in it!"[14]

Living out what one learns, appropriating what he appreciates, can result in renewed spiritual vitality, renewed excitement about the Word of God and the God of the Word, renewed spiritual vigor because of dealing with sin, renewed spiritual impact on a lost world, and renewed spiritual power.

In 1742 John Albert Bengel wrote a verse-by-verse commentary on the New Testament in which he emphasized the spiritual and the devotional along with exegesis. He wrote, "Apply yourself wholly to the text, and apply the text wholly to yourself." That summarizes the essence of a theological seminary: to be engaged in an academic *and* a spiritual enterprise. "Be ye doers of the Word and not hearers only" (James 1:22, KJV).

14. Warfield, p. 70.

THOMAS L. CONSTABLE (Diploma, Moody Bible Institute; A.B., Wheaton College; Th.M., Th.D., Dallas Theological Seminary) is director of D.Min. studies and associate professor of Bible exposition at Dallas Theological Seminary.

What Prayer Will and Will Not Change

Thomas L. Constable

"Why did God not answer our prayers? Our son had suffered from a liver problem since he was injured in an automobile accident when he was only a small boy. But a few months ago he died. He was only nineteen and our only child. We prayed so hard for him. Why did God allow him to die?"

A middle-aged couple confronted me with this question after I had finished preaching one Sunday morning in their church. Their question has been asked by many men and women. Most people have wondered why their petitions are granted in some cases, but not in others.

Christians look at that ubiquitous motto that is perhaps the most popular of all, Prayer Changes Things, and think, "Yes, I believe prayer changes things; I have experienced many answers to prayer. But sometimes prayer does not change things. And I do not understand why."

Most believers do not have to search their memories long to remember some things God gave them in answer to their prayers: wisdom in some difficult decision, safety in travel, good health, the salvation of a loved one, and many more. The Bible itself contains many examples of God's granting the petitions of people who prayed. Hannah received a son (1 Sam. 1), David obtained pardon from his heinous crimes (Ps. 51), Peter was released from prison (Acts 12), and Paul was delivered from his enemies and kept safe so that he could continue to preach the gospel (2 Tim. 4).

But we can also think of many other situations in our own lives or in the lives of others in which God did not grant our requests. The Scriptures also contain such examples. God did not grant Jeremiah's petition to spare Judah and not send her into captivity in Babylonia (Jer. 7:13-16; 14:11-12). The Christians to whom James wrote his epistle were not receiving answers to their prayers (James 4:3). Even the Son of God seems to have been denied a request by His Father (Luke 22:42).

When will prayer "change things?" What things will it change and not change? How can a believer tell if God will grant his request or not?

A DEFINITION OF PRAYER

God's Word uses the term *prayer* to refer to the thoughts and feelings expressed to God. Prayer does not include God's response to our words; that is His answer. In the Bible prayer refers specifically to all expressions addressed toward deity. It is used to describe the heathen praying to idols as well as believers praying to the true God (Isa. 45:20). Any expression to a being or concept conceived of as a god in the mind of the person praying is regarded as prayer in Scripture.[1] This definition is not explicitly stated in the Bible; the Word of God does not define prayer. But by noting how God uses the term *prayer* in His Word we can construct such a definition inductively.

The Bible contains examples of many different kinds of prayer. They include prayers of inquiry, personal petition, intercession, confession, praise, thanksgiving, complaint, and general narration. The problem discussed in this article, however, deals only with prayers that ask God for something: petitions for ourselves or for others (intercession). Petitions may be for specific action or for information (inquiries). Again these categories, like the definition of prayer itself, are based on what God has revealed about prayer in His Word.[2]

CHANGES PRAYER DOES EFFECT

Basically there are three types of changes that prayer effects when Christians pray to God. The only prayer of a non-Christian that God promises to answer is a prayer calling on Him for salvation on the basis of the finished work of Christ (Acts 2:21; Rom. 10:13). Of course, God hears all prayers; He is omniscient. And sometimes He graciously grants the petitions of unbelievers according to His will. But the only prayer of an unbeliever that God has promised always to answer is one calling on Him for salvation.

---

1. Thomas L. Constable, "The Doctrine of Prayer" (Th.D. dissertation, Dallas Theological Seminary, 1969), pp. 3-7.
2. Ibid., pp. 7-24.

SUBJECTIVE CHANGE IN THE PERSON PRAYING

Almost everyone agrees that prayer changes the person who prays. Even skeptics who deny that prayer accomplishes anything objectively concede that the practice of praying has beneficial effects on the person who prays.[3]

Prayer benefits anyone who practices it in his spirit. As one prays his thoughts turn Godward, and he is motivated to live a better life. Scripture records several examples of this kind of change taking place in the lives of believers. For instance, when the early Christians prayed about their persecutors, they were encouraged to continue testifying for Christ boldly (Acts 4:23-31).

Not only does prayer provide spiritual benefit for the person praying; it also helps him psychologically. Studies have been done indicating that praying results in greater mental and emotional stability.[4] When a person experiences psychological peace, his physical condition also improves. So praying contributes to the general physical well-being of the person who prays.

OBJECTIVE CHANGE IN THE WORLD

The Scriptures indicate that praying can result in other significant changes in addition to those mentioned above. Not only does prayer change the person who prays, it can also bring about changes in the people and situations about which he has prayed. One might come to this conclusion on the basis of experience alone, but the Bible also clearly teaches it. It seems significant that those who deny the power of prayer to effect objective change often repudiate the Bible. "The objections raised by skeptics against [prayer] . . . for the most part reject the authority of Scripture."[5]

However, there are also many Christians who submit to scriptural authority but who nevertheless have problems believing that prayer can bring about change in the world. These individuals cite biblical teaching on other subjects that seems to contradict the idea that prayer really does change things. To harmonize the teaching of Scripture on prayer one must first study what the Bible teaches about God and His ways. In many

3. William James, *The Varieties of Religious Experience* (New York: Mentor Books, 1958), p. 353; Michael R. Austin, "Can Intercessory Prayer Work?" *The Expository Times* 89 (1978):335-39.
4. Friedrich Heiler, *Prayer: A Study in the History and Psychology of Religion*, trans. Samuel McComb (New York: Oxford U., 1932); Donald Capps, "The Psychology of Petitionary Prayer," *Theology Today* 39 (July 1982):130-41.
5. B. M. Palmer, *Theology of Prayer* (Richmond: Presbyterian Committee of Publication, 1894), p. 347.

places the Bible teaches that God is sovereign. "Sovereignty is not a property of the divine nature, but a prerogative arising out the perfections of the Supreme Being."[6] God has the right to rule over all because of who He is.

The doctrine of providence rests on the doctrine of sovereignty. By divine providence we mean that God does rule in all affairs. "God's works of providence are his most holy, wise, and powerful, preserving and governing all his creatures and all their actions."[7] "In sum, the doctrine of providence tells us that the world and our lives are not ruled by change or by fate but by God."[8]

The doctrine of divine decree is built on God's works of providence. Whereas sovereignty says God has the right to rule and providence says that He does indeed rule, the decree sets forth that He has a plan for ruling. "The decrees of God are, his eternal purpose, according to the counsel of his will, whereby for his own glory, He hath foreordained whatsoever comes to pass."[9] As Chafer has noted:

> There is one comprehensive plan in which all things have their place and by which they proceed . . . .
>
> The term *decree of God* appears first in the singular, since God has but one all-inclusive plan . . . . For convenience, the separate features of this plan may be called the *decrees of God:* but there should be no implication in this that the infinite understanding of God advances by steps or in a train.[10]

William G. T. Shedd has also highlighted the importance of God's all-inclusive plan. "The most important aspect of the Divine decree is, that it brings all things that come to pass in space and time into a *plan.*"[11]

The doctrine of foreordination builds on the decree. It explains in part how God's plan operates. In particular God has ordained beforehand whatever comes to pass.

---

6. Charles Hodge, *Systematic Theology,* 3 vols. (New York: Scribner's, 1887), 2:440.
7. Ibid., 1:575.
8. T. H. L. Parker, "Providence," *Baker's Dictionary of Theology,* ed. Everett F. Harrison, p. 427; cf. John Calvin, *Institutes of the Christian Religion,* ed. John McNeill, trans. Ford Lewis Battles, vols. XXI and XXII: The Library of Christian Classics (Philadelphia: Westminster, 1960), 1:197-210.
9. "The Westminster Shorter Catechism," answer to question 7, *The Confession of Faith of the Presbyterian Church in the United States,* rev. ed. (Richmond: Board of Christian Education, 1965), p. 289.
10. Lewis Sperry Chafer, *Systematic Theology,* 8 vols. (Dallas: Seminary Press, 1947), 1:228.
11. William G. T. Shedd, *Systematic Theology,* 2 vols. (Edinburgh: T. & T. Clark, 1889), 1:398.

Before dealing with our understanding of how prayer fits into the divine decree we should first explain the relationship between other doctrines that grow out of foreordination. *Foreknowledge* refers to God's knowledge of all things *before* they occur. Some theologians equate foreknowledge with foreordination and argue that if God knows something before it happens, it is thereby foreordained.[12] Others separate them, contending that foreknowledge does not necessitate foreordination. *Predestination* refers to God's predetermining the eternal destiny of individuals. *Election* is God's choice of some for salvation.

The problem that prayer raises with these various doctrines is this: If God has a plan that includes whatever comes to pass, what good will it do to pray? Will not an event come to pass if it is part of God's plan or not come to pass if it is not part of His plan, regardless of whether a believer prays about it?[13] This problem confronts what the Bible teaches about foreordination most directly.

In what sense does God determine beforehand what will come to pass? One answer is that He determined every detail of life directly.[14] That is, He is personally involved in an immediate relationship with every activity down to the smallest and most insignificant event, such as the decomposition of a scrap of plastic in the middle of the Sahara Desert. Those who take this position find support for it in passages such as Matthew 10:29-30.

However, Scripture seems to indicate that even though God does ordain whatever comes to pass, in many cases He does so indirectly. Frequently He does not personally intervene but works through secondary agents or causes, much as an efficient administrator would do. Thus God can be said to foreordain all things generally, though He does not always do so directly. This recognition of secondary causation in the decree of God seems essential to the harmonization of prayer and foreordination.

Prayer is one of the means that God has foreordained and by which His plan finds fulfillment in history. Other means include human government and witnessing. In other words God has given human beings a measure of freedom. It is limited, but significant and genuine. Man's exercise of his freedom never carries him beyond what God has foreordained.

This answer to the problem of the relationship between prayer and foreordination suggests that foreordination looks primarily at the big picture.

12. Ibid., 1:545; Chafer, 8:158; Augustus Hopkins Strong, *Systematic Theology* (Westwood, N.J.: Revell, 1970), p. 356.
13. John Bretherton, *The Purpose of Prayer* (London: SCM, 1920), p. 82.
14. Calvin, 1:225-27.

Nothing has ever taken place or will take place that does not harmonize with the ultimate purposes of God. It is not that God preplanned every detail of every individual's personal history but that every detail is controlled by God to the extent that it ultimately harmonizes with His plans and priorities. It is His larger purposes that are the focus of statements concerning God's predetermining control.

Another way to answer the question of the relationship between prayer and foreordination is to insist that foreordination refers to the details of the decree and that indications of varying levels of divine determination mean something else. But if God determines everything that comes to pass with the same degree of volition, the many statements in Scripture that portray God as doing otherwise seem to be misleading. When God said He swore by Himself that He would do something, was He really saying nothing more than if He had simply said He would do it? And when He said if His people disobeyed Him He would discipline them, was He really saying that their actions would have no effect whatsoever on His actions? These conclusions seem unwarranted. If we really have no freedom, God would simply be playing games with us and leading us to believe things about our relationship with Himself that are not true.

That God can and does employ means demonstrates the greatness of His power. We would regard a parent who demands the right to make all his childrens' decisions for them as inferior to one who allows them significant freedom and still maintains control over them and brings his will to pass through a measure of indirect control. So the greatness of God's sovereignty and decree are seen in His employment of secondary causes and the granting of freedom to His creatures.

God's will can still be accomplished even though He allows people to influence Him through prayer to bestow certain benefits, withhold others, and alter His timing of some events. In fact, in some cases failing to pray results in God's not granting what He would give if we did pray (James 4:2). The person who prays becomes a partner with God in the execution of His plans and the accomplishment of His will on earth.

The Scriptures ascribe many objective changes to prayers. God gave Joshua many extra hours of daylight in answer to his request (Josh. 10:12-14). God added fifteen years to King Hezekiah's life (1 Kings 20:1-6). Paul's prayers for the saints in the various churches testify to his belief in the objective effects of prayer (e.g., Eph. 1:15-23; 3:14-19; Phil. 1:3-6; Col. 1:3, 9-12).[15]

15. Oscar Cullmann, "Paul in Prayer: Practice and Theology," *Theology Digest* 31 (Summer 1984):119-22.

OBJECTIVE CHANGE IN GOD

Not only does prayer change both the person who prays as well as situations and individuals for whom he prays, but the Scriptures state that prayer has occasionally "changed" God's mind (Ex. 32:14; Num. 14:12, 20). But can prayer actually change God's intentions? It is one thing to say that God accomplishes His will as we pray; it is quite another to say that God "changes" His intentions in response to prayer. Yet this is what the Bible teaches.

Some Christians find such passages hard to reconcile with the scriptural teaching that God is immutable (cf. Ps. 102:24-27; Isa. 46:9-10; Mal. 3:6; James 1:17).[16] But these passages assert only that God's essential character and ultimate purposes do not change. They do not teach that God never takes a different relationship or attitude toward specific situations or individuals. There are many instances in Scripture where God altered His attitude or intended action in response to certain conditions (Gen. 6:6-7; Ex. 32:14; Num. 14:20; Deut. 32:36; Judg. 2:18; 1 Sam. 15:11; 2 Sam. 24:16; 1 Chron. 21:15; Pss. 90:13; 135:14; Jer. 18:8; 26:3, 13, 19; 42:10; Hos. 11:8; Joel 2:13-14; Amos 7:3, 6; Jonah 3:9-10; 4:2; Rev. 2:15-22).

But what about the verses that say God does not change His mind? There are several of these in the Bible (cf. Num. 23:19; 1 Sam. 15:29; Ps. 110:4 [also quoted in Heb. 9:21]; Rom. 11:29). The point of these statements is that God does not change His mind as man changes his. God is not fickle or capricious, nor will His ultimate purposes change. God will not change His mind with respect to the major aspects of His decree. He has, however, changed His mind with regard to minor negotiable matters.

The parent-child analogy is again helpful. There are some things about which a good father who is in control of his family will not change his mind no matter how hard his child may try to convince him. "No, you may not play on the highway. You may as well stop asking me because there is nothing you can say that will convince me to let you do that." But there are other things about which he is open to influence. "Yes, you may have a chocolate ice cream cone rather than strawberry, if you prefer." Or, "Since you have done what I asked you to do, I am going to take you to the baseball game this weekend."

Another objection could be raised. Perhaps God is not really changing. Could the Bible just be using terminology that is designed to help believers

16. Theodore J. Kondoleon, "The Immutability of God: Some Recent Challenges," *The New Scholasticism* 58 (Summer 1984):293-315.

understand God's actions even though the expressions do not literally represent what is taking place?[17] Phenomenological language, the language of appearance, is common both in Scripture usage and in modern usage. For example, we speak of the sun rising, but we know that the sun does not literally rise. We are simply describing a situation as it appears to us, not scientifically. Could not these descriptions of God changing His mind be written in phenomenological language?

God uses many analogies and figures to help His finite creatures grasp the infinite. Most of the descriptions of God Himself, for example, are analogies—including the one that God has a "mind." But recognizing anthropomorphisms for what they are does not solve our problem; it just begs the question. The question still remains, Does God really change His attitudes and actions in response to people's petitions?

The scriptural evidence suggests that He does change on the negotiable levels of His decree. To deny this requires us to say that passages like Exodus 32:14 and Numbers 14:20 are simply not true. To deny these verses means we must deny that God altered His attitudes and action in response to Moses' intercession, even though that is what the text clearly seems to say. It is not just a matter of redefining or reinterpreting these verses as we could do, for example, by interpreting the term "sunrise" as the beginning of a new day. It is, rather, a denial of the assertion that a new day began at all, or that God really changed His attitude.

We have seen that prayer can change several things. It can change the person who prays just because he prays, and it can also change the circumstances about which he prays. It can even change God's attitude toward a particular course of action and result in His acting or permitting action to take place in a different fashion than He had previously intended. And in all these changes God still is God because He remains in control. His foreordained purposes are being accomplished, and He knew beforehand what would happen.

CHANGES PRAYER DOES NOT EFFECT

GOD'S FIXED PURPOSES

We must now turn to those situations that prayer does not change. Before beginning the subject of God's fixed purpose one must pause to remember that God is a person. "He is not a cold abstraction, but a living,

17. Calvin, *Institutes,* 1:225-27.

loving person, near at hand, and that His people may feel this more and more as He makes prayer the condition upon which He puts forth His power."[18] The Bible describes God manifesting characteristics that are observed in other people. This is part of mankind's being made in God's image; our personalities reflect His.

One of the characteristics of human personalities that the Bible teaches God also possesses is volition (cf. Gen. 1:26; John 3:16). When we observe God's volition at work in the Scriptures, we discover that He wills very much as we do. He is, of course, greater than man, but the characteristics of His volition are the same as man's. For example, no healthy human being is equally determined about everything in his life. We determine to do some things with more steadfastness than others. I am determined, with God's help, to remain faithful to my wife. I also plan to keep my car for at least three more years. And I would like to bring milk with my lunch today; though if I cannot drink milk, I will be just as satisfied to drink something else. Here are three levels of volitional determination, and there are many others. The point is that we are not equally or entirely committed to everything we plan to do.

The evidence in Scripture indicates that God is the same. There are some things to which He has committed Himself, and nothing will turn Him from His purpose. God affirmed that He would bless Abraham and his descendants greatly. God's covenants with His people were solemn commitments that He would indeed bring to pass what He had promised (cf. Gen. 15; Ex. 24:1-11). Many of God's promises will be fulfilled regardless of other people's reactions to them (cf. Gen. 2:16-17; 8:20-22; John 6:47; 1 Thess. 4:15-17).

Second, there are other purposes that God has not willed as strongly. For example, He said that certain of His actions would be dependent on other conditions. If the Israelites would obey Him, He would bless them; but if they disobeyed, He would discipline them (Deut. 27-28; Josh. 8:30-35). If Christians walk in loving obedience to the Lord, He will cause them to increase and abound in their spiritual benefits (Eph. 3:14-19; Col. 2:6-7). So there are things God has purposed to do regardless of men's actions and other things He has said He may do depending on their actions.

Third, there are those decisions that God allows an individual to make that are so inconsequential that He gives liberty to choose whatever he or

18. T. W. Chambers, "Prayer," *Concise Dictionary of Religious Knowledge,* ed. Samuel Maenuley Jackson (1891), p. 738.

she might wish. Whether I drink a glass of water within the next five minutes is not something toward which God takes the same volitional relation as some of His more important purposes. At least there is no indication in Scripture that He imposes His will on us in every one of these decisions; the evidence points in the other direction. God is aware of and cares about the most insignificant events in life (Matt. 10:29-31), but He does not exercise the same amount of control in every case.

Fourth, there are also things God desires but does not determine. He desires that no one should perish but that all should come to a full knowledge of the truth (1 Tim. 2:4). However, the Bible clearly teaches that universal conversion will never come to pass (Matt. 25:46; Rev. 20:10).

God does not exercise the same degree of volition in every aspect of life. Some of the things He has willed will take place regardless of any human action, whereas others may or may not take place depending on human action. There are some things God has willed that believers need never pray about because no amount of praying will alter His purpose (e.g., Josh. 7:6-13; Jer. 7:13-16; 14:11-12). Many of these things have been revealed in Scripture, but others have not. In some cases we do not know whether God will change His mind. In this sense prayer is sometimes a mystery; we may not know, by scriptural revelation, whether God can be influenced to grant our request. But Scripture does give us insight into God's plans and purposes to the extent that we can be aware of what His response may be in some of these situations.

God has a set of priorities. The manifestation of His glory is His ultimate priority (1 Cor. 15:20-28). It is important to God that His creatures be allowed to live with a degree of freedom (Josh. 24:15). This priority seems to take precedence over His desire that all men come to repentance in this life and be saved (2 Peter 3:9), since He permits people to choose to reject a relationship with Himself. He also desires that all people enjoy life as much as possible on this earth (cf. Prov. 1:1-7; Eccles. 2:24; 3:12-13; 5:18-19), but this priority obviously ranks below the preceding three. These and other priorities of God's that are revealed in Scripture indicate that God does not purpose everything with the same degree of volition.

God has established procedures by which He administers the world. In some situations He is directly involved in the affairs of the world. Some examples of this are God's personal relations to individuals and groups throughout history (Gen. 12:1-3; cf. Heb. 1:1-2). In other situations He took a less direct approach, as when He sent a human messenger with His message rather than delivering it Himself (cf. Jer. 32:1). In still other situations He took an even less direct approach. For example, after giving the Mosaic law, God left His people alone and expected them to carry it out. God's use of a variety of procedures in administering the affairs of the world suggests that from God's viewpoint everything is not equally significant.

Another reason God may not grant our petitions is related to individual freedom. Sometimes we ask God to change another person—to save him, move him to adopt a particular course of action, or influence him to have a change of attitude. Why are our requests granted in some cases but not in others? A significant factor in this problem is that one of God's high volitional priorities is to permit human beings a measure of freedom (cf. Luke 13:34-35). This is even more important to God than that all do what He wants them to do, namely, be blessed and ultimately go to heaven (John 1:12). Why is this so important to God? Because it will somehow result in greater glory for Him, since the glory of God is His ultimate priority.

God allows people freedom in making choices—so much freedom that He can justly hold them responsible for their decisions (John 3:36). He does not coerce people, though He does bring circumstances to bear on them and thereby influences their decisions. It is for this reason that we cannot pray for the salvation of a particular person, for example, and be absolutely certain that that individual will be saved. God leaves the choice up to the individual, but God may bring influences to bear on him through our prayers that will lead him to make the right decision.

> The purpose of prayer is not to force or coerce his will; never that. It is to free his will from the warping influences that now twist it awry. . . . To pray for the salvation of others is not to interfere with the exercise of their freedom, but to prevent sin from perpetually holding their will in bondage.[19]

That our prayers can move God to influence others in their choices seems clearly revealed in Scripture. The apostles prayed, and people were saved (Acts 4:24-31). Paul considered the prayers of the Christians to whom he wrote his epistles essential to the success of his missionary labors (Rom. 15:30-32). Experiences confirm the teaching of Scripture. Many believers have seen God change people's hearts in response to prayer. The spiritual awakenings that have taken place throughout history have nor-

19. Bretherton, pp. 218, 221.

mally been preceded by periods of intense prayer by God's people.[20]

Is it wrong to "claim" the salvation of a person for whom we pray? Can we really be sure that a given individual will be saved when he has not yet trusted in Christ? The only way we can be sure something will happen is if God has promised that it will. Unfortunately He has not *promised* that any single individual will be saved. He has said it is His *desire* that all be saved (2 Pet. 3:9), but He has also revealed that it is not His *purpose* that all will be saved (Matt. 25:41). The most we can be assured of is that as we pray and work for the salvation of a given individual, we know that we are doing what God desires and commands. If this particular individual's salvation is within the purpose of God, God will bring him to salvation sooner or later, preferably sooner.

Ultimately it is really God who determines whether a person is saved (Eph. 1; Rom. 9). But how can man be genuinely free and still be subject to God's sovereign will? This is a mystery that we may comprehend to some extent but that we cannot fully understand. The Bible teaches both that man is responsible for his choices (cf. John 1:12) and that God has chosen some people for salvation (cf. Rom. 9:18). These two facts appear contradictory, but actually they are both taught in Scripture and are reasonable. The reconciliation of the apparent contradiction evidently lies beyond the ability of man, since no one has yet been able to offer an explanation that has proved completely satisfying, though many have tried.

Scripture reveals that man has a measure of freedom. And because of this freedom God allows us to pray to Him to influence others, but within limits. Since those limits are not clearly defined we are tempted to become confused. In some cases the limits are broad, and this should encourage us to pray. But in other cases the limits are narrow, and this has caused many believers to become discouraged.

Another difficulty we face in thinking about human freedom is reconciling it with divine omniscience.[21] How is it possible for God to know everything if some of what happens is determined by free human choice? One suggestion is that omniscience applies only to the actions and choices of God Himself, not those of other persons, and that what God foresees is what the consequences of each free choice would be for the individual

---

20. Richard F. Lovelace, *Dynamics of Spiritual Life* (Downers Grove, Ill.: InterVarsity, 1979), pp. 151-60.
21. David Basinger, "Why Petition an Omnipotent, Omniscient, Wholly Good God?" *Religious Studies* 19 (March 1983):25-41.

making the choice, rather than what the choice will be.[22] This explanation seems to limit God's knowledge somewhat. A second suggestion is that God knows all things possible as well as all things actual. Omniscience so defined is broad enough to include choices and actions that are genuinely free.[23]

A third suggestion seems to offer the best means of reconciling human freedom and divine omniscience. This third proposal to the problem of omniscience and freedom holds that God is outside of time (there is no past, present, or future with respect to God). What we take to be past, present, and future are equally present to God. According to this view God does not predict the future on the basis of evidence but knows it in some more immediate way that does not logically entail the predetermination of events so known.[24]

MAN'S FAILURES

A third factor in explaining why our petitions are not always granted is perhaps the most obvious. We do not pray as we should. We hinder our own effectiveness in prayer.[25] In some cases we have an improper attitude toward prayer. We may become discouraged and conclude that prayer will not work, so we do not pray (Luke 18:1-8). But prayer does work, and it often results in significant change (James 5:17-18). If we do not pray, we will fail to receive from God what we would otherwise obtain (James 4:2).

Prayer is not a lever that we can use to force God to act. The power in prayer is the same type of power that one individual can bring to bear on another through conversation. Neither is prayer a substitute for obedience (Josh. 7:6-13). Sometimes we should be praying prayers of confession rather than prayers of petition. Prayer should also be accompanied by action when we can do something within the will of God to expedite our request —like witnessing to the person we are asking God to save, giving money to the person for whom we are asking God to provide, or diligently studying the Scriptures that we are asking God to help us understand. God expects us to use all the resources and opportunities He gives us to secure the good results for which we pray. Working need not indicate a lack of faith; it should demonstrate the genuineness of faith (James 2:22).

22. Axel D. Steuer, "The Freedom of God and Human Freedom," *Scottish Journal of Theoloy* 36 (1983):176.
23. Chafer, 1:192.
24. Steuer, p. 178.
25. Constable, pp. 153-80.

We hinder the effectiveness of our prayers to God when we fail to listen carefully to the Scriptures (John 15:7). If we show no concern for God's Word to us, we should not be surprised if He gives little regard to our words to Him (Jer. 7:13-16). A self-centered attitude and lack of concern for what will glorify God definitely hinder effective praying (James 4:3). Pretentiousness in prayer—trying to impress others—drew Jesus' criticism and warning (Matt. 6:15). Even an unforgiving spirit can block our prayers (Ps. 66:18; Matt. 11:25).

Several specific actions are identified in the Bible as hindrances to effective prayer. These include oppression of others (Mic. 3:1-4), lack of consideration for one's spouse (1 Pet. 3:7), and empty ritualism (Matt. 15:1-9). Flagrant disobedience and persistent sinning (1 Sam. 15:11; Jer. 11:11) are also significant handicaps to prayer.

CONCLUSION

This essay has sought to point out that our concept of God is important in our praying. The more a person knows about God and His ways as they are revealed in Scripture the better he will understand how to relate to God in prayer and how and why God responds to prayer as He does. Therefore if one would understand the mysteries of prayer, he should first give his attention to the study of God and His ways as they are revealed in the Bible.

Many of the problems we have with prayer arise out of an unbiblical concept of God. God has used a relational model to communicate Himself, His will, and ways to us.[26] He has not used mechanical or philosophical categories. The Bible is not a book of philosophy, though scholars have used Scripture in the study of philosophy. Nor did God reveal Himself by giving us an "owner's manual" that tells us step-by-step what to do so that we will be able to cope with life and obtain salvation. Rather, He has chosen to give us a record of His dealings with people. We see there one Person relating to others, and we learn not only how to cope with life but also how important our relationship with God is to Him.

It is significant that when Jesus' disciples asked Him to teach them to pray, the first thing He told them was to conceive of God as their Father (Matt.6:9). He did not tell them to address God as Sovereign (though He is that), or Master, Shepherd, Bridegroom, or Friend (though He is all these,

---

26. Milton Ferguson, "Prayer and Providence," *Southwestern Journal of Theology* (1972):19-28.

too). By telling them to address Him as Father, Christ was saying that thinking of God in that relationship was most appropriate and helpful in view of the possibilities and problems connected with prayer. Our relationship as children to our heavenly Father is one of the most important and helpful revelations God has given us. It helps us understand why God does and does not grant our requests. Why does an earthly father grant or not grant the requests of his children? Why does he respond in some cases and not in others? Why can he be persuaded to take a course of action different from what he had intended in some situations but not in others? This earthly relationship was intended to teach us a lot about our relationship with God.

We also need to remember the ultimate purposes of God as He has made them known. The manifestation of God's glory is His highest priority. The significant freedom of His creatures is below this priority, but that freedom takes precedence over God's desire to establish a personal relationship with every individual. When we order these priorities as God does we will be able to understand better why God grants answers to some of our prayers but not to others.

WILLIAM D. LAWRENCE (B.S., Philadelphia College of Bible; Th.M., Th.D., Dallas Theological Seminary) is associate
professor of pastoral ministries at Dallas
Theological Seminary.

The Traitor in the Gates: The Christian's Conflict with the Flesh

William D. Lawrence

INTRODUCTION

Nothing is more treacherous than traitors. They earn the trust of their countrymen and then use it to destroy them. The designations given traitors throughout history show the pain that such betrayal brings. The phrase *traitor in the gates,* for example, comes from the river gate in the Tower of London through which traitors were committed to prison as a kind of high dishonor for their position and crime.[1] Later the name *Benedict Arnold* became synonymous with treason.

During these more apocalyptic days a new term has come into use. In the language of the CIA, the KGB, and the MI5, traitors are called "moles," for they burrow deep within the organization they profess to serve and do their dirty work as enemy agents. Perhaps the best example of this is Kim Philby. Son of a privileged British family, Philby became a Communist at Cambridge University, was recruited into the KGB, and at the same time became a member of the British counter-intelligence agency known as MI5.[2] His purpose was to become a mole and infiltrate MI5, earning the trust of his countrymen while doing the dictates of his Russian masters. Philby accomplished his purpose. At one point he actually served as head

---

1. *The Compact Edition of the Oxford English Dictionary,* 2 vols. (Oxford U., 1971), 2:3, 375.
2. Bruce Page, David Leitch, and Phillip Knightley, *The Philby Conspiracy,* (Garden City, N.Y.: Doubleday, 1968), p. 61.

of the anti-Russian section, assisting the very enemy he was supposed to resist.[3]

How tragic to trust a traitor! He is the most dangerous, deceptive, and destructive of enemies. What is true in the political realm is equally true in the spiritual realm. Every believer has a traitor in the gates,[4] a mole burrowed deep within his essential being who opens the way for the world and the devil. The name of this enemy is the flesh.

THE DANGER OF THE FLESH

THE DECEPTIVENESS OF THE FLESH

The deceptiveness of the flesh is the first characteristic that makes it so dangerous. No committed Christian would ever trust the world or the devil, but all of us trust the flesh: it is self, the self in which we have placed confidence all our lives. Therefore, we like the flesh; it is our friend. Furthermore, the flesh is not just a sensuous, ugly kind of thing. It is often committed, dedicated, and religious—undeniably religious. The problem with the flesh is never religion; the problem with the flesh is always righteousness. From the many gods of animism to the no god of Communism the flesh displays itself as incurably religious. But from the many gods of animism to the no god of Communism the flesh is incurably unrighteous. Like the mole Kim Philby the flesh is burrowed deep inside the believer, the head of the anti-sin section, deceiving the believer into trusting it as it assists the enemy master it claims to resist.

THE DESTRUCTIVENESS OF THE FLESH

From its position of control within us, the flesh, having deceived us, begins its work of destruction. It opens the door of our beings to the call of the world and the wiles of the devil. In our fleshly dedication to Christ we become concerned about the Lord's work *and* our honor, about opportunity to serve Him *and* influence for ourselves. We build structures that enable us to serve *and* succeed; we create titles that identify us as successful servants. Like the disciples we are deceived into thinking that success in ministry means sitting at the right and the left of the King. With our minds we serve the Lord, but with our emotions we seek the flesh. This enables Satan to move in on us, producing discouragement due to our inabil-

3. Kim Philby, *My Secret War* (New York: Grove, 1968), p. 125.
4. C. Leslie Mitton, *The Epistle to the Ephesians* (Oxford: Clarendon, 1951), p. 84.

ity to accomplish success as we define it, distress because others do not recognize us, despair of ever being all we can be, and even doubt of God's goodness. The flesh has opened the way to the world and the devil exactly as its master, sin, directs it to do.

In short, the danger of the flesh lies in its deceptiveness and destructiveness. William Barclay summarizes this danger well when he states, "The flesh is the great enemy of . . . the Christian life . . . the bridgehead through which sin invades the human personality. The flesh is like the enemy within the gates who opens the way to the enemy who is pressing in through the gates."[5] Why are so many believers deceived and therefore destroyed by the flesh? Because they do not understand what the flesh is or how to defend against it. The primary aim of this study is to define the flesh; a secondary aim is to show how to defend against it.

THE DEFINITION OF THE FLESH

THE TERMS *BĀSĀR* AND *SARX*

The meaning of these terms. The Bible uses two key terms for flesh, *bāsār* in the Old Testament and *sarx* in the New. In order to define the concept of the flesh it is necessary to understand the meaning and use of these two words.

Literally, *bāsār* describes "the material of the living body, the soft muscular covering of the bones, whether of man or animal."[6] It also describes flesh as the food of men,[7] including the sacrifices offered to God.[8] Further, the word speaks of blood relationship[9] as seen in the phrase "bone of my bone and flesh of my flesh,"[10] which emphasizes the common source of physical substance. "This striking formula is also used in the OT to emphasize an existing blood relationship and to stress the responsibilities that this implies."[11] From these literal meanings *bāsār* developed certain figurative meanings through synecdoche, that is, the use of a part for the whole. "The flesh being the most outstanding part of the living creature, covering

---

5. William Barclay, *Flesh and Spirit* (Grand Rapids: Baker, 1962), pp. 21-22.
6. Samuel Lewis Johnson, "Survey of Biblical Psychology in the Epistle to the Romans" (Th.D. dissertation, Dallas Theological Seminary, 1949), pp. 65-66.
7. *The New International Dictionary of New Testament Theology* (1975), by A. C. Thiselton, s.v. "Flesh," 1:672.
8. H. H. Wendt, "Dr. Wendt on the Old Testament Usage," in William P. Dickson, *St. Paul's Use of the Terms Flesh and Spirit* (Glasgow: Maclehose, 1883), p. 404.
9. *Theological Dictionary of the New Testament*, s.v. "sarx," by Friedrich Baumgartel, 7:106.
10. Wendt, p. 404.
11. *The Theological Dictionary of the Old Testament*, s.v. "bāsār," by N. P. Bratsiotis, 2:328.

the bones and containing the blood, it naturally came to be used, the part being taken for the whole, of the living creature in general."[12] When used in this manner *bāsār* speaks of the whole body (Job 6:12; 21:6),[13] the person (Pss. 16:8-9; 27:2), of all living beings generally, as in "all flesh"[14] (Gen. 6:12; Isa. 40:6; 49:26; 66:23), and of human frailty in contrast to God's power. "The word thus denotes living beings *with the connotation of the absolute weakness and perishableness of their nature in distinction from the power and living operation of God.*"[15]

Thus *bāsār* has a physical and nonphysical sense; it describes flesh as food, human flesh, animal flesh, the human body, the whole man, all mankind,[16] and particularly man in his weakness in contrast to God in His power. "The things about man that are emphasized in particular in connection with the word *bāsār* are his creatureliness, his absolute dependence on God, his earthly nature, and his weakness, inadequacy, and transitoriness."[17]

The New Testament uses *sarx* in similar ways to *bāsār*. *Sarx*, of course, has a history very different from *bāsār*, but in the New Testament *bāsār* exercises more influence on the meaning of *sarx* than in either classical Greek or Hellenism. As in so many other instances of New Testament terminology, Old Testament usage reflected in the Septuagint translation has greater control on the meaning of the term than does its usage in secular Greek. In relation to *sarx* Greek thinkers had developed a dualism that saw all that is physical as evil and all that is nonphysical as good. "The evil of the body became one of the dominant ideas of Greek thought. *Soma sema,* the body in a tomb, ran the Orphic jingle. The body, said Philolaus, is a house of detention in which the soul is imprisoned to expiate its sin."[18] Furthermore, the Epicureans saw the *sarx* as the seat of the desire, a view that was misunderstood as advocating unbridled lust,[19] and which seems to influence the modern misconception that the flesh is only sensuous.

Nothing could be further from the New Testament perspective of the physical. The Scripture never equates the physical with evil; God created the physical and said it was good (Gen. 1:31). The physical is *not* inherent-

---

12. A. B. Davidson, *The Theology of the Old Testament* (Edinburgh: T. & T. Clark, 1904), p. 188.
13. *Theological Dictionary of the Old Testament*, 2:325.
14. Wendt, p. 406.
15. Ibid., p. 408 (italics his).
16. *New Testament Theology,* 1:672.
17. *Theological Dictionary of the Old Testament*, 2:328.
18. Barclay, p. 10.
19. *Theological Dictionary of the Old Testament*, 7:103-4.

ly evil in the Bible, and the New Testament does not describe the flesh in this way. There is no Platonic dualism in which flesh and soul are irreconcilably opposed to each other in the Bible. Instead, the Old Testament sees man as a twofold entity made up of flesh and soul (*bāsār* and *nepesh*) "which is expressed by a distinct consciousness of unity."[20]

Paul would not draw his understanding of the flesh from Greek philosophy. As a Pharisee he was unalterably opposed to Hellenism; he had no confidence in the wisdom of men to bring people to Christ (1 Cor. 1:20-31); his dependence was on the Holy Spirit, not on the wisdom of men, to substantiate his gospel (1 Cor. 2:1-5); and he was far more interested in fusing Judaism and Christianity than he was in harmonizing Christianity and Greek thought.[21] When it comes to the use of *sarx*, both the New Testament and Paul stand on Old Testament ground.[22]

In the New Testament *sarx* is used in the fully physical sense to describe the muscular covering of the bones of both men and animals,[23] by synecdoche of the body[24] as in Galatians 2:20, to describe kinship (cf. Rom. 1:3),[25] and to speak of human nature.[26] When *sarx* speaks of human nature it does not speak of sin, since Christ became flesh (John 1:14), but it does speak of frailty even as *bāsār* did in the Old Testament. " 'Flesh' not only means man, but man dependent upon God."[27]

There is one new element in *sarx* that is not fully present in *bāsār*, the element of sin, the ethical element that makes the flesh the traitor in the gates. This aspect of the flesh is a shadow in the Old Testament, an undeveloped implication, a bud that bears full fruit in the New Testament, especially in the writings of Paul. It will be helpful to trace the development of the ethical concept of the flesh through a study of selected key passages from the Old and New Testaments. Once this step is taken it will be possible to define the flesh and learn how to defend against it.

THE DEVELOPMENT OF THE ETHICAL CONCEPT OF THE FLESH

The ethical concept foreshadowed in the Old Testament. Though the

20. Ibid., 2:326.
21. M. Scott Fletcher, *The Psychology of the New Testament* (London: Hodder and Stoughton, 1912), pp. 130-31.
22. Dickson, p. 203.
23. Johnson, pp. 65-66.
24. Ernest De Witt Burton, "Spirit, Soul, and Flesh," *American Journal of Theology* 20 (1916):596.
25. Fletcher, p. 116.
26. Ibid., pp. 118-24.
27. Ibid., p. 122.

ethical concept of the flesh was not fully developed in the Old Testament, it was foreshadowed. Paul did not arbitrarily apply the idea of flesh ethically; he had a biblical base for such thinking as a survey of the key passages shows.

Before beginning this survey, however, it is necessary to make one point about the use of *bāsār*. *Bāsār* is never used in relation to God, a key to understanding the ethical dimension of the word. "The OT always emphasizes that God is not *bāsār*, and sharply distinguishes him from all *bāsār*. Whenever *bāsār* is connected with God, it simply emphasizes the immense distance and difference of flesh from God, the complete dependence of flesh on God, and the striking antithesis between flesh and God."[28]

Even before the Fall the term *bāsār* possessed an ethical connotation when it described the marriage relationship as "one flesh" (Gen. 2:24). Though sin was not yet present, there can be no doubt that the word assumed ethical implications as soon as sin infected marriage, since Genesis 2:24 referred to monogamy[29] and all the moral responsibilities involved in the husband-wife relationship.

Following the Fall, *bāsār* had a negative connotation as can be seen in Genesis 6:13. "It cannot be denied that in this passage sin is intimately connected with *bāsār* and that it is also used to denote the ethical aspect of man."[30] In Genesis 6:13 *bāsār* possessed an ethical perspective. God declared the end of "all flesh" because of the violence that filled the earth. Flesh is more than mere weakness; it is moral weakness, although the concept is not as fully developed as in Paul. Nonetheless, a passage like this could form the foundation for Paul's thinking.

In 2 Chronicles 32:8 a pattern of contrast is established between the flesh and the Lord or the flesh and the spirit that continues in other passages. As the passage explains, Hezekiah was surrounded by Sennacherib's army, a massive Assyrian force superior to the army of Jerusalem. Yet the king understood the reality between dependence on the "arm of flesh" and the Lord God, the contrast between the apparent strength of the flesh and its true weakness when compared to God.[31] The arm of flesh appears to be powerful and certain of victory, but it is human frailty in rebellion against God and doomed to failure. The flesh appears to be powerful, but the reality of its weakness is seen in the fact that the Lord struck down 185,000

---

28. Ibid.
29. *Theological Dictionary of the Old Testament*, 2:328.
30. Ibid., 2:329.
31. Ibid., 2:330.

soldiers in the camp of the Assyrians (Isa. 37:36).

Isaiah 31:3 continues this contrast and makes it even stronger, first through the structure of the passage: men and flesh are contrasted with God and spirit (the Hebrew *'ādām lō' ēl,* "men not God," is synonymous with *bāsār lō' rûaḥ,* "flesh not spirit").[32] Second, the point of the passage is clearly to show that an alliance with Egypt (forbidden by God in Deut. 17:16)[33] was useless, since Egypt was men and flesh rather than God and spirit.[34] Finally, Isaiah 31:3 goes beyond this to develop the thought that men wrongly place the same kind of trust in the flesh that they ought to place in God (Isa. 31:1). Men depend on the flesh to sustain them and provide them with a strength and power they do not possess in themselves. As a result they have an attitude of dependence on human resources that can never meet their needs and replace God in their lives. This becomes one of the greatest problems with the flesh when it is viewed ethically: it replaces God as a source of confidence and power and becomes a place of trust and faith for those who refuse to depend on God. Men count on the weakness and frailty of the visible in preference to the power of the invisible.

Jeremiah 17:5 not only continues the contrast between flesh and God (*'ādām* and *bāsār,* "man" and "flesh," are in contrast to Yahweh, "Lord")[35] but also emphasizes the folly of trusting in the former. The prophet pronounces a curse on those who rely on mankind and make flesh their strength because their hearts turn away from the Lord. From this it may be observed that the heart is closely related to the flesh, and it is the heart that creates the problem of trust. The flesh reflects the heart, and unless there is a change in heart there can be no control of the flesh. The foolishness of placing faith in the flesh is seen in the way the word "trust" (*bāṭaḥ,* which describes a sense of security resulting from confidence in someone) is used in Isaiah 36:6. The Old Testament uses *bāṭaḥ* in contrast to the confidence that comes from dependence on something other than God.[36] In Isaiah 36:6 Israel's misplaced confidence in Egypt is pictured as reliance on a crushed reed that pierces the hand of the one who leans on it. Egypt (flesh) is as useful as a crushed reed to a person with a broken leg. What could be weaker?

In summary, *bāsār* had ethical significance even before the Fall (Gen.

---

32. Ibid.
33. Alfred Martin and John A. Martin, *Isaiah: The Glory of the Messiah* (Chicago: Moody, 1983), p. 88.
34. Dickson, pp. 120-21.
35. *Theological Dictionary of the Old Testament,* 2:330.
36. *Theological Wordbook of the Old Testament,* s.v "*bāṭaḥ,*" by John N. Oswalt, 1:101.

2:24) and was associated with sin soon after (Gen. 6:3, 13). As the ethical dimensions of *bāsār* unfold in the Old Testament, a contrast between the weakness and frailty of the flesh and the power of God becomes increasingly evident (2 Chron. 32:8; Isa. 31:3; Jer. 17:5). Though such weakness is neither moral nor immoral in itself, it rapidly assumes an ethical connotation because of the issue of trust. To trust in anything other than God is to disobey and to sin. Though the flesh itself is not inherently sinful in these passages, it is but a short step to Paul's conclusion that sin is master of the flesh. "Even in the Old Testament *bāsār* does not only mean the powerlessness of the mortal creature but also the feebleness of his faithfulness and obedience to the will of God . . . it is not the Qumran texts . . . that are moving for the first time towards the Pauline recognition that 'nothing good dwells in my flesh.' "[37]

Before leaving this survey of the ethical concept of the flesh in the Old Testament it is important to note that all is not bleak. There are two rays of hope. The first is Psalm 78:38-39 in which God's compassion toward the weakness of the flesh and the resultant iniquity is stated. The second is Ezekiel 11:19 and 36:26, in which God promises to deal with the root issue by replacing the heart of stone with a heart of flesh, that is, by exchanging a hardened heart for a tender heart.[38] These rays of hope combined with the promise of the Spirit in Joel 2:28 lead naturally into the New Testament where the ethical concept of the flesh is fully developed as God fulfills His promise.

The ethical concept brought to fruition in the New Testament. John 3:6 is the bridge between the Old Testament and the New on this topic because it is in this passage that the developing ethical concept of the flesh enters the New Testament. Here the Son of God introduced both the Old Testament contrast between the flesh and the Spirit and the folly of faith in the flesh when He told Nicodemus, "That which is born of the flesh is flesh and that which is born of the Spirit is spirit (NASB)." "Flesh" here *must* have an ethical implication.[39] Nicodemus, a Jew, naturally thought that his racial descent was adequate to give him a right relationship with God, but Christ was telling him that even *Abraham's* flesh was deficient in this regard. Only that which is born of the Spirit is acceptable to God, since (1)

37. Hans Walter Wolff, *Anthropology of the Old Testament* (Philadelphia: Fortress, 1974), p. 31.
38. *Theological Dictionary of the Old Testament*, 2:332.
39. John Calvin, *The Gospel According to St. John, John 1-10,* Calvin's Commentaries, trans. T. H. L. Parker (Grand Rapids: Eerdmans, 1959), p. 65.

there is not evolution from the flesh to the Spirit, and[40] (2) each nature generates its own substance.[41]

In John 3:6 Christ brings the revelation of the Old Testament into sharp focus and prepares the way for the revelation of the New. The flesh is more than human weakness, more than moral weakness even; ethically considered it is evil, incapable of entering into a relationship with God. In other words, the flesh considered *ethically* is inherently sinful. This must be so. Nothing about the flesh from a physical perspective keeps it from fellowshiping with God. Weakness does not separate man from God. And as noted above, the physical is never regarded as inherently evil in the Scriptures; in fact, the body will be redeemed, resurrected, and renewed in heaven (Rom. 8:18-30). Furthermore, there is a definite distinction between the body and the flesh *(sōma* and *sarx)* in the Bible. "The body can become the instrument of the service and the glory of God; the flesh cannot. The body can be purified and even glorified; the flesh must be eliminated and eradicated."[42] Clearly our Lord was not talking about physical birth in John 3:6; He must be speaking of the ethical implications of being born of the flesh.

It is but a short step to Paul's conclusion concerning the flesh found in Romans 7:1—8:17; Galatians 5:16-24; and Philippians 3:4-6. Since these passages have received more than adequate attention both in commentaries and journals, this essay intends only to survey those points that most contribute to the definition of the ethical concept of the flesh.

In Paul the contrast between the flesh and the Spirit and the foolishness of confidence in the flesh merge together to show why the flesh is the traitor in the gates. The flesh is the exclusive sphere of the unbeliever, the only resource he has for spiritual power (Rom. 7:5). But the believer no longer is in the flesh (cf. the imperfect *ēmen* of Rom. 7:5), though he is subject to its control unless he defends himself by the Spirit. This is clear from Paul's personal testimony in Romans 7:14-25 where he describes his experience in struggling with the flesh after becoming a believer. The flesh is sold (perfect passive participle, *pepramenos)* into bondage to sin, the permanent slave of sin, committed to doing its bidding in every circumstance no matter how dedicated the believer may be to obey God. It is this

40. Leon Morris, *The Gospel According to John,* The New International Commentary on the New Testament (Grand Rapids: Eerdmans, 1975), p. 219.
41. Marcus Dods, "The Gospel of St. John," in *The Expositor's Greek Testament,* ed. W. Robertson Nicoll, 5 vols. (Grand Rapids: Eerdmans, n.d.), 1:714.
42. Barclay, p. 20.

reality that brought such pain to Paul when he tried to keep God's law in the power of the flesh. To his regret he discovered that there is nothing good in the flesh (Rom. 7:18)—that, in fact, the weakness of the flesh limits all efforts to obey the law by believer and unbeliever alike (Rom. 8:3). Only the Holy Spirit can control the flesh (Gal. 5:16), but the flesh, because it is permanently enslaved to sin, always resists the Spirit (Gal. 5:17). As a result believers face both the constant potential of the works of the flesh and the continuous peril of warfare between the flesh and the Spirit.

Because of this threat from the flesh, the most destructive thing the believer can do is to put his confidence in it, no matter what basis he may have to do so (Phil. 3:4). Paul demonstrates the futility of such confidence by pointing out that it results in the production of spiritual rubbish and in the loss of ever knowing Christ and His resurrection power (Phil. 3:7-11). By his personal witness in Romans 7 and Philippians 3 Paul shows both the deceptiveness and destructiveness of the flesh. It deceived him into thinking he could obey God in its power and then destroyed all spiritual gain in his life. Similarly, the flesh is the traitor that deceives us into thinking we can obey God in our own power, bringing the destructiveness of failure into our lives. When this occurs Satan has the believer where he wants him, discouraged and disheartened in the shame of the flesh.

In summary, according to the New Testament the flesh ethically conceived is permanently enslaved to (Rom. 7:14) and fully identified with sin (Rom. 7:17), having nothing spiritually good in it (Rom. 7:18). Its weakness limits all efforts to keep the law (Rom. 8:3). It resists the Spirit (Gal. 5:17) and brings only the loss of resurrection life (Phil. 3:4-11). In particular the New Testament adds two major elements to the Old Testament view of the flesh. It makes the flesh an indwelling, inherent force within human beings, and it identifies flesh with sin, moving the flesh from the sphere of moral weakness to essential evil. What remains is to formulate a definition of this ethical concept of the flesh.

THE DEFINITION OF THE ETHICAL CONCEPT OF THE FLESH

The ethical concept of the flesh defined. The flesh ethically defined is that anti-God, self-reliant aspect of all human beings (saved and unsaved alike) that is the seat of sin, engaged in unremitting resistance to the Holy Spirit. "The flesh is human nature as it has become through sin. . . . It has made him [man] such that he can neither avoid the fascination of sin nor resist the power of sin. The flesh is man as he is apart from Jesus Christ and his Spirit."[43] The flesh is the independent effort of man and "refers to what man is, or can do, apart from God."[44] The unbeliever can only live in the flesh; the believer must live according to the flesh when he chooses not to live according to the Spirit.

In essence the flesh ethically considered is man as he is in his moral weakness and independence apart from God and His resources. We tend to speak of the flesh as a specific part of us in much the same way we would speak of the heart or lungs. However, the flesh is not a particular segment of man, but the whole of the human personality apart from the Holy Spirit. The Scriptures do not break the human personality into such discernible parts that it can be diagrammed the way anatomy can, and we make a serious mistake when we speak of the flesh in that manner. The flesh as an aspect of my being touches every element of me. It is what I am—body, soul, and spirit, mind, will, and emotion—apart from the Holy Spirit. Though my identity as a believer is drawn from Christ and I can claim my right as a child of God to be free from sin's control, I continue to have the aspect of my inherent being called flesh for as long as I live. Our Lord made this clear when He stated, "That which is born of the flesh is flesh (John 3:6)." The flesh never changes, it is sold in slavery to sin, and it infects every aspect of one's being apart from the Spirit's control.

Confusion has come at this point, a confusion that can result in the denial that the flesh is an inherent aspect of the believer. In his influential work entitled *Birthright*, David C. Needham has made an important contribution to current thinking, emphasizing that Christians are actually new creatures who have a birthright of freedom from sin through their identification with Christ. Unfortunately, Needham is not adequately clear concerning the concept of flesh: he fails to distinguish between its physical and ethical dimensions. Viewed physically the flesh is morally neutral. But viewed ethically the flesh is inherently evil, plaguing the believer as long as he lives. The only freedom from the control and works of the flesh is through the supernatural power of the Holy Spirit, and the believer must always be aware of this indwelling traitor that will take control of his physical flesh whenever it can.

Needham is confusing because he does not adequately recognize the different ways in which the word "flesh" is used in Scripture. Concerning Paul's use of *sarx*, he quotes James S. Stewart, who says that the flesh is

---

43. Ibid., p. 22.
44. J. Dwight Pentecost, *The Divine Comforter* (Chicago: Moody, 1963), pp. 200-201.

human nature in its frailty, weakness, and need for God's help, but it is not in itself evil.[45] At this point Needham appears not to distinguish the physical and ethical uses of *sarx*. The same problem occurs later when Needham declares, "He [God] never wants us to forget that we are for a while inseparably linked to unredeemed flesh. Our bodies are mortal. Not just the bones and muscles, glands and senses, but mind and emotions as well."[46] Here he seems to equate unredeemed flesh and the physical body, also including within the physical aspects of man elements that are normally regarded as immaterial. The failure to distinguish these elements from the body while equating unredeemed flesh with the physical is confusing and gives the impression that the ethical element of the flesh is primarily physical. Further, Needham states that "flesh includes the physical, mental, and emotional parts of me—my whole psycho-physical self."[47] This gives every evidence of confusing the physical and ethical aspects of the flesh with the result that we are not able to determine exactly what the flesh is. In his concern to protect the positive birthright of the believer, Needham has introduced confusion concerning the flesh that could lead to a denial that it is part of who I am. That is something the Scriptures never do. It is evident from the passages discussed in John 3; Romans 7-8; Galatians 5; and Philippians 3 that the ethical dimension of the flesh is an inherent part of me, the product of my "of flesh" birth, which continues to be active in me unless it is brought under the Spirit's control.

Needham not only confuses the physical and ethical elements of the flesh, he also implies that the believer is not the one who sins when the flesh acts. "He [Paul] stated that when a Christian sins *'it is no longer I who do it, but it is sin living in me that does it.'* And where is it dwelling in me? Paul answers, *'in my flesh'* . . . operating *'in the members of my body'* (Romans 7:18-25 [Needham's italics])."[48] Based on this interpretation of Paul's words there is not identification between the believer and his own sin; he does not do it—the flesh does. Further, the believer is *not* the flesh in his deepest identity because the flesh dwells in the members of his body and because the believer has only one nature, which is righteous.[49] Needham does not hold to sinless perfection[50] nor to a denial of responsibility

45. David C. Needham, *Birthright* (Portland: Multnomah, 1979), p. 36.
46. Ibid., p. 79.
47. Ibid., p. 125.
48. Ibid., p. 78.
49. Ibid.
50. Ibid., p. 81.

for sin; but if I am not my flesh in my identity, it is only a short step to a denial that I (in my true identity) am sinning. In fact, Needham does deny the presence of anything inherently evil within the believer when he finds meaning as he should. "Yet when that determinative search for meaning flows out of the deepest self, empowered and directed by the Holy Spirit, there is at that point *nothing inside of me* that is essentially evil,"[51] even though the believer is responsible for the flesh in the broadest sense of his personhood. All of this is confusing at best, and it certainly gives the appearance of denying responsibility for the actions of the flesh.

It would seem that Needham misunderstands the point of Romans 7:18-25 when he appears to imply that Paul denies responsibility in his innermost being for sinning. Paul is neither excusing himself for his sin nor disassociating himself from the sinful acts. Rather he speaks as a man baffled by his actions. To paraphrase Paul's point he says, "This is not what I wished to do, not what I intended to accomplish." *Thelō* in Rom. 7:16, 19, and 20 emphasizes desire in contrast to determination; the apostle discovers that his desires cannot determine what he actually does.[52] "I did the sin, of course; but it was not I in terms of my desires or my plans or my longings. My will power is simply not strong enough to free me from sin." Paul speaks similarly from the opposite perspective in 1 Corinthians 15:10, where he says that the grace of God worked in him to accomplish his labors. There is no doubt that Paul performed the actions to which he refers in that passage, but the power that worked through him was God's. The same is true in Romans 7:18-25, only the resource is the power of sin. If this is not the case, then Paul did neither the sin nor the righteousness, which is utter nonsense.

> As no one supposes that the labours and life here spoken of were not the labours and life of the apostle, or that they did not constitute and express his moral character; so no Christian supposes that the greatness and power of his sin frees him from its responsibility, even when he expresses his helpless misery by saying . . . "It is not I, but sin. . . ."[53]

It becomes clear from the above discussion that the ethical concept of the flesh must be clearly defined or serious confusion will occur. To main-

51. Ibid.
52. William Sanday and Arthur C. Headlam, *A Critical and Exegetical Commentary on the Epistle to the Romans*, The International Critical Commentary (Edinburgh: T. & T. Clark, 1902), p. 182.
53. Charles Hodge, *Commentary on the Epistle to the Romans* (Grand Rapids: Eerdmans, 1976), p. 232.

tain such clarity two factors must be noted: (1) the physical and ethical aspects of the flesh continue to be an inherent part of the believer—this could be denied, with the result that sin is identified with the body in an inappropriate way; (2) the reality that the believer in his essential identity is the one who sins must be accepted, or there could be a disastrous denial of personal responsibility for sin.

These two factors are closely connected: when one sees the flesh as a part of his essential being, he also sees his responsibility for the flesh most clearly. Through the new birth the believer is identified with Christ; through old birth he has the flesh. These will be the two most essential realities about the believer as long as the effects of his two births continue—the flesh until he dies and the Spirit throughout eternity.

Implications arising from the ethical concept of the flesh. Five significant implications arise from the ethical concept of the flesh, implications that we must consider if we are to be fully aware of the impact of the flesh in our lives.

First, unless we understand the flesh and how it works in us we can never be free from sin. Richard Lovelace has observed that "much of the church's warfare today is fought by blindfolded soldiers who cannot see the forces ranged against them, who are buffeted by invisible opponents and respond by striking one another."[54] The flesh is self-centered and divisive; it is deceptive and can even be dedicated to God and His service. But the flesh is sin's slave, and unless it is brought under the Spirit's control it will do sin's bidding whenever it has the opportunity to act. Ignorance in this area of spiritual reality is deadly, as Lovelace has shown so well.

Of the three enemies that the believer faces, the world, the flesh, and the devil, two (the world and the devil) are external, and one (the flesh) is internal. Satan will not be able to work his wiles through the world system within the believer if his "mole" is discovered and brought under control. When the believer faces the flesh in the power of the Spirit, he frees himself not only from the flesh but also from the indirect attack of Satan and the world. It is imperative that we understand how the flesh works if we are to be free from sin, Satan, and the world. Unless this happens, the Scriptures state, the believer will know only the works of the flesh and the defeat of Romans 7.

Second, the flesh will never change, because it is permanently sold in slavery to sin (Rom. 7:14, *pepramenos*). This means that the flesh will al-

---

54. Richard F. Lovelace, *Dynamics of Spiritual Life* (Downers Grove, Ill., InterVarsity, 1979), p. 18.

ways and only do what sin, under the control of Satan, directs it to do. All efforts to change the flesh are futile; the only thing that can be done with the flesh is to bring it under the control of a greater power. As long as we try to improve ourselves apart from dependence on God's Spirit we are condemned to a life of futility, frustration, and failure.

Third, there can never be an integration of Christianity and psychology without dealing with the flesh and its unchanging nature. Christopher Lasch has observed that "the contemporary climate is therapeutic, not religious,"[55] that "the 'psychological man' of the twentieth century seeks . . . peace of mind. . . . Therapists, not priests or preachers of self-help . . . become his principal allies . . . he turns to them in the hope of achieving the modern equivalent of salvation, 'mental health.' "[56] Christianity is not exempt from this desire for peace of mind or from the influence of psychology. Such influence can be for good but not when it fails to integrate the reality of the flesh with its solutions for life. In a sense the diagnosis of psychology is actually a study of the flesh and how it develops its destructive course in the life of humanity. Unless psychology recognizes this reality and incorporates the biblical perspectives concerning the unchanging nature of the flesh and the need for spiritual resources to overcome it, there will be neither a Christian psychology nor a spiritual triumph.

Fourth, we must accept the negative realities of the flesh in order to enjoy the positive realities of grace. Martin Lloyd-Jones states that "you must be made miserable before you can know true Christian joy."[57] The flesh is a most painful reality to face, particularly when we realize it will never change. As a result every effort is made to deny its presence in us and to reject its product through us. However, as long as we refuse to face the flesh we also refuse to grow in grace; it is only as we face the flesh that we realize our need for God's grace and discover that God already knows the worst about us and loves us anyway. Only the believer who is willing to face the flesh can grow in grace.

Fifth, the flesh is not merely sensuous or sexual but also spiritual and social, even good when measured by human standards. Galatians 5:19-21 shows that the sexual accounts for only three of the fifteen characteristics listed there, and Philippians 3:4-6 shows that the flesh can be religious, dedicated to the good and to obeying God. An awareness of this truth de-

---

55. Christopher Lasch, *The Culture of Narcissism* (New York: Warner Books, 1979), p. 33.
56. Ibid., p. 42.
57. D. Martyn Lloyd-Jones, *Spiritual Depression: Its Causes and Cure* (Grand Rapids: Eerdmans, 1968), p. 28.

mands that the believer learn how to defend against the deceptiveness of the flesh.

THE DEFENSE AGAINST THE FLESH

Lewis Sperry Chafer defined the basic issue when he observed the fact that most sermons could be reduced to two words: be good. But few sermons tell people how to be good.[58] Lovelace declares that most Christian congregations are saturated with the dead goodness that is motivated by the flesh rather than by the Holy Spirit.[59] In view of the fact that the flesh has such a grip on the church and that so few know how to be good, it is essential to remember that the one way to be free from the flesh is to walk by the Spirit as emphasized in both Romans 8 and Galatians 5.

"Walking by the Spirit" is an image used in Scripture to show that only an attitude of conscious and deliberate dependence on the Holy Spirit can free believers from the control of the flesh. To walk by the Spirit is to depend on the Holy Spirit rather than self for freedom from the flesh and obedience to righteousness. It is a mental attitude, a mind-set, a conscious determination to rely only on the resources of the Spirit for the power needed to obey God, and it is accomplished through Bible study, worship, fellowship with other believers, and the Spirit Himself. It could also be described as yielding to the Spirit. The words walking by the Spirit suggest an illustration that best pictures it. As we grow older the principle of physical death may work in our bodies until we reach the time when we cannot walk by our own power. At such a time we must count on the power of another if we are to walk; otherwise, we can take no steps. This physical truth pictures the spiritual reality caused by the flesh. Even after salvation, no believer can reach God's standard of righteousness in his own power, because the flesh cripples spiritually even as old age does physically. As a result we need a power greater than ours if we are to live righteously. Just as the physically weak person must depend on another to walk, so we who are spiritually weak must depend on the Holy Spirit to walk God's way. When we, spiritually speaking, place our hand on the arm of the Spirit and walk by His power, we are free from the flesh, delivered from the reigning power of sin, and enabled to be righteous. As Chafer observed, "One must learn better *how* to 'walk in the Spirit': but he will never come to a moment in this life when he will need to walk *less* by the Spirit. The divine resources

58. Lewis Sperry Chafer, unpublished class lectures, Dallas Theological Seminary.
59. Lovelace, p. 92.

for a moment by moment triumph in Christ are limitless; but the utter need of the helpless creature never ceases."[60]

CONCLUSION

The flesh is the traitor in the gates, the Benedict Arnold, the "mole" that claims to assist the believer in righteousness but is actually sold to sin and will resist God at every turn. Because of this treachery the flesh is the most dangerous enemy the believer faces—the deceptive, destructive fifth column that opens the door to the world and the devil and destroys every effort at righteousness. As observed long ago, "Man enters into the world at traitor's gate; born in sin and conceived in iniquity."[61] Only the Holy Spirit frees the believer from the flesh, and this happens only when the believer faces the flesh directly, assumes responsibility for its deviousness, and denies its control through walking by the Spirit. All believers must choose between the works of the flesh and the fruit of the Spirit. Colin Brown describes this choice well when he states, "To live according to the flesh is to travel into the cul-de-sac which ends in death; to live according to the Spirit is to enter life."[62] This, then, is the significance of the flesh, the traitor in the gates: death or life.

---

60. Lewis Sperry Chafer, *He That Is Spiritual* (Grand Rapids: Zondervan, 1918), p. 43.
61. *Oxford English Dictionary,* 2:3375.
62. *Dictionary of New Testament Theology,* 1:682.

J. RONALD BLUE (A.B., University of Nebraska; Th.M., Dallas Theological Seminary; Ph.D. candidate, University of Texas at Arlington) is chairman and associate professor of world missions at Dallas Theological Seminary.

Reach the World in One Generation

J. Ronald Blue

"Reach the world in one generation? You have to be kidding!" Pastor Carter was well informed. He knew that the population of the world was close to 5 billion people. To think that every one of those people could be touched with the gospel in the short span of thirty to forty years seemed both idealistic and unrealistic. "Impossible!" His conclusion was uttered with a tone of absolute finality.

Carter's missionary friend was not easily swayed. "If it is an impossibility, why did the Lord command us to do it? Is it not our responsibility to disciple all nations? Are we not to preach the gospel to every creature?" Jones had a good point.

"You missionaries are all alike. You need to get out of the clouds and face the realities of life." Carter was half joking. But there was another half to his jovial remark that was dead serious. "It is mathematically impossible for the church to reach the whole world in one generation."

Was Pastor Carter right in his conclusion? Is it mathematically impossible to reach the world's billions in one generation? Before exploring the answer to this penetrating question, it might be of interest to trace the origin of the high-sounding "one generation" missionary slogan.

HISTORICAL ORIGIN

The slogan Reach the World in One Generation can be traced to a student movement that began more than a hundred years ago. As early as 1877 the Young Men's Christian Association named a full-time secretary in the United States to work exclusively among university students. The newly named secretary, Luther Wishard, traveled from campus to campus not only to encourage evangelism and discipleship but to arouse missions interest as well. In fact, Wishard was on the verge of departing for overseas ministry when he was tapped for the collegiate assignment with the YMCA.[1]

Wishard found ready response to world missions on several key campuses. At Princeton a group of students under the leadership of Robert Wilder, son of one of the early missionaries to India under the American Board of Commissioners, formed what they called the Princeton Foreign Missionary Society. At Cornell University God used J. E. K. Studd, brother of C. T. Studd of the famous Cambridge Seven that had ignited a new missions thrust in England, to influence a sophomore named John R. Mott to a deep concern for world evangelism.[2]

In the summer of 1885 Luther Wishard of the YMCA, Robert Wilder of Princeton, J. E. K. Studd of Cambridge, and John R. Mott of Cornell persuaded Dwight L. Moody to sponsor a student Bible conference. In July 1886, 250 students from about one hundred colleges and universities gathered at Moody's conference grounds in Mt. Hermon, Massachusetts, for a month of fellowship, prayer, and Bible study.[3] At the opening of the conference Moody announced that they had no program planned but rather would simply emphasize the Bible, music, and prayer.[4]

As the students engaged in group Bible study, corporate worship, and continued prayer, God began to work. On July 16 A. T. Pierson, editor of *The Missionary Review of the World* and a renowned Bible teacher, was asked to address the group on "God's Providence in Modern Missions." In his address Pierson "supported by convincing arguments and striking proposition that 'all should go, and go to all.' This was a keynote which set many to thinking and praying."[5]

Following Pierson's powerful sermon, most of the students continued in prayer through the night. There emerged from that meeting the slogan that soon became the watchword for Christian students all over the

1. See C. Howard Hopkins, *History of the Y. M. C. A. in North America* (New York: Association, 1951).
2. David M. Howard, "The Road to Urbana and Beyond" *Evangelical Missions Quarterly* 21 (January 1985):10-11. For one of the best historical surveys of the Student Volunteer Movement, see David Howard's *Student Power in World Evangelism* (Downers Grove, Ill.: InterVarsity, 1970).
3. Robert Flood, "Moody Bible Institute: History on Every Side" *Moody Monthly* (February 1985), pp. 28-29.
4. Ruth Wilder Braisted, *In This Generation: The Story of Robert Wilder* (New York: Friendship, 1941).
5. Hopkins, p. 15.

country: The Evangelization of the World in This Generation.[6]

The slogan was not empty boast. Students were ready to yield their lives to achieve the goal. One hundred of those at the conference signed a declaration indicating their desire to go to the unevangelized portions of the world. Furthermore, the vision did not die at the end of the conference. Two of the students, Robert Wilder and John Forman, were commissioned to travel to college campuses and spread the vision. During the 1886-87 school year Wilder and Forman visited 162 schools and saw 2,106 students sign missionary volunteer declarations. Among those who signed were Samuel Zwemer and Robert E. Speer.[7]

In order to provide structure to the growing movement the students formed the Student Volunteer Movement for Foreign Missions, officially incorporated in 1888. John R. Mott was named chairman and Wilder traveling secretary. Their watchword, "The evangelization of the world in this generation," swept the continent. Mott later wrote of the impact this simple slogan had on his life: "I can truthfully answer that next to the decision to take Christ as the Leader and Lord of my life, the watchword has had more influence than all other ideals and objectives combined to widen my horizon and enlarge my conception of the Kingdom of God."[8]

Not everyone shared Mott's optimism, however. The slogan was openly criticized by some. The German mission historian and theologian Gustav Warneck, for example, considered "the evangelization of the world in this generation" an arrogant statement. He branded the idea that all the world be Christianized as superficial and naive. William R. Hogg, however, correctly assessed the misunderstanding by those who opposed the watchword.

> The majority of its detractors (most of them Continentals) apparently failed to grasp its true meaning. It did not prophesy nor suggest as possible the *conversion* of the world in this generation. . . . The overwhelming majority of students to whom it was meaningful understood by it the *responsibility* to each generation to make the gospel known to all mankind in that generation. None other can repeat that eternal message to a particular generation. Its own members alone can do that.[9]

6. John R. Mott, *Five Decades and a Forward View* (New York: Harper, 1939), p. 8.
7. Howard, p. 12.
8. *Christian Students and World Problems: Report on the Ninth International S. V. M. Convention, Indianapolis, 1924* (New York: Student Volunteer Movement, n.d.), p. 64. Quoted by David Howard in *Student Power,* p. 87.
9. William R. Hogg, *Ecumenical Foundations* (New York: Harper, 1952), p. 88.

Thousands of students responded to the call to reach the entire world in their generation. "By 1945, at the most conservative estimate, 20,500 students from so-called Christian lands, who had signed the declaration, reached the field, for the most part under the missionary societies and boards of the Churches."[10]

Sadly, however, the Student Volunteer Movement became increasingly concerned about social needs and ecumenical goals and suffered a painful demise. The Student Volunteer Movement merged with the United Student Christian Council and the Interseminary Movement and later with the Roman Catholic National Newman Student Federation to form the University Christian Movement. In 1969 a remnant of twenty-four students voted that "the UCM cease to exist as a national organization."[11] The movement that had mobilized thousands of students to move out with a burning desire to evangelize the entire world in their generation died before the proposed goal had been met.

Could it be that the goal to evangelize all of the world's peoples in one generation was overly idealistic? Was it an impossibility that simply could not be achieved? Was it naive to believe that in a span of thirty to forty years every person on the globe could be afforded the opportunity to hear the good news of the Lord Jesus Christ? These burning questions did not die with the Student Volunteer Movement. They need to be addressed anew in the light of Scripture.

SCRIPTURAL CONSIDERATION

The global goal of the visionaries of the Student Volunteer Movement may have seemed idealistic by some, but it was founded in the Word of God.

The Great Commission texts clearly emphasize the universal scope of the gospel. Matthew recorded Christ's command to "make disciples of all the nations" (Matt. 28:19). Mark stressed the Lord's order to "go into all the world and preach the gospel to all creation" (Mark 16:15). Luke wrote that "repentance for forgiveness of sins should be proclaimed . . . to all the nations" (Luke 24:47) and that Christ's disciples would be witnesses "to the remotest part of the earth" (Acts 1:8). John revealed the world-encom-

10. Ruth Rose and Stephen C. Neill, *A History of the Ecumenical Movement.* 1517-1948 (Philadelphia: Westminster, 1967), p. 328.
11. *News Notes,* Department of Higher Education, National Council of the Churches of Christ in the U.S.A., New York, 15, no. 3, March 1969.

passing assignment when he quoted Christ's words "As the Father has sent Me, I also send you" (John 20:21). The Lord's assignment was clearly worldwide in its scope.

It is not evident, however, whether there was a possibility of completing the assignment in the time span of one generation. In fact, it appears that Christ's promise was to assist His witnesses in the evangelization and discipleship process "even to the end of the age" (Matt. 28:20).

It was not the *scope* of their vision but the idealistic *timing* of the Student Volunteer Movement that was most criticized by those who questioned their objectives. To reach the whole world in one generation seemed absurd.

Were the objectives to the watchword legitimate? It seems reasonable to determine if indeed each generation could fulfill its responsibility of world evangelization. The Student Volunteer Movement did not propose to finish the task for all generations. They only sought to reach the world of *their* generation. Were they wrong? Were they chasing after the wind in a hopeless pursuit?

It is the purpose of this article to show that it was neither naive nor impossible to fulfill the dream that motivated the youth of the Student Volunteer Movement. They were right on target. They were clearly in line with the intent of Scripture. It is lamentable that their global thrust was diffused into nonevangelistic endeavors. A movement that might have continued to mushroom in fulfillment of Christ's worldwide assignment was cut short. Worse yet, with the demise of the Student Volunteer Movement the church lapsed into a state of complacency that is still woefully evident. Christians remain skeptical about missions. They give part-time attention to world evangelism and dedicate only surplus funds to what they see as an impossible task.

CHRIST'S COMMISSION

The Lord Jesus Christ did not present a Great Commission that was impossible to achieve. He never intended for His children to surrender so easily.

With the command to "make disciples of the nations" Christ outlined the means to achieve the goal (Matt. 28:19-20). Each believer is to "go" and *reach* people who need the good news of salvation. He then must bring people to Christ and by "baptizing" them *root* them in the Word and in fellowship with other believers. Finally, he is to build up each new believer by "teaching" him to obey God's Word and thus *ready* him to in turn reach others.[12]

The plan outlined by Christ was one of continuous multiplication. It was an assignment for every Christian of each generation. The command was not limited to the apostles who heard Christ's words and then saw Him ascend into heaven. In fact, when the process began in the early church, the outreach into Judea and Samaria was not accomplished by the apostles but by the other believers.[13]

The world-wide assignment could hardly be limited to the first generation of Christians. Just as the Father had sent Christ into the world "to seek and to save that which was lost" (Luke 19:10), so the Son sent the church into the world. Each generation must carry on the assignment given by the Lord. The multiplication of disciples is to continue until the "end of the age" (Matt. 28:20).

PAUL'S INSTRUCTION

Few of the early believers seemed to understand the assignment better than the apostle Paul, and nowhere does he more clearly outline God's plan than in his last letter recorded in the Word of God. Of the thirteen epistles in the Bible written by Paul one of the most heart-warming, and at the same time challenging and convicting, is his second letter to Timothy.

Very likely writing during his final imprisonment, Paul realized that death was near. He wrote, "The time of my departure has come." Paul continued, "I have fought the good fight, I have finished the course, I have kept the faith" (2 Tim. 4:6-7). He wanted Timothy to be able to follow his example and to be as effective in ministry as he had been.

In chapter 2 Paul specifies the multiplication process that Timothy is to follow so that the assignment Paul has received from the Lord will be completed in each succeeding generation. Paul wrote, "You therefore, my son, be strong in the grace that is in Christ Jesus. And the things which you have heard from me in the presence of many witnesses, these entrust to faithful men, who will be able to teach others also" (2 Tim. 2:1-2).

Anyone who has been involved with an organization that stresses discipleship is very well acquainted with what is sometimes referred to as "two-

---

12. See David J. Hesselgrave, "Confusion Concerning the Great Commission" *Evangelical Missions Quarterly* 15 (October 1979):197-204.
13. Acts 8:1, "They were all scattered throughout the regions of Judea and Samaria, *except the apostles.*"

two-two," that is, 2 Timothy 2:2. Many of those who are so aware of 2 Timothy 2:2, however, fail to focus on 2:1. Herein is an example of the importance of considering all Scripture in context. The process outlined in verse 2 cannot be accomplished without the provision revealed in verse 1.

Paul stressed a dynamic relationship far more than he did the discipleship responsibility. In fact, what Paul writes in 2:1 may be considered a summary statement of what he presents to Timothy in chapter 1. "You therefore, my son, be strong in the grace that is in Christ Jesus" captures the thrust of Paul's opening remarks in this epistle. In chapter 1 the apostle challenged Timothy with three commands. First he wrote, "Kindle afresh the gift of God which is in you" (1:6). Next he said, "Retain the standard of sound words which you have heard from me" (1:13). Finally Paul declared, "Guard, through the Holy Spirit who dwells in us, the treasure which has been entrusted to you" (1:14). Timothy was instructed to give attention to the *sovereign worth* found in him, the *sound words* given to him, and the *Spirit's work* accomplished through him.

Paul emphasized the spiritual dimension and the relational dynamic of life. He encouraged Timothy to find in God the source of power, love, and discipline needed to fulfill the ministry (1:8).

"Therefore," Paul concluded, "be strong in the grace that is in Christ Jesus" (2:1). The command was not issued with cold indifference. Paul gave the order in a direct, personal, loving manner. He addressed Timothy as his "son," or more literally, his "child." With the love and authority of a father, Paul instructed Timothy to find his strength in the unsurpassed sufficiency and unmerited satisfaction of the Lord Jesus Christ. The dependency on the Lord can be seen in the passive voice of the verb *endunamou*, which might better be translated "be strengthened." Furthermore, it is to be a continual dependency, for the verb is in the present tense.

Perhaps the greatest problem in the discipleship process is the disciple who is too weak spiritually to disciple others. Far too many Christians have lost contact with the power source and are simply too weak to multiply. It is little wonder Paul stressed the Source of strength and the contact with that Source.

In God's sovereignty He has chosen the weak vessels called humans to evangelize the world. Each generation must bear the responsibility for that task. Nothing can be accomplished, however, unless those humans who have been saved *by* God's grace continue to find their spiritual strength *in* His grace. To every Christian Paul's inspired command has relevance, "Be strong in the grace that is in Christ Jesus."

In a practical way Paul's admonition means that every Christian must learn to rely on Christ's power. One way to live in Christ's power is to be disciplined enough to plug into that power every day. A daily appointment with the Lord can be one of the most effective means of insuring daily reliance on His strength. Appointments are made for every other activity of life. Certainly this one should be a priority. It is incredible that each Christian should have immediate access to the Creator of the universe through the Lord Jesus Christ. It is even more incredible that the majority of Christians take so little advantage of this contact.

Perhaps the greatest hindrance to the evangelization of the world in this generation is not the lack of contact with the lost but the lack of contact with the Lord. It must be remembered that the explosion of world evangelization of the Student Volunteer Movement began with attention to Bible study and prayer.

After encouraging Timothy to take advantage of God's provision of spiritual strength found in the Lord, Paul outlined God's plan to accomplish successfully the work of the Lord. The multiplication process is found in "two-two-two," a key verse in the Word of God. "And the things which you have heard from me in the presence of many witnesses, these entrust to faithful men, who will be able to teach others also."

Paul wanted to be sure that his diligent service for the Lord would not die when he died. He could see his last lap ending, but he knew that the race was still on. Paul passed the baton to Timothy and then instructed the young runner to do likewise. Timothy was to be a part fo the "P.I.0. League," as Guy King calls it—a league to "Pass It On."[14]

Paul's assignment to Timothy was verified by "many witnesses" *(pollōn marturōn),* who may have been "the presbyters who were present and assisted at Timothy's ordination"[15] or the other disciples whom Paul taught. Whoever the witnesses were, the command is clear. Timothy must take what Paul taught him and entrust it to others.

The assignment was not one of merely repeating to others what Paul has said. The verb "entrust" *(parathou)* means "to deposit as a trust."[16] The idea is "to entrust something to another for safekeeping."[17] It is clear that

14. N. A. Woychuk, *An Exposition of Second Timothy* (Old Tappan, N.J.: Revell, 1973), p. 41.
15. Charles T. Ellicott, *The Pastoral Epistles of St. Paul* (London: Longmans, Green, and Co., 1883), p. 122.
16. Kenneth S. Wuest, *The Pastoral Epistles* (Grand Rapids: Eerdmans, 1952), p. 128.
17. Donald Guthrie, *The Pastoral Epistles* (Grand Rapids: Eerdmans, 1957), p. 138.

Paul was as concerned about the reception of the truth as he was about the transmission.

The truth was to be entrusted to selected individuals. Timothy was not directed to scatter the seed indiscriminately across the open fields. He was to plant the seed carefully among the faithful. The selection was to be based on one supreme quality: faithfulness. It is the person who demonstrates a consistent and reliable pattern of life who is a candidate for effective discipleship. The good-looking, talented, intelligent, and so-called sharp people all too often drop out before the race is won. Effective and lasting discipleship will best be achieved by focusing on the faithful, not the flashy.

Finally, Paul turned to the goal of the discipleship plan. The faithful men to whom Timothy was to entrust the truth must then be "able to teach others also." The multiplication process is clear. What Paul has given to Timothy, Timothy was to deposit in faithful men who in turn would reproduce in others.

God's provision of spiritual strength to accomplish His plan of successive multiplication does, nonetheless, carry with it some prerequisites. Paul sounded some precautions in the verses that follow. He wanted Timothy to understand that discipleship was not some small exercise that took little effort to accomplish. The apostle emphasized three prerequisites of character that would be essential for anyone engaged in the reproduction process. To make the needed characteristics abundantly clear, Paul used three vivid examples.

First, Paul pointed to the soldier (2:3-4). "Suffer hardship with me, as a good soldier of Christ Jesus" (v. 3). Paul frequently used military metaphors, probably because the military might of the Roman Empire was in such high profile.[18] Paul did not call on Timothy to engage in something that the apostle himself was not willing to endure. The verb "suffer hardship together" *(sugkakopathēson)* clearly denotes participation and could be rendered "take your share of suffering."[19]

Paul continued, "No soldier in active service entangles himself in the affairs of everyday life, so that he may please the one who enlisted him as a soldier" (v. 4). Good soldiers exhibit *discipline.* They are ready to go through anything, whether they feel like it or not, in order to fulfill their

---

18. Some examples of Paul's military metaphors may be found in Romans 6:13; 7:23; 1 Corinthians 9:7; and Ephesians 6:11-18.
19. The preposition *sun* in the composite verb *sugkakopatheō* indicates the participatory aspect of the suffering. See 2 Timothy 1:8, "Join with me in suffering for the gospel."

duty to their commander and their country. N. A. Woychuk gives a touching example: "A French soldier once lay sorely wounded on the field of battle. When the surgeons were probing the wound in the breast to find the bullet, the soldier remarked, 'A little deeper, gentlemen, and you will find the emperor.'"[20]

Such singleness of purpose keeps a soldier from getting entangled in the affairs of life, or as William F. Arndt and F. Wilbur Gingrich translate the phrase, "become entangled in civilian pursuits."[21] Paul's point is clear. To be an effective discipler, a person must be disciplined like a good soldier. He cannot win the conquest without engaging in the conflict.

Second, Paul turned to the athlete. "If anyone competes as an athlete, he does not win the prize unless he competes according to the rules" (2:5).[22] When Paul wrote this letter Greek athletes were probably as prevalent as Roman soldiers. To be a winning athlete the participant had to be fully dedicated to his sport.

The rules to which Paul referred were not simply the rules of the game. They dealt with the rules of the athlete. In the *Dictionary of Antiquities,* Galen outlines some of the regulations.

> Every candidate had to prove that he was of pure Hellenistic descent. He was disqualified by certain moral and political offences. He was obliged to take an oath that he had been ten months in training, and that he would violate none of the regulations. The usual course was to eat bread for the morning meal and meat for the evening. After the morning meal their exercise continued until the evening. Bribery was punished by severe fines. The candidate had to practice again in the gymnasium immediately before the games, under direction of umpires, who were themselves for some ten months instructed in the details of the games.[23]

Anyone who has been involved in athletics knows that to succeed demands the utmost in *dedication.* It is especially impressive to see the dedication of nonprofessional athletes. They pour their lives into the pursuit of excellence and drive their bodies to the utmost in order to win the event in

---

20. Woychuk, p. 42.
21. William F. Arndt and F. Wilbur Gingrich, *A Greek-English Lexicon of the New Testament* (Chicago: U. of Chicago, 1957), p. 236. The verb "entangle," *empleketai,* is used only here and in 2 Peter 2:20.
22. The verb "compete," *athleō,* "to engage in a contest" or "strive in the games," is used only here in the New Testament.
23. Galen, quoted by Woychuk, pp. 48-49.

which they are engaged. Their material reward is nominal. The crown Paul mentioned was a mere wreath of leaves.[24] The medal or trophy amateur athletes receive today is of limited value as well. The athlete's dedication is deep and demanding. It is winning that counts, and he will not win the crown unless he competes.

Third, Paul wrote about the farmer (2:6). "The hard-working farmer ought to be the first to receive his share of the crops." There could be no better example of *diligence*. The word here translated "hard-working" vividly depicts "labor carried to the point of great weariness and exhaustion."[25] Discipleship demands work—hard work. As someone has wisely stated, the only place success comes before work is in the dictionary. If a farmer expects a crop, he must expend the back-breaking energy required in cultivation. If a discipler plans to see any spiritual fruit, he too must engage in faithful cultivation.

The apostle Paul could not have made it clearer. He pointed to the *provision* of spiritual strength in the grace that is in Christ Jesus. He outlined the *plan* of multiplication that must be pursued generation after generation. He highlighted the *prerequisites* of personal character that must be evident in the discipler—the discipline of a soldier, the dedication of an athlete, and the diligence of a farmer.

Lest there remain any misunderstanding or confusion, Paul concluded, "Consider what I say, for the Lord will give you understanding in everything" (2:7). The apostle was not so naive as to believe that just because he wrote it down everyone would understand, much less obey. He trusted in the Lord to insure the results.

But what does all this have to do with reaching the world in one generation? It has everything to do with reaching the world in one generation. The simple process of multiplication outlined by the Lord Jesus Christ in the Great Commission and further delineated by Paul in his letter to Timothy is the answer to the skeptics who still consider the watchword of the Student Volunteer Movement idealistic and unrealistic. It is neither. The goal to reach the world in one generation is real and attainable *if* believers of each generation follow the instruction from the Word of God.

MATHEMATICAL VERIFICATION

A pocket calculator can be used to prove mathematically that the entire

24. The "crown," *stephanoutai*, is a wreath and is distinct from the "diadem" of royalty.
25. Homer A. Kent, Jr., *The Pastoral Epistles*, rev. ed. (Chicago: Moody 1982), p. 261.

world can be evangelized in but one generation. Through the biblically prescribed process of multiplication the seemingly unattainable goal is a reasonable target.

The problem is that far too many Christians continue to focus on adding people to the church rather than multiplying witnesses to the world. A simple mathematical exercise will clearly show the fallacy of addition and will support the biblical accuracy of multiplication. Too many people focus on evangelistic decisions rather than on effective discipleship.

Contrast two Christians, one named Gordon, the other Fred. Gordon is a zealous believer who through aggressive personal evangelism succeeds in leading a person to Christ every single week, year after year. Needless to say, most Christians would rightfully look upon this "super star" with much favor and admiration.

Fred is a more average believer who over the course of a year's time brings a friend of his to the Lord. Certainly faithful Fred seems a more plausible model than "flash" Gordon, the "one-a-week" wonder. Faithful Fred continues to work with his newly converted friend and through the year grounds him in the Word and encourages him to reach out to his friends who also needs to know the Lord. The multiplication process continues in like manner year after year.

Who will evangelize the world in one generation—"flash" Gordon or faithful Fred? The calculator provides the answer. Consider the results:

	"Flash" Gordon Wins one person each week—	Fred Disciples one person each year—
1 year	53	2
2 years	105	4
3 years	157	8
4 years	209	16
5 years	261	32
6 years	313	64
7 years	365	128
8 years	417	256
9 years	469	512

In but nine years faithful Fred surpassed the production of the amazing "flash" Gordon.

Continue the process for thirty-two years, or the approximate time-span of one generation. At the conclusion of thirty-two years Gordon will have brought 1,665 people to the Lord, providing he did not miss a single week in his ambitious effort to win one a week.

And what about faithful Fred who has systematically discipled one person a year and has seen his disciples follow the same process with others year after year? Fred will have been instrumental in bringing 4,294,967,296 to the Lord. That is right. More than 4 billion would be reached in a mere thirty-two years by means of the multiplication process.

There is no intent to discredit zealous soul-winners who are active in evangelism. Ideally the most desired believer would be a combined Gordon and Fred, one who was continually communicating the gospel *and* faithfully discipling new converts. The point, however, is clear. Evangelism without edification is insufficient. Reproduction must occur.

Conclusion

It is mathematically feasible to reach the entire world in but one generation. The vision of the Student Volunteer Movement was not irrational and unrealistic. Every generation needs to recapture the vision of those students. Their vision is God's vision.

The Lord has commanded the church to world-wide evangelization. He has promised to provide the necessary power to fulfill His purpose. The Lord has clearly outlined the plan to follow to achieve His global goal. The only obstacle is the self-satisfied, self-sufficient, self-serving believer who pronounces the goal unreasonable and unattainable and sits, soaks, and sours in his skepticism and self-righteousness.

May God grant a whole new breed of Christians who will raise the banner with confidence and inspire thousands to march again toward God's goal—*the evangelization of the world in this generation!*

Part 3

Things to Come:
Themes from Prophecy

Donald K. Campbell (A.B., Wheaton College; Th.M., Th.D., Dallas Theological Seminary) is president and professor of Bible exposition at Dallas Theological Seminary.

The Church in God's Prophetic Program

Donald K. Campbell

In the mind of this writer a prophetic program for the church is based on the primary distinction between Israel and the church, an essential mark of dispensationalism. Robert L. Saucy declares:

> The consistent witness of Scripture is to the distinctiveness of Israel and the church. Israel is an elect nation called to witness to the glory of God as a nation among nations and serve a distinct phase in the kingdom program. The church, on the other hand, is a people called out from every nation as "a people for his name" (Acts 15:14). . . . Having noted this distinction, it is necessary to guard against a dichotomy which fails to see the place of the church as an integral part of God's program along with Israel and thus a coheir of the promises (Gal. 3:29).[1]

Contemporary dispensationalists affirm that the church participates in the blessings of the Abrahamic covenant by inheriting the promise of justification by faith (Gal. 3:6-9, 29) and in the blessings of the New Covenant of Jeremiah 31 by experiencing regeneration, the indwelling Spirit, and so on. This participation, however, does not fulfill or abrogate the remaining covenant promises of a national nature, which will find their fulfillment for Israel following Christ's second advent.

The distinction between Israel and the church extends beyond the present age into the future. Some dispensationalists make a sharp distinction between Israel as God's earthly people and the church as God's heavenly people, both continuing as such throughout eternity. Others favor a blur-

1. Robert L. Saucy, *The Church in God's Program* (Chicago: Moody, 1972), pp. 73-74.

ring of such distinctions in eternity. Charles C. Ryrie states, "The redeemed in the Body of Christ, the Church of this dispensation, are the con-
tinuation of the line of redeemed from other ages, but they form a distinct
group in the heavenly Zion (Heb. 12:22-24)."[2]

This article pursues the future of the church as a distinct entity and discusses selected aspects of her relation to the second advent, the Millennium, and eternity.

THE CHURCH AND THE SECOND ADVENT

ISRAEL AND THE TRIBULATION

A recognition of the distinction between Israel and the church supports
the belief that the church will be removed from the earth before the Tribulation at the rapture, the first phase of Christ's return. This is true because
the Tribulation primarily concerns Israel, a fact cogently argued by J.
Dwight Pentecost. He affirms that although this period will see the wrath
of God poured out on the entire earth, the period relates particularly to Israel. In support he cites Jeremiah 30:7, which calls this span "the time of
Jacob's trouble." He comments further:

> The events of the seventieth week are events of the "Day of the Lord" or
> "Day of Jehovah." This use of the name of deity emphasizes God's pecu-
> liar relationship to that nation. When this period is being anticipated in
> Daniel 9, God says to the prophet, "Seventy weeks are determined upon
> thy people and upon thy holy city" (v. 24). This whole period then has
> special reference to Daniel's people, Israel, and Daniel's holy city,
> Jerusalem.[3]

THE CHURCH AND THE TRIBULATION

It is not possible within the limitations of this article to review the arguments for and against the church's pretribulation rapture. That has already
been amply and adequately done by such eschatological experts as Pentecost, Ryrie, and John F. Walvoord. Recently, however, two landmark articles have appeared dealing with this issue and, in the opinion of this writer, they make a positive contribution toward a resolution of this debate.
The articles are "The Rapture in 1 Thessalonians 5:1-11," by Zane C. Hodges,[4]

2. Charles C. Ryrie, *Dispensationalism Today* (Chicago: Moody, 1965), p. 154.
3. J. Dwight Pentecost, *Things to Come* (Findlay, Ohio: Dunham, 1958), p. 195.
4. Zane C. Hodges, "The Rapture in 1 Thessalonians 5:1-11," in *Walvoord: A Tribute*, ed. Donald K.
   Campbell (Chicago: Moody, 1982), pp. 67-79.

and "The Rapture in Revelation 3:10," by Jeffrey L. Townsend.[5]

It has been sometimes said even by pretribulationists that their view has no clear or explicit textual support but is based more on theological considerations. Without minimizing the latter, we can be grateful for recent exegetical studies of the type cited above that support the doctrine of the pretribulational rapture of the church.

1 Thessalonians 5:1-11. Hodges states, "For the truth that the church is destined for rescue from the woes of the Tribulation, no passage has more to offer to exegetical scrutiny than does 1 Thessalonians 5:1-11."[6] He develops his argument as follows:

First, 1 Thessalonians 1:9*b*-10 is labeled "the key passage." It describes the conversion of the Thessalonian believers who "wait for His Son from heaven, whom He raised from the dead, that is Jesus, who delivers us from the wrath to come." The reference is obviously to the future return of Christ and the phrase "the wrath to come" is "redolent with eschatological overtones." From this future wrath Jesus "delivers us."[7]

Second, Hodges finds 1:9*b*-10 to contain a summation of the rest of the epistle. The expression "how you turned to God from idols" refers to the Thessalonians' past, and Paul addresses those early days in chapters 2 and 3. The phrase "to serve a living and true God" points to their present lifestyle and anticipates Paul's discussion in 4:1-12. The words "to wait for His Son from Heaven . . . who delivers us from the wrath to come" points to the future, and that is the subject of the eschatological portion of the epistle in 4:13—5:11.[8]

Third, in 5:1-3 Paul indicates what the Thessalonians knew about the prophetic programs. The "wrath to come" referred to in 1:10 is here described as the "birthpangs" of the familiar day of the Lord; and it is from this wrathful period that the Thessalonians are promised deliverance (1:10).[9]

Fourth, the apostle next makes clear that his Christian readers stand in a different relationship to these eschatological woes than does the unregenerate world around them. The unsaved are of the "darkness" and "will

5. Jeffrey L. Townsend, "The Rapture in Revelation 3:10," *Bibliotheca Sacra* 137 (July-September, 1980):252-66.
6. Hodges, pp. 67-68.
7. Ibid., p. 68.
8. Ibid., pp. 68-69.
9. Ibid., pp. 70-71.

not escape." In contrast the *believers* belong intrinsically to the "light" (5:3-5).[10]

Fifth, Paul follows his explanation with a strong appeal for the Christians to arm themselves against spiritual lethargy and unwatchfulness by putting on the "breast-plate of faith and love, and as a helmet, the hope of salvation" (5:8). The helmet of hope is the expectation of deliverance from "the wrath to come." Is that hope valid? Can it be relied on? The promise of deliverance is reaffirmed in the language of 1:10, "For God has not destined us for wrath, but for obtaining salvation [i.e., deliverance] through our Lord Jesus Christ" (5:9). Therefore Christ at His coming will deliver believers from the eschatological woes at their outset so that they might live forever with him.[11]

"Thus," concludes Hodges, "the truth that the church will escape the Tribulation by means of the rapture has firm roots in the New Testament exegesis."[12]

Revelation 3:10. It has been said that Revelation 3:10 is "probably the most debated verse in the whole discussion about the time of the Church's rapture."[13] All agree that the church at Philadelphia was promised protection from "the hour of testing." The debate concerns the nature of that protection. Will it be an external preservation by means of the rapture or an internal preservation or protection as the church goes through the Tribulation?

Townsend ably defends the former by a careful exegesis of Revelation 3:10. First, he deals with the Lord's promise that He will keep them from the hour of testing. The words "keep from" (*tēreso ek*), whatever their meaning, pose a great problem for the posttribulationist because according to the book of Revelation the saints are not protected or preserved during the Tribulation, but rather face fierce persecution and martyrdom. Townsend examines the preposition *ek* ("out of" or "from within") in classical literature, the Septuagint, Josephus, and the New Testament. His conclusion is instructive.

> This study of *ek* throughout its linguistic history and especially its usage in the New Testament has shown that the preposition may sometimes indicate outside position (whereas other times it means removal

10. Ibid., pp. 73-74.
11. Ibid., pp. 75-77.
12. Ibid., p. 78.
13. Robert H. Gundry, *The Church and the Tribulation* (Grand Rapids: Zondervan, 1973), p. 54.

from within). In relation to the interpretation of *tēreō ek* in Revelation 3:10, this finding establishes the pretribulational position as a bona fide grammatical possibility. To understand *tēreō ek* as indicating preservation in an outside position is well within the bounds of the linguistic history and usage of *ek*.[14]

Second, Townsend examines the meaning of "the hour of testing." The preservation promised the Philadelphian Christians related to a particular period of time, a well-known hour of trial, the seven-year period of tribulation that precedes Christ's return to earth. Christ's specific promise is that He will keep the church from the *time* of testing and not only from the testing itself. This requires removal from the dimension of time to that of eternity. "Since the church is to be preserved outside a period of time which encompasses the whole world, preservation by a pretribulation rapture is again seen to be a logical inference from the context. Only a rapture to heaven removes the church from the earth and its time continuum."[15]

Third, Townsend discusses the purpose of the "hour of testing." The hour is designed "to test those who dwell upon the earth." The testing is not localized but comes upon the "whole world," an expression that cannot legitimately be restricted to the Roman world of John's day and its well-known persecution of Christians. Rather careful studies have demonstrated that *oikoumenē* ("whole world") may refer to mankind as a whole.[16] Earth's population will face a final test during the Tribulation period, and it will be clearly shown that they deserve the judgments the Lord will carry out on His return.[17]

Thus we have in Revelation 3:10 what some consider to be the best proof of the pretribulation rapture of the church, for although the verse does not mention the rapture specifically, it shows the church outside the hour of testing, a position that could only be realized by a pretribulation rapture. W. Robert Cook also gives a careful and thorough exegesis of Revelation 3:10 and concludes, "On the basis of these facts, it would seem reasonable to conclude that Revelation 3:10 is *clear* support for a pretribulation rapture."[18]

But what of those who minimize the significance of this promise because it was made to only one church that no longer exists? First, several

14. Townsend, "The Rapture in Revelation 3:10," pp. 257.
15. Ibid., pp. 259-61.
16. Ibid., pp. 265-66.
17. Ibid., p. 261.
18. W. Robert Cook, *The Theology of John* (Chicago: Moody, 1979), p. 170.

verses in the first chapter of Revelation (cf. 1:4, 11) indicate that the seven letters were for all the churches, showing that 3:10 is not an exclusive promise. Second, each letter closes with the appeal "He who has an ear let him hear what the Spirit says to the churches." Many Bible students believe that the seven churches represent seven types of churches that always exist in this age, making the promise of 3:10 relevant to the universal church. Third, even though the promise was given to a first-century church that is now defunct, it must be remembered that the author was dealing with an imminent event, yet one that could not be precisely dated. "If the promise to the Philadelphians is invalid because the church has not survived, so are related promises made to the Thessalonians (1 Thess. 4:13-18) and the Corinthians (1 Cor. 15:52-53)."[19]

THE CHURCH AND THE MILLENNIUM

THE PRINCIPLE OF LITERAL INTERPRETATION

Another foundational principle of dispensationalism, in addition to maintaining the distinction between Israel and the church, is the insistence that the Bible must be interpreted literally. When the Bible is interpreted in this fashion, it demands an earthly reign of Christ and a future millennial age. Amillennialist Floyd Hamilton wrote, "Now we must frankly admit that a literal interpretation of the Old Testament prophecies gives us such a picture of an earthly reign of the Messiah as the premillennialist pictures."[20] This observation was also made by Dutch theologian Gerrit C. Berkower.

> Time was when most theologians regarded Chiliasm as a fantastic, earthbound eschatology. . . . A remarkable change has taken place. . . . While the critics of Chiliasm find its description of the millennial times objectionable and unacceptable, the same critics praise the Chiliast's fidelity to God's purpose for the earth. It is this motif, they say, that has made Chiliasm a current that has never been wholly set aside in the church. The Chiliast's hope for Christ's kingdom on earth is sometimes called the anti-spiritualistic motif in millennialism. It is the faith that God's salvation has meaning not only for heaven, but for earth as well. For this earth![21]

19. Jeffrey L. Townsend, "Views of the Rapture in the Book of Revelation." Paper delivered in a doctoral seminar, Dallas Theological Seminary, October 15, 1982, p. 11.
20. Floyd E. Hamilton, *The Basis of the Millennial Faith* (Grand Rapids: Eerdmans, 1952), p. 38.
21. G. C. Berkower, "Review of Current Religious Thought," *Christianity Today,* 6 (27 October 1961), p. 40.

A majority of early church Fathers including Papias, Barnabas, Iren-aeus, Justin Martyr, and Tertullian held that a kingdom would be inaugu-rated by Christ at His second advent and that it would be within history on this earth. This doctrine was attacked in the third century by such Alexan-drian Fathers as Dionysius, Clement, and Origen, and later by Augustine, who in his *City of God* equated the church with Christ's earthly kingdom.

THE LITERAL DEBATE

The two opposing viewpoints of premillennialism and amillennialism are still with us, though some modifications are taking place. Some pre-millennialists now view the present age as the first phase of the fulfillment of the promised messianic kingdom in that believers now experience the *spiritual* aspects of that kingdom such as the blessings of the New Cove-nant.[22] Of course premillenarians have always recognized more than one aspect of the kingdom.

> It should be obvious, however, that the millennial kingdom, though in some respects the consummation of much kingdom truth in Scripture, is not the sum total of God's kingdom purpose. . . . Though there is a rule of God in the present age which can properly be described by the word *kingdom*, it is not the fulfillment of those prophecies that pertain to the millennial reign of Christ upon the earth.[23]

Whereas the majority of amillennialists continue to see the church in the present age as the only fulfillment of the kingdom promises, a few among them, such as Arthur Lewis in *The Dark Side of the Millennium* and Anthony Hoekema in *The Bible and the Future,* see a real if not literal fulfillment of the kingdom promises in the eternal state. In this view the Millennium is to be identified with the present age, and the messianic age with the eternal state.

THE CRUCIALITY OF REVELATION

Once again, reference can be made to the contribution of two significant articles that address the present versus future millennial kingdom issue, particularly from the viewpoint of Revelation 20. The articles are "Premil-

22. Robert L. Saucy, "Contemporary Dispensational Thought," Theological Students Fellowship Bul-letin (March-April 1984), p. 11.
23. John F. Walvoord, *The Millennial Kingdom* (Findlay, Ohio: Dunham, 1959), p. 297.

lennialism in Revelation 20:4-6," by Jack S. Deere[24] and "Is the Present Age the Millennium?" by Townsend.[25]

In order to discuss the relation of the church to the future Millennium it must first be shown that the Millennium is indeed future and not to be equated with the present church age. Four key interpretive issues in Revelation 20 will be addressed in this connection.

First is the question of the chronology of Revelation 19-20. Though all of the book of Revelation is not in strict chronological order, chapters 19 and 20 appear to be. Deere summarizes the evidence:

> Not only do the parallels with Daniel 7 and the exegetical connections with 19:11-21 argue for a futuristic interpretation of Revelation 20:4-6 but also its setting in a context that is completely futuristic before and after argue for a yet-future fulfillment. Unless there are compelling exegetical reasons to the contrary, Revelation 20:4-6 must be viewed as chronologically following the Second Advent and as therefore future.[26]

The Millennium is future and cannot be identified with the present age.

The second issue concerns the length of the millennial reign of Christ. Six times in Revelation 20:2-7 the messianic kingdom is said to last a thousand years. But are the thousand years to be taken literally or symbolically? John J. Davis affirms that numbers "should always be taken at face value and understood as conveying a mathematical quantity unless there is either textual or contextual evidence to the contrary."[27] Alva J. McClain declares that of twenty-five time references in Revelation 4-20 only two (6:17; 15:7) are used symbolically.[28] Finally, Deere states what whenever the Hebrew and Greek words for "year" are used with a numeral, the reference is always to literal years.[29] Since, therefore, the words "a thousand years" were used by John to describe a definite time span, the Millennium cannot be the present age, which is an indefinite period of time.

The third key interpretive issue in this passage is the binding of Satan. To support their view that the Millennium is in existence today, amillennialists equate what the New Testament says about the limitations of Satan

---

24. Jack S. Deere, "Premillennialism in Revelation 20:4-6," *Bibliotheca Sacra* 135 (January-March, 1978):58-73.
25. Jeffrey L. Townsend, "Is the Present Age the Millennium?" *Bibliotheca Sacra* 140 (July-September, 1983): 206-24.
26. Deere, p. 62.
27. John J. Davis, *Biblical Numerology* (Grand Rapids: Baker, 1968), p. 155.
28. Alva J. McClain, *The Greatness of the Kingdom* (Chicago: Moody, 1959), pp. 493-94.
29. Deere, p. 70.

in the present age (e.g., Matt. 12:29; Luke 10:18; John 12:31; 2 Thess. 2:7) with the "binding" of Satan in Revelation 20:1-3. They do not, on the other hand, adequately consider the present power and activity of Satan (cf. Acts 5:3; 1 Cor. 7:5; 2 Cor. 12:7; 1 Thess. 2:18; 1 Pet. 5:8) nor do they give due consideration to the absolute terms of Satan's binding in Revelation 20. That "binding" is spoken of in strong terms: he is bound with a great chain for a thousand years; he is thrown into the abyss; the abyss is shut, locked, and sealed. Robert H. Mounce summarizes, "The elaborate measures taken to insure his custody are most easily understood as implying the complete cessation of his influence on earth (rather than a curbing of his activities)."[30]

The Millennium cannot be equated with the present age because Satan is energetically active on the earth now, whereas in the Millennium Satan will be imprisoned and cut off from the earth.

The fourth interpretive issue in the Revelation 20 passage is the meaning and significance of the first resurrection. Since the section at hand (20:4-6) focuses on events during the Millennium, its proper understanding will enable us to determine whether the Millennium parallels the present age. In order to make the passage fit the present rather than the future, amillennialists have defined the first resurrection as the soul's regeneration, as a symbolic resurrection, or as the entrance of the soul into heaven following death. Townsend ably summarizes the evidence that the language of Revelation 20:4-6 requires that the first resurrection be understood as a premillennial, bodily resurrection of saints.

> At issue is whether the word *ezesan* ("came to life") means a literal, bodily resurrection or . . . a resurrection of the soul at death. Several arguments strongly support the premillennial view that *ezesan* (Rev. 20:4-5) refers to physical resurrection. Most interpreters . . . agree that *ezesan* in 20:5 refers to bodily resurrection at the great white throne judgment. It would seem natural, then, to take the same bodily meaning for *ezesan* in 20:4-5. This understanding is fortified in 20:5-6 where the coming to life is plainly referred to as the first resurrection. The word John employs is *anastasis*. In over 40 uses in the New Testament, with only one clear exception (Luke 2:34), *anastasis* always refers to bodily resurrection.[31]

---

30. Robert H. Mounce, *The Book of Revelation,* The New International Commentary on the New Testament (Grand Rapids: Eerdmans, 1977), p. 353.
31. Townsend, "Is the Present Age the Millennium?" p. 219.

Also in favor of the premillennial understanding of this passage is the location of the saints' reign—on the earth and not in heaven. Supporting
this are the following facts: (1) Christ is seen as personally present on the
earth after His return (19:11-16); (2) the saints are still on the earth after
the thousand years, for this is the place Satan attacks them (20:9); (3) Revelation 5:10 indicates the reign of the resurrected saints is on the earth;
and (4) messianic prophecies in the Old Testament anticipate an earthly
kingdom.[32]

Is the present church age the Millennium, or do we look for a future
thousand-year reign of Christ on the earth? A careful examination of Revelation 20 shows that the events of the thousand-year period simply do not
fit the present age. The premillennial understanding of the Millennium as
future is much to be preferred, and we therefore now consider the relation
of the church to that age.

THE CHURCH AND THE MILLENNIUM

Though recognizing the distinct blessings of a restored and regenerated
Israel in the millennial kingdom in fulfillment of the promises of the Abrahamic and Davidic covenants, it must be noted that the church, too, will
share in the rule of that kingdom. Erich Sauer described the church as the
"ruling aristocracy, the official administrative staff, of the coming
kingdom."[33]

Several New Testament passages describe the role of the church in the
millennial kingdom. Prior to His death Christ told the disciples they would
reign with Him in His kingdom over the twelve tribes of Israel. Matthew
19:28 records, "And Jesus said to them, 'Truly I say to you, that you who
have followed Me, in the regeneration when the Son of Man will sit on His
glorious throne, you also shall sit upon twelve thrones, judging the twelve
tribes of Israel." Paul rebuked Corinthian believers for not solving mundane quarrels among themselves without going to law courts by remind-
ing them that when the kingdom comes they will judge the world. He
wrote, "Or do you not know that the saints will judge the world? And if the
world is judged by you, are you not competent to constitute the smallest
law courts?" (1 Cor. 6:2). In writing to Timothy near the end of his ministry, Paul declared, "If we endure, we shall also reign with Him" (2 Tim.
2:12). The apostle John affirmed four times in the book of Revelation that

---

32. Deere, p. 69.
33. Erich Sauer, *From Eternity to Eternity* (London: Paternoster, 1954), p. 93.

saints will join with Christ in His reign on the earth (Rev. 1:6; 3:21; 5:10; 20:6). The latter verse is particularly significant: "Blessed and holy is the one who has a part in the first resurrection; over these the second death has no power, but they will be priests of God and of Christ and will reign with Him for a thousand years" (Rev. 20:6). Since it is generally agreed that the first resurrection is not a single event but an order of resurrections that includes the saints of all ages, we discover from this passage that all resurrected saints will have some part in the government of the millennial earth. Even though some dispensationalists have taught that only church saints will reign with Christ, such a view is obviously not in keeping with this passage. Since the twelve disciples will have a special assignment in the kingdom, perhaps the same will be true of other groups of saints. At any rate, the church saints will certainly reign along with and not apart from the saints of other ages.

Questions have been raised concerning the abode of the church during the Millennium. Some have postulated that the New Jerusalem descends and is suspended over the earth, thus providing a house for glorified saints during the kingdom age. This requires that Revelation 21:1-8 relate to eternity, whereas the verses immediately following refer back to the Millennium. In the view of this writer a plain reading and interpretation of the text does not yield this view. The more natural interpretation would seem to be to maintain the chronological progression begun in 19:11 with the return of Christ to the earth, thus seeing the New Jerusalem descending to the new earth at the onset of eternity. Although some will object that this would require glorified and nonglorified beings to live together during the Millennium, such intermingling is not without precedent in the New Testament. The risen Christ in His glorified body associated with believers in nonglorified bodies prior to His ascension. Cook argues, "Both the glorified Christ and glorified saints will meet with nonglorified beings all during the millennium; and if any contact at all is sustained between the two groups, an argument for a special abode loses its urgency."[34]

THE CHURCH AND ETERNITY

INHABITANTS OF THE NEW JERUSALEM

The Scriptures make clear that the church will inhabit the New Jerusalem in eternity. But she will not dwell in that city exclusively. The writer to

34. Cook, p. 237.

the Hebrews asserts: "But you have come to Mount Zion and to the city of the living God, the heavenly Jerusalem, and to myriads of angels, to the general assembly and church of the first-born who are enrolled in heaven, and to God, the Judge of all, and to the spirits of righteous men made perfect, and to Jesus, the mediator of a new covenant" (Heb. 12:22-24a). Thus, five distinct groups can be identified as eternal inhabitants of the New Jerusalem: (1) the angels; (2) the church; (3) God, the Judge; (4) the spirits of righteous men made perfect; and (5) Jesus, the mediator. Only the fourth group is not clearly identified in the text; however, most Bible students believe the "spirits of righteous men made perfect" refers to Old Testament saints. It could justifiably be argued that tribulational and millennial saints are included in this category, for even though not a part of the church they are certainly "righteous men made perfect." Thus, this group would include the saints of all ages exclusive of the church.

It is important to observe that there is a heavenly hope and future for Israel. Old Testament believers will be in the heavenly city along with the church. But this is not to deny Israel's role as God's earthly people. Pentecost explains:

> The conclusion to this question would be that the Old Testament held forth a national hope, which will be realized fully in the millennial age. The individual Old Testament saint's hope of an eternal city will be realized through resurrection in the heavenly Jerusalem where, without losing distinction or identity, Israel will join with the resurrected and translated of the church age to share in the glory of His reign forever.[35]

UNITY AND DIVERSITY IN THE NEW JERUSALEM

Though some believe there will be a progressive blurring of the distinction between Israel and the church in the Millennium and eternal state, the biblical evidence seems to indicate that each group of saints will retain its identity (cf. Heb. 12:22-24). This can be inferred also from the fact that the names of the twelve tribes of Israel will be inscribed on the gates of the heavenly city and the names of the twelve apostles of the church will be inscribed on the city's foundation (Rev. 21:12, 14).

> While the saints of all ages are included in the New Jerusalem, their separate identity is maintained, that is, Old Testament saints are still classi-

35. Pentecost, p. 546.

fied as such. Those who are members of the church, the body of Christ, are so described, angels are still angels, and God also retains His identity. This at once provides for the unity and diversity of God's program, the unity in the common salvation experienced by all the saints, the diversity in their peculiar character and dispensational background.[36]

In short, in the eternal kingdom there will be one family of God with a diversity of members.

The saints in eternity will find their highest joy in serving God. Described as *douloi* (bondservants), they will always be submissive to the divine will and under the sovereignty of God, and the Lamb will reign forever (Rev. 22:3,5).

CONCLUSION

The church of Jesus Christ has a glorious future. Her destiny includes being taken out of this world before the Tribulation woes to be with Christ (John 14:1-3), being a part of the "ruling aristocracy" on earth during Christ's millennial reign, and serving God along with other members of His family in the New Jerusalem for all eternity. All of this, and more, was made possible because "Christ loved the church and gave Himself up for her" (Eph. 5:25b).

36. Walvoord, p. 326.

Louis A. Barbieri, Jr. (A.B., Westmont College; Th.M., Th.D., Dallas Theological Seminary) is dean of students and assistant professor of Bible exposition at Dallas Theological Seminary.

The Future for Israel in God's Plan

Louis A. Barbieri, Jr.

INTRODUCTION

May 14, 1948, is a day that is burned into the mind of every citizen of the state of Israel. On that day a significant event occurred—a nation that had disappeared for almost two thousand years reappeared as a distinct entity.

A MODERN-DAY MIRACLE

Israel's rebirth was the culmination of a movement to reclaim the land of Palestine and make it the homeland for Jews that began in the previous century. That movement was aided by a number of dramatic events, including two world wars. During the second of these wars, John F. Walvoord notes, "due to the world-wide sympathy aroused for the people of Israel because of the slaughter of six million Jews under Nazi domination, the feeling became widespread that Israel should have a homeland to which its refugees could come and establish themselves."[1] In 1948 Palestine was under British control. On May 14 British control was withdrawn, and Israel proclaimed itself an independent state within boundaries established by the United Nations. Before the day was over, however, war broke out, and Israel was attacked on all sides by surrounding Arab nations. A series of truces followed until on January 7, 1949, a general armistice was arranged that permitted Israel to retain the additional land she had gained during the conflict. That original plot of land was greatly expanded in the

---

1. John F. Walvoord, *Israel in Prophecy* (Grand Rapids: Zondervan, 1962), p. 18.

Six-Day War of June 1967. In the fighting, Israel regained her ancient capital, Jerusalem, and pushed her borders outward on every side. Although some of that land has been returned to Egypt, Israel has maintained her borders and lived in relative peace, even though she is surrounded by enemies.

Truly Israel's return to the land is a modern-day miracle, one the prophet Ezekiel more than five hundred years before the time of Christ apparently predicted would occur. As recorded in Ezekiel 37, that prophet had a vision of a valley of dry bones in which the bones came together, "and behold, sinews were on them, and flesh grew, and skin covered them; but there was no breath in them" (37:8). By way of explanation God declared to Ezekiel that "these bones are the whole house of Israel" (37:11) and further that "I will open your graves, and cause you to come up out of your graves, my people; and I will bring you into the land of Israel. Then you will know that I am the Lord, when I have opened your graves and caused you to come up out of your graves, My people" (37:12-13). The condition of modern-day Israel seems to be precisely what Ezekiel saw in this vision. Israel, dead for almost two thousand years, has returned from the grave.

But what is her spiritual condition? It would be hard to conclude that Israel as a whole recognizes that her restoration is the result of the hand of God. For whereas a small portion of the nation considers itself "orthodox," the greatest portion would admit to being "agnostic." When visiting Israel this author has talked with many Israelis. The overwhelming conclusion among them is that what has happened has been brought about by human hands, and that God, if He truly exists, has had little to do with Israel's victories. That, too, fits Ezekiel's prophecy, for God also said that, after He has brought the nation back to the land, "I will put my Spirit within you, and you will come to life, and I will place you on your own land" (37:14). Yes, Israel possesses the land today, but she clearly is not there in belief. The promise of God is that the nation *will* believe. That path, however, is filled with great suffering and death.

WILL ISRAEL SURVIVE?

Looking at Israel's present situation, one cannot help wondering if the nation can indeed survive, surrounded as she is by enemies who wish to see her destroyed. And even though most Israelis are not concerned with spiritual matters, the nation is nevertheless "pro-God," which means Satan's forces are also opposed to her. If "holy war" were ever declared on Israel by her Arab neighbors, it is doubtful from a human perspective that she could survive. The sheer numbers of her enemies are against it.

The tendency one must avoid when writing on prophecy is to become a prophet. This author does not know what is going to happen to the state of Israel in the immediate future. It could have many days of relative peace or be attacked at any time. However, it seems clear from biblical prophecies that there will be a Jewish nation in existence when the prophetic events detailed in the Scriptures begin. Therefore the nation as it is known today will probably survive in some form in order to fulfill the details of the biblical texts.

ISRAEL IN TRIBULATION

THE CHARACTERIZATION

A number of Scriptures indicate that a future time of Tribulation is coming on the earth far more intense than the suffering and persecution known by God's people at any other period in history. Jeremiah stated, "I have heard a sound of terror, of dread, and there is no peace. Ask now, and see, if a male can give birth. Why do I see every man with his hands on his loins, as a woman in childbirth? And why have all faces turned pale? Alas! for that day is great, there is none like it; and it is the time of Jacob's distress" (30:5-7). "The time of Jacob's distress" is God's description of this period, and it is a time in which God is going to accomplish a significant work among the Jews. The period is also known as the seventieth week of Daniel, a future seven-year period that closes with intense persecution (Dan. 9:27). In another passage Daniel described the period as "a time of distress such as never occurred since there was a nation until that time" (12:1). Finally, Christ characterized it by saying, "There will be great tribulation, such as has not occurred since the beginning of the world until now, nor ever shall. And unless those days had been cut short, no life would have been saved" (Matt. 24:21-22).

When one reads the descriptions of death that occur in the Tribulation, it is no wonder that Jesus said that unless those days be cut short no one would survive. Zechariah indicated that during this period two-thirds of the people of Israel would die (13:8-9). The judgments recorded in the book of Revelation also indicate widespread death. At the breaking of the fourth seal, for example, one-fourth of the earth's population will be destroyed (6:7-8), and when the sixth trumpet sounds one-third of those remaining will be annihilated (9:13-21). This coupled with the other notations of death in the seal, trumpet, and bowl judgments substantiates the fact that death will be widespread during this seven-year period. To give some idea of the extent of the destruction, if one applies those fractions to the present world population, the number of men dying during these seven years could approach three billion, even if allowance is made for the removal of true believers in the rapture. Is it any wonder that the Bible describes this time as a period of distress such as the world has never known?

INAUGURATION

Not only are the general characteristics of the Tribulation described in Scripture, the time of its institution is also clearly indicated. I believe in a pretribulation rapture of the church, but it is not the rapture per se that begins the Tribulation. Following the rapture of the saints there will be a period of time in which a number of significant world events will occur. As Daniel revealed in his prophetic visions, a ruler will arise out of the nations that were once part of the ancient Roman Empire. Daniel called this man by various titles throughout his book: "another horn, a little one" (7:8), "a king" (8:23), "the prince who is to come" (9:26), and "the king [who] will do as he pleases" (11:36). In the New Testament Jesus referred to him as "the abomination of desolation" (Matt. 24:15), Paul as "the man of lawlessness" (2 Thess. 2:3), and John as "a beast coming up out of the sea" (Rev.13:1-10). It is this world leader who will make a "firm covenant" with the "many" for the final seven-year "week" in Daniel 9:27. The "many" must be a reference to the Jews, for according to Daniel 9:24 the entire seventy-week period was decreed for Daniel's people and his holy city. Daniel's "people" were the Jews and his "holy city" was Jerusalem. It is the enactment of this covenant in 9:27 that marks the beginning of the seventieth week, the final seven-year period in God's dealing with Israel designed to accomplish the six things promised in Daniel 9:24.[2] Through the seventy weeks all six things will be fulfilled. Here is perhaps one of the strongest reasons for believing that the present state of Israel must endure. If Israel is to enter into an agreement with a powerful Western leader, Israel as a nation must exist.

---

2. For an explanation of the six things, see Donald K. Campbell, *Daniel: Decoder of Dreams* (Wheaton, Ill.: Victor, 1977), p. 109, and J. Dwight Pentecost, *Things to Come* (Findlay, Ohio: Dunham, 1958), pp. 241-42.

The Tribulation is precisely described in Scripture. Herman A. Hoyt states that the identification of the Tribulation with the seventieth week of Daniel's prophecy "makes it clear that it is seven years in length. . . . This period of seven years is divided into two smaller periods of three and one-half years each (Dan. 9:27), referred to as 'a time, and times, and half a time' (Rev.12:14; cf. Dan. 12:7). The length of each period is also declared to be forty-two months (Rev. 11:2; 13:5), and 1,260 days (Rev. 11:3; 12:6)."[3] It appears from biblical descriptions that the first three-and-one-half years of the Tribulation period will be a time of relative peace for Israel. Israel will have entered into a covenant with the leader of the Western nations. This man will rise to power and present himself to the world as a great man of peace. John described him as the rider on a white horse who will emerge when the first seal is broken (Rev. 6:1-2). As a man of peace he rides forth in the color of peace with a bow but no arrows. He is crowned as a king, and he conquers through peaceful means. Commenting on his conquests, Charles C. Ryrie has said, "His method of conquest, however, is not by open hostilities. In modern parlance, we would call his method 'cold' war. This description exactly coincides with the picture of the beginning of the Tribulation given in 1 Thessalonians 5:3—it will be a day when men are talking about peace and safety."[4] The Antichrist is supported in his efforts by the world-wide church that will arise following the rapture of true believers (Rev. 17:3-7). Richard W. DeHaan adds that "this political genius will pose as a friend of the Jews for three and one half years. He will apparently settle the Arab-Israeli controversy by granting Israel undisputed possession of Palestine, and the Jews in the land will be guaranteed protection from all foes. Thus the people of Israel will live in their land with a feeling of complete security."[5] Israel will feel so secure that she will live in "unwalled villages" (Ezek. 38:11). This will be the situation in the first half of the Tribulation.

Shortly before the midpoint of the Tribulation period, in this author's view, the events of Ezekiel 38-39 will occur. After biding their time the forces of the north and south (Dan. 11:40) will challenge the promise of

3. Hermon A. Hoyt, *The End Times* (Chicago: Moody, 1969), pp. 139-40.
4. Charles C. Ryrie, *The Bible and Tomorrow's News* (Wheaton, Ill.: Scripture Press, 1969), p. 146.
5. Richard W. DeHaan, *Israel and the Nations in Prophecy* (Grand Rapids: Zondervan, 1968), p. 129.

peace that the Western leader has made to Israel. In seeking to pinpoint the timing of their invasion, DeHaan notes that "inasmuch as this attack will come from the north when 'they [Israel] shall dwell safely, all of them . . . dwelling without walls, and having neither bars nor gates. . .' (Ezek. 38:8,11), it must occur sometime *after* the Beast [Antichrist] makes this covenant with Israel and *before* he turns against them. This places it during the first half of the Tribulation period, Daniel's seventieth week."[6] Though there has been much debate about the identification of Gog, Magog, Rosh, Meshech, and Tubal, it is safe to conclude that these refer to peoples that occupied the area to the north of Israel. Ryrie has stated that "the names listed in Ezekiel 38:39 are identified in Genesis 10:2 as sons of Japheth. The Japhethites migrated, after the Flood, from Asia Minor to the north, beyond the Caspian and Black Seas. They settled in the area we know today as modern Russia. 'Gog' and Magog,' therefore, may refer to the people who lived north of Palestine in Russia."[7] If God chooses to set in motion all of these prophecies in this century, the forces of Russia clearly are in view here. If God delays, Russia may no longer exist, but there will still be a "king of the north." These combined forces (north and south) will invade the land of Israel. By so doing they will be attacking the Western king because he has made a covenant of protection with Israel. In effect the kings of the north and south will be saying, "Let's see you back up your claim. We will overrun Israel before you are able to lift a finger." According to Ezekiel 38:9 they will come like a storm, "like a cloud covering the land, you and all your troops, and many peoples with you." Israel, dwelling in unwalled villages, will feel safe in the power of the Western ruler. The invading kings will believe that Israel is easy prey and that they will be able to overrun her quickly.

THE SOVEREIGN INTERVENTION

The Lord, however, is aware of what is happening. In fact, as one reads Ezekiel 38 it is clear that the Lord is ultimately the One behind the invasion. It is the Lord who brings these kings against the land of Israel "in order that the nations may know Me when I shall be sanctified through you before their eyes, O Gog" (38:16). From various verses it appears that God sovereignly intervenes in the midst of this invasion from all sides by destroying the invading forces with "fire" from heaven (39:6). The destruction

6. Ibid., p. 103.
7. Ryrie, p. 153.

is so complete it will take the people of the land seven months to dispose of all the bodies left behind (39:12).

THE RESULTS OF THE BATTLE

Conversion of the multitudes. It is declared several times in Ezekiel 38 and 39 that the outcome of the destruction of the invading forces will be a demonstration that the Lord is God and that the nations will believe in Him: "I shall bring you against My land, in order that the nations may know Me when I shall be sanctified through you before their eyes, O Gog" (38:16); "And I shall magnify Myself, sanctify Myself, and make Myself known in the sight of many nations; and they will know that I am the Lord" (38:23); "And My holy name I shall make known in the midst of My people Israel; and I shall not let my holy name be profaned anymore. And the nations will know that I am the Lord, the Holy One in Israel" (39:7); "And I shall set My glory among the nations; and all the nations will see My judgment which I have executed, and My hand which I have laid on them. And the house of Israel will know that I am the Lord their God from that day onward" (39:21-22). Clearly one result of God's sovereign intervention will be the conversion of a multitude of people, both Jews and Gentiles. This dramatic event will supplement the preaching of the 144,000 Jews who were appointed as God's spokesmen (Rev. 7:1-8).

Ascension of the world dictator. With the removal of the military forces of the north and south, the one who has risen to power over the Western nations suddenly will find himself without military opposition. Sensing that the time is ripe, he will assert himself and move into the Holy Land, coming by way of North Africa through Libya, Ethiopia, and Egypt (Dan. 11:41-43). As he moves into the Holy Land, he will establish his headquarters in Jerusalem and seek to rule the world from there (Dan. 11:45). It is at this time that he will break the covenant of protection and religious freedom (Dan. 9:27) previously made with Israel, ending the worship that the Jews have reestablished in a reconstructed Temple, destroying all religion (Rev. 17:16-17), and demanding that he alone be worshiped. His "image" will be set up in the Temple, and all will be required either to worship the image or be killed (Rev. 13:14-15). Walvoord summarizes the activity of the world ruler by noting, "The future world ruler of the time of the great tribulation will not only take to himself absolute political power but will demand the worship of the entire world, will blaspheme the true God, and persecute the saints (Rev. 13:4-7)."⁸ Perhaps the world ruler will attempt to take credit for the destruction of the invading forces. Obviously he will not be pleased with those placing their faith in Jesus Christ, so his persecution will be intense. Multitudes will die for their faith (Rev. 7:9). The final three-and-one-half years of the Tribulation will be a horrible time for the inhabitants of the earth. Regenerated people will live in constant fear for their lives. Even the followers of the world dictator will not escape the worldwide famine, death, and destruction.

THE FINAL BATTLE

As the days of the Tribulation draw to a close there will be one final great battle. An army numbering 200 million will converge on the Holy Land, coming from the east as the waters of the Euphrates River are dried up permitting them to cross (Rev. 9:13-16). These eastern forces have remained inactive through the early years of the Tribulation, but now their presence will be felt. As rumors from the east and the north (Dan. 11:44) begin to disturb the world dictator, he will go forth to meet the approaching army. All of the military forces will gather in one place, "which in Hebrew is called Har-Magedon" (Rev. 16:16). Before they have the chance to engage one another in battle, however, "the sign of the Son of Man will appear in the sky, and then all the tribes of the earth will mourn, and they will see the Son of Man coming on the clouds of the sky with power and great glory" (Matt. 24:30). The armies realize they have a common enemy and join forces to fight against the Lord. But it will be too late. The returning King will take the Western leader and his false prophet and cast them alive into the lake of fire. "And the rest were killed with the sword which came from the mouth of Him who sat upon the horse" (Rev. 19:21). Through this great battle at Har-Magedon the Lord Jesus Christ will return to establish His earthly millennial kingdom.

THE CONVERSION OF ISRAEL

The Tribulation period will mark the conversion of a multitude from the nation of Israel. As noted earlier, the apostle John recorded the sealing of the 144,000 Jewish believers (Rev. 7:1-8). These individuals will be marked in some special way by God so that they cannot be harmed during the Tribulation. This group is seen again in Revelation 14:1-5 in millennial

---

8. John F. Walvoord, *Daniel: The Key To Prophetic Revelation* (Chicago: Moody, 1971), p. 236.

glory, demonstrating that God is faithful to His promise to bring them safely through the Tribulation. But other Jews will also come to faith in the Messiah during the Tribulation. Many of them will die for their faith, but others will live through the entire period and enter the kingdom. The prophet Zechariah recorded the fact that the Spirit would be poured out on the house of David and on the inhabitants of Jerusalem, "the Spirit of grace and supplication, so that they will look on Me whom they have pierced; and they will mourn for Him, as one mourns for an only son, and they will weep bitterly over Him, like the bitter weeping over a first-born" (12:10). Throughout the land there will be great weeping and mourning as both individuals and families recognize their guilt. "In that day a fountain will be opened for the house of David and for the inhabitants of Jerusalem, for sin and for impurity" (Zech. 13:1). This is the kind of repentance Peter declared would be necessary before the Messiah could return to the nation (Acts 3:19-20). The nation that once turned from Jesus and said, "We have no king but Caesar" (John 19:15) will turn in belief and acknowledge their rightful ruler.

THE REGATHERING OF ISRAEL

The theme of the regathering of Israel is prominent throughout the Old Testament. When Moses instructed the children of Israel concerning God's requirements for faithfulness, he indicated they would not obey and that God would remove them from the land. But Moses also indicated that the Lord would bring Israel back to the land when they remembered the Lord and turned to Him (Deut. 30:1-5). God, through the prophet Amos, promised, "I will also plant them on their land, and they will not again be rooted out from their land which I have given them" (9:15). Ezekiel added that the Lord would restore His people from the lands of their enemies and "leave none of them there any longer" (39:28). When the Lord restores Israel to her land of promise, she will truly be at rest. Though she thought she had peace under the false messiah, her rest will occur only when the true Messiah places her in her land.

THE JUDGMENT ON ISRAEL

The resurrection of Old Testament saints. Though not all premillennial interpreters of Scripture agree on the time of the resurrection of Old Testament saints, it seems best to place it at the second advent of Jesus Christ when He comes to reign on David's throne. It is clear from the book of Revelation that the resurrection of the wicked dead does not occur until the end of the millennial age when they appear before the great white throne for judgment (Rev. 20:11-15). Daniel, however, speaks of the resurrection of the saints as occurring after the time of the Tribulation (12:2). Walvoord concludes that "the passage [Dan. 12:2] then becomes a statement that subsequent to the tribulation all the dead will be raised, but in two groups, one group to everlasting life and the other group to everlasting contempt."[9] Believers must be in view in 12:3 for Daniel speaks of the righteous who will "shine brightly like the brightness of the expanse of heaven, and those who lead the many to righteousness, like the stars forever and ever." The Lord will resurrect and reward Old Testament saints before the institution of the Millennium in order that they may share in the blessings of the kingdom. Daniel himself is an illustration of this, for he was told, "Go your way to the end; then you will enter into rest and rise again for your allotted portion at the end of the age" (Dan. 12:13). An assigned portion was guaranteed to Daniel, and he will be restored to this position. As part of His judgment on Israel the Lord will resurrect the righteous and reward them so that they may enter His earthly kingdom to enjoy His reign.

The evaluation of living Jews. When Jesus Christ returns in glory and triumph to the earth, He will carefully evaluate the heart condition of all the living. Not everyone will die in the Tribulation judgments or be part of the armies gathered for battle with the returning Lord. A multitude of Jews and Gentiles will survive. But not all will have trusted in Jesus Christ during the Tribulation. Before His kingdom can be instituted on earth the Lord must judge all who still are alive to determine who will be permitted entrance. The judgment on living Gentiles is clearly taught in Matthew 25:31-46. The judgment on living Israelites is seen in Ezekiel 20:34-38. After the Lord gathers Israel from the lands where they have been scattered the people will "pass under the rod," an analogy to the work of a shepherd. "As a shepherd's staff is employed to count the sheep (Jer. 33:13), so the Lord will bring the entire flock under the rod, this time with the purpose of separating the godly from the wicked. The godly will be brought more firmly into the bond of the covenant, whereas the rebels will be purged out; those who have transgressed against the Lord will be brought out of the land of their sojourn but denied admission to the land of promise."[10] Although the Scripture does not say directly what happens to these rebels,

    9. Walvoord, *Israel,* p. 117.
    10. Charles Lee Feinberg, *The Prophecy of Ezekiel* (Chicago: Moody, 1969), p. 115.

it appears that they are killed. In my opinion the same picture of judgment on the Jews is seen in the story Jesus told of the ten virgins, five of whom were wise and five of whom were foolish (Matt. 25:1-13). The wise virgins had made adequate provision and were awaiting the arrival of the bridegroom. They entered the wedding feast (the millennial age), but the foolish virgins were denied access. When the kingdom then is instituted on earth, the subjects of the kingdom will all be righteous, either in glorified bodies (Old Testament saints, church saints, and Tribulation martyrs) or saved individuals who have lived through the Tribulation and the judgment of the Lord Himself.

ISRAEL IN THE MILLENNIUM

THE INSTITUTION OF THE KINGDOM

A number of biblical texts support the idea that the Messiah of Israel will establish a kingdom with His capital in Jerusalem and rule over all the nations. The prophet Isaiah described the nations coming to Zion to worship the God of Jacob and to be taught in His ways. They would submit because "the law will go forth from Zion, and the word of the Lord from Jerusalem" (2:3). In commenting on Isaiah 2:2-4 Walvoord says, "From this passage it is evident that Jerusalem is to be the capital of the world, that from Zion the law will go forth, and all nations will be under the sway of this righteous government."[11] The psalmist also indicated that the Son of God will reign over the nations: "He [God the Father] said to Me, 'Thou art My Son, today I have begotten Thee. Ask of Me, and I will surely give the nations as Thine inheritance, and the very ends of the earth as Thy possession. Thou shalt break them with a rod of iron, Thou shalt shatter them like earthenware' " (2:7b-9). Finally, Daniel presented the institution of this kingdom in his interpretation of Nebuchadnezzar's dream (Dan. 2). The great image in the dream was a succession of four great Gentile empires, Nebuchadnezzar's being the first. In the final stage of this Gentile domination a "stone" struck the image and brought it crashing down. This "stone" then became "a great mountain and filled the whole earth" (2:35). Daniel's interpretation of this imagery was that "the God of heaven will set up a kingdom which will never be destroyed, . . . it will crush and put an end to all these kingdoms [the Gentile kingdoms], but it will itself endure forever" (2:44). Walvoord points out that this symbolism originated with God rath-

11. Walvoord, *Israel*, p. 121.

er than with man. "The effect is that the fifth kingdom, the kingdom of God, replaces completely all vestiges of the preceding kingdoms, which prophecy can only be fulfilled in any literal sense by a reign of Christ over the earth."[12] The truth concerning the succession of Gentile world powers was repeated by Daniel in chapter 7. In that vision the Gentile powers were pictured as four "beasts" that arose from the sea. After the four beasts appeared Daniel saw "One like a Son of man" (7:13), who came to the "Ancient of Days" and received from Him "dominion, glory and a kingdom, that all the peoples, nations, and men of every language might serve Him. His dominion is an everlasting dominion which will not pass away; and His kingdom is one which will not be destroyed" (7:14).

The concept of the Messiah establishing His kingdom over the nations is also a New Testament teaching. Jesus said that immediately after the period of Tribulation, "the powers of the heavens will be shaken, and then the sign of the Son of Man will appear in the sky, and then all the tribes of the earth will mourn, and they will see the Son of Man coming on the clouds of the sky with power and great glory" (Matt. 24:29b-30). The apostle John presents a similar scenario in Revelation 19-20. The One who will return from heaven in power and glory cannot be identified as anyone other than Jesus Christ, for "on His robe and on His thigh He has a name written, 'King of kings, and Lord of lords'" (19:16). Following Christ's return, His kingdom will be instituted on the earth. This period will be the fulfillment of the Old Testament prophecies of Messiah's reign over His people Israel and all the nations of the world.

PHYSICAL CONDITIONS IN THE KINGDOM

Topographical changes. It is clear from a reading of the prophet Zechariah that the return of the Messiah will bring about dramatic changes in the topography surrounding Jerusalem. In his last "burden" concerning Israel (chaps. 12-14) Zechariah describes the effects of the nations coming against Israel in the Tribulation. When the nations are gathered against Jerusalem for battle, the Lord will intervene to save His people. "And in that day His feet will stand on the Mount of Olives, which is in front of Jerusalem on the east; and the Mount of Olives will be split in its middle from east to west by a very large valley, so that half of the mountain will move toward the north and the other half toward the south" (Zech. 14:4). De-Haan explains, "A great earthquake brings about a radical transformation

---

12. Walvoord, *Daniel,* p. 76.

of the entire land. The mountains that now surround Jerusalem will be flattened into a plain, and Jerusalem will be elevated above the rest of the terrain. The city which is now nestled between the mountains will be situated on a high hill."[13]

In Ezekiel 40-48 the prophet describes the building of a large temple during the Millennium—the location of that temple seems to be slightly to the north of the present city of Jerusalem. He also describes a river that will flow from the temple toward the east and empty into what is known as the Dead Sea, transforming it into a place of such fertility that men will spread their fishing nets on its shores (47:8, 10). Anyone familiar with the topography surrounding Jerusalem realizes that in order for these verses to find fulfillment tremendous changes will be necessary.

The curse lifted. After describing the judgments of the Tribulation in chapter 34, Isaiah turns to talk of the glories of the kingdom in chapter 35. "The wilderness and the desert will be glad, and the Arabah will rejoice and blossom; like the crocus it will blossom profusely and rejoice with rejoicing and shout of joy" (35:1-2a). He continues, "Then the eyes of the blind will be opened, and the ears of the deaf will be unstopped. Then the lame will leap like a deer, and the tongue of the dumb will shout for joy. For waters will break forth in the wilderness and streams in the Arabah" (35:5-6). Physical death will not be completely eliminated during the kingdom age, but death will be the exception rather than the rule. Isaiah quoted God's words when he declared, "No longer will there be in it [millennial Jerusalem] an infant who lives but a few days, or an old man who does not live out his days; for the youth will die at the age of one hundred and the one who does not reach the age of one hundred shall be thought accursed" (65:20).

Increased longevity will produce the population explosion predicted by Jeremiah as he quoted the Lord, "'And I will multiply them, and they shall not be diminished; I will also honor them, and they shall not be insignificant. Their children also shall be as formerly, and their congregation shall be established before Me'" (Jer. 30:19b-20a). Robert E. Baughman has written concerning this population explosion, "The long life, low death rate, plentiful food supply, and favorable conditions will cause the population to expand rapidly. . . . At the end of the millennial era, the world will probably have its record population. It seems probably that there will be

13. DeHaan, p. 101.

more people living at that time than the total who have lived from Adam to the kingdom"[14]

A tremendous change will take place in the animal realm as well. The barrier that exists today because of the ferocity of animals will be done away in the millennial age. Isaiah described the change in the following manner: "And the wolf will dwell with the lamb, and the leopard will lie down with the kid, and the calf and the young lion and the fatling together; and a little boy will lead them. Also the cow and the bear will graze; their young will lie down together; and the lion will eat straw like the ox, and the nursing child will play by the hole of the cobra, and the weaned child will put his hand on the viper's den. They will not hurt or destroy in all My holy mountain, for the earth will be full of the knowledge of the Lord as the waters cover the sea" (Isa. 11:6-9). Such dramatic changes in the effects of the curse placed on the earth following Adam's fall will bring about a radically changed life-style in the kingdom age.

Reestablishment of the tribal portions. It was noted previously that both Amos and Ezekiel spoke of Israel's return to the land sworn to Abraham, Isaac, and Jacob. Amos added a thought in the conclusion of his prophecy as he quoted directly from the Lord. "'I will also plant them on their land, and they will not again be rooted out from their land which I have given them,' says the Lord your God" (9:15). Ezekiel also quoted the word of the Lord directly when he said, "Then they will know that I am the Lord their God because I made them go into exile among the nations, and then gathered them again to their own land; and I will leave none of them there any longer" (39:28). When the Lord restores His people, He will permanently place them in the land of promise. The details of the settling of the land in the millennial age are provided in Ezekiel 47:13—48:29. After a detailed explanation of the boundaries of the land, Ezekiel presented the tribal portions to the north (48:1-8) and to the south (48:23-29) of the city of Jerusalem.[15]

SPIRITUAL CONDITIONS IN THE KINGDOM

The work of the Holy Spirit. Several passages from the Old Testament illustrate that there will be a vital ministry of the Holy Spirit directed toward people living in physical bodies in the millennial kingdom. In a mil-

---

14. The tribal portions in the Millennium have been well illustrated by Ray E. Baughman, *The Kingdom of God Visualized* (Chicago: Moody, 1972), p. 237.

15. Ibid., p. 206.

lennial context Isaiah communicated the words of the Lord: "For I will pour out water on the thirsty land and streams on the dry ground; I will pour out My Spirit on your offspring, and My blessing on your descendants; and they will spring up among the grass like poplars by streams of water. This one will say, 'I am the Lord's'; and that one will call on the name of Jacob; and another will write on his hand, 'Belonging to the Lord,' and will name Israel's name and honor" (Isa. 44:3-5). A similar thought was presented by Ezekiel. "And I will put My Spirit within you and cause you to walk in My statutes, and you will be careful to observe My ordinances. And you will live in the land that I gave to your forefathers; so you will be My people, and I will be your God" (36:27-28). In commenting on this passage Baughman has said, "There isn't any reason to believe that this promise is exclusively for the Jews, for the Lord will give the Holy Spirit unto Gentiles as He does in this age."[16] The ministry of the Spirit will be necessary for the kingdom people in physical bodies, for they will still be subject to the effects of the Fall. Those born in the kingdom will need to be regenerated by the Spirit; and all in the kingdom will need the power of the Spirit to live victoriously, just as today.

The worship in the temple. Following the establishment of the kingdom on earth, a temple will be erected just to the north of the present city of Jerusalem from which Jesus Christ will rule the world. Extremely accurate information concerning this building is given in Ezekiel 40:1—42:20. Charles L. Feinberg notes, "The competent opinion of architects who have studied the plan given here is that all these dimensions could be drawn to scale to produce a beautiful sanctuary of the Lord."[17] Baughman has given a floor plan of the temple.[18]

There would certainly be no reason for God to provide such an accurate description of this building if He did not intend to build it. Ezekiel not only gave the accurate description of the building, he also presented the priesthood, the sacrificial system, and the worship days for the rebuilt temple (44:1—46:24). The reinstitution of sacrifices has been a problem to some biblical scholars. Clearly these sacrifices are not expiatory in any way, for the work of Jesus Christ on the cross has completed the work of salvation once for all. Ralph H. Alexander has pointed out that "the millennial worship appears to be pictorial lessons to everyone in the Millennium, just as it should be to us today (Rom. 15:4; 1 Cor. 10:1-12). They are to remind

16. Ibid., p. 234.
17. Feinberg, p. 242.
18. Baughman, p. 228.

believers (and those in the Millennium) of the work which Christ performed for them and the life which believers are to live. They are commemorative in the same manner as the Lord's table (cf.1 Cor. 11:23-26)."[19] It does appear that the entire world will be subject to the rule of the Messiah and will participate, at least outwardly, in the worship of Him. However, men have been known to conform outwardly while inwardly being in a state of rebellion.

THE FINAL REBELLION

Even so, outwardly all is in conformity to the King during the Millennium, but there will be people born during the kingdom who will not accept Him. Why this will be the case is not explained in Scripture. One wonders how anyone born in a perfect society with no external form of spiritual opposition could rebel against the visible displays of God's grace and power. Yet one of the purposes of the millennial age will be to demonstrate the wickedness of the human heart. No one born in the kingdom will have any excuse for turning away from the King except for his own wickedness and stubborn refusal to accept the King's authority. John in writing the book of Revelation described the effect of the release of Satan from "the abyss" in which he had been imprisoned for the thousand year reign of Christ. When he was released, Satan went into the four corners of the earth "to gather them together for the war; the number of them is like the sand of the seashore" (Rev. 20:8). The eternal optimist, Satan believes that he will win. He will try one last time to overthrow the Lord's anointed by gathering all the "rebels" from the kingdom. But his attempts will be futile. When they come up against the city of Jerusalem to engage in battle, the Lord will destroy them (Rev. 20:9). No specific nations are mentioned in this final rebellion, but it is reasonable to conclude that representatives from all nations will constitute this army assembled by Satan.

THE FINAL JUDGMENT

Following the final revolt of Satan and his "rebels," John pictured the final great judgment on man commonly called "the great white throne judgment" (Rev. 20:11-15). The wicked from all ages (including Jews and Gentiles) will be raised to life to appear before the Lord. They will be judged "according to their deeds" (Rev. 20:13), with the result that all who

---

19. Ralph H. Alexander, *Ezekiel* (Chicago: Moody, 1976), pp. 132-33.

are present at this judgment will be cast into the lake of fire for eternity (Rev. 20:15).

ISRAEL IN THE ETERNAL STATE

THE NEW HEAVENS AND EARTH

Scripture seems to indicate that, following the judgment of all the wicked Jesus Christ will hand over the kingdom to His Father. Paul declared, "Then comes the end, when He delivers up the kingdom to the God and Father, when He has abolished all rule and all authority and power. For He must reign until He has put all His enemies under His feet" (1 Cor. 15:24-25). It should not be concluded, however, that Christ's reign will cease. As Alva J. McClain has pointed out, "this does not mean the end of our Lord's regal activity, but rather from here onward in the unity of the Godhead He reigns with the Father as the eternal Son. There are no longer two thrones: . . . there is but one throne, and it is 'a throne of God and the Lamb' (Rev. 22:3)."[20] Though it cannot be dogmatically asserted, it appears that at this time there will be a total remaking of the present world system. The words of Peter are pertinent: "Looking for and hastening the coming of the day of God, on account of which the heavens will be destroyed by burning, and the elements will melt with intense heat! But according to His promise we are looking for new heavens and a new earth, in which righteousness dwells" (2 Pet. 3:12-13). Regenerated people in physical bodies who did not follow Satan in his rebellion could not survive such an intense refinement of the earth. Although the Bible does not say what will happen to these people while this process is taking place, it is reasonable to conclude that they will experience a "rapture" into the heavenly city, Jerusalem. In order for these people to enter the heavenly city, they must experience a change from human bodies to glorified bodies. John made clear that "nothing unclean and no one who practices abomination and lying, shall ever come into it [the heavenly city], but only those whose names are written in the Lamb's book of life" (Rev. 21:27). With the completing of these events all mankind will be in one of two places: either eternally separated from God in the lake of fire, or eternally present with God in glorified bodies in the new heaven and the new earth.

---

20. Alva J. McClain, *The Greatness of the Kingdom* (Chicago: Moody, 1968), p. 513.

S. LEWIS JOHNSON, JR. (A.B., College of
Charleston; Th.M., Th.D., Dallas Theo-
logical Seminary) is a teaching elder at
Believers Chapel, Dallas, Texas, and was
professor of systematic theology at Dallas
Theological Seminary.

Paul and "The Israel of God": An Exegetical and Eschatological Case-Study

S. Lewis Johnson, Jr.

In spite of overwhelming evidence to the contrary, there remains persistent support for the contention that the term *Israel* may refer properly to Gentile believers in the present age. Incidental support for this is claimed in such passages as Romans 2:28-29; 9:6; and Philippians 3:3; but the primary support is found in Galatians 6:16 where Paul writes, "And those who will walk by this rule, peace and mercy be upon them, and upon the Israel of God" (NASB). The rendering of the NIV illustrates the point, for it has, "Peace and mercy to all who follow this rule, even to the Israel of God." It is obvious from this rendering that the term "the Israel of God" is to be equated with "all who follow this rule," that is, with believers in the present age, whether Jew or Gentile.

This rendering of the verse serves quite well the purpose of those who would like to find New Testament justification for the practice of the spiritualization of Scripture, that is, the habit of taking Old Testament texts regarding ethnic Israel and referring them to the New Testament church.[1]

I cannot help but think that dogmatic considerations loom large in the interpretation of Galatians 6:16. The tenacity with which this application

---

1. For a defense of the hermeneutical practice see Albertus Pieters, "Darbyism vs. the Historic Faith," *Calvin Forum* 2 (May 1936):25-28; Martin J. Wyngaarden, *The Future of the Kingdom in Prophecy and Fulfillment: A Study of the Scope of the "Spiritualization" in Scripture* (Grand Rapids: Baker, 1955), p. 167. Another familiar illustration of spiritualization is found in Oswald T. Allis's *Prophecy and the Church* (Wayne, Pa.: Presbyterian and Reformed, 1974), p. 149, where in the discussion of Acts 15:12-21 Allis refers the rebuilding of the tabernacle of David to the ingathering of the Gentiles in the church age.

of "the Israel of God" to the church is held in spite of a mass of evidence to the contrary leads one to think that the supporters of the view believe their eschatological system, usually an amillennial scheme, hangs on the reference of the term to the people of God, composed of both believing Jews and Gentiles. Amillennialism does not hang on this interpretation, but the view does appear to have a treasured place in amillennial exegesis.

In speaking of the view that the term refers to ethnic Israel, a sense that the term *Israel* has in every other of its more than sixty-five uses in the New Testament and in its fifteen uses in Paul, in tones almost emotional William Hendriksen, the respected Reformed commentator, writes, "I refuse to accept that explanation."[2]

I am reminded of the comment of Irving Kristol, John M. Olin Professor of Social Thought at the New York University Graduate School of Business. In another connection he once said, "When we lack the will to see things as they really are, there is nothing so mysterious as the obvious."

It is often said by New Testament and Old Testament scholars that systematic theologians do not pay enough attention to the text and its exegetical details. The claim is too frequently justified, but there is another side to the question. It may also be said that biblical scholars often unwittingly overlook their own theological presuppositions, logical fallacies, and hermeneutical errors. What I am leading up to is expressed neatly by D. W. B. Robinson in an article written about twenty years ago: "The glib citing of Gal. vi:16 to support the view that 'the church is the new Israel' should be vigorously challenged. There is weighty support for a limited interpretation."[3] We can say more than this, in my opinion. There is more than weighty support for a more limited interpretation. There is overwhelming support for such. In fact, the least likely view among several alternatives is the view that "the Israel of God" is the church.

I propose to review the present status of the interpretation of Galatians 6:16, then offer an analysis grammatically, exegetically, and theologically of the principal suggested interpretations. A few concluding comments will bring the paper to its termination.

2. William Hendriksen, *Exposition of Galatians,* New Testament Commentary (Grand Rapids: Baker, 1968), p. 247.
3. D. W. B. Robinson, "The Distinction Between Jewish and Gentile Believers in Galatians," *Australian Biblical Review* 13 (1965):29-48.

GALATIANS 6:16 IN CONTEMPORARY INTERPRETATION

VIEW ONE: "THE ISRAEL OF GOD" IS THE CHURCH

A few words will suffice for the context of the text in Galatians, for there is general agreement regarding it. Whereas others boast of their conquests and their statistics in winning adherents to their legalistic cause, Paul would confine his boasting to the cross of Christ, by which he had been severed from the world and its spirit. In Christ and in the church of Christ the circumcision issue has lost its relevance. He lives in the realm of the new creation where walking by the Spirit prevails. For those who walk accordingly there is the blessing of peace and mercy, and that also touches the Israel of God. His scars in the service of Jesus, not circumcision, certify and authenticate his confession that his master is the Lord. And, fittingly, picking up the note of grace with which he began his letter (cf. 1:3), a benediction concludes the epistle. So much for Galatians 6:11-18.

Three principal interpretations have characterized the exegesis of Galatians 6:16. The first is the claim that "the Israel of God" is simply a term descriptive of the believing church of the present age. The term is linked with the preceding words, "And those who will walk by this rule, peace and mercy by upon them," by an explicative *kai* (NASB, "and"; NIV, "even"), given practically the sense of apposition. The Israel of God is the body who shall shall walk by the rule of the new creation, and they include believing people from the two ethnic bodies of Jews and Gentiles.

It is well-known that Justin Martyr in his *Dialogue with Trypho* is the first author to claim an identification of the term *Israel* with the church.[4] Of the commentators, Chrysostom is one of the earliest to identify apparently the church with Israel, affirming that those who keep the rule are "true Israelites."[5] Others who follow this view include Daniel C. Arichea, Jr., and Eugene Nida,[6] Ragnar Bring,[7] John Calvin,[8] R. A. Cole,[9] N. A.

---

4. *Dialogue with Trypho* 11:1-5, etc.
5. *Commentary on the Epistle to the Galatians and Homilies on the Epistle to the Ephesians of S. John Chrysostom*, new rev. ed. (London: Walter Smith [Late Mosley], 1884), p. 98.
6. Daniel C. Arichea, Jr., and Eugene A. Nida, *A Translator's Handbook on Paul's Letter to the Galatians* (Stuttgart: United Bible Societies, 1975), pp. 158-59. Very disappointing help is provided for the translator here.
7. Ragnar Bring, *Commentary on Galatians*, trans. Eric Wahlstrom (Philadelphia: Muhlenberg, 1961), p. 291.
8. John Calvin, *The Epistles of Paul the Apostle to the Galatians, Ephesians, Philippians and Colossians*, ed. David W. Torrance and Thomas F. Torrance, trans. T. H. L. Parker (Grand Rapids: Eerdmans, 1965), p. 118. Calvin contends that the term *Israel of God* "includes all believers, whether Gentiles or Jews."
9. R. A. Cole, *The Epistle of Paul to the Galatians: An Introduction and Commentary* (Grand Rapids: Eerdmans, 1965), pp. 183-84. A cursory treatment in which the author appears to consider the key term as simply another way of saying "the people of God."

Dahl,[10] Donald Guthrie,[11] William Hendricksen,[12] Robert L. Johnson,[13] M. J. Lagrange,[14] Hans K. LaRondelle,[15] R. C. H. Lenski,[16] J. B. Lightfoot,[17] Martin Luther,[18] Herman Ridderbos,[19] Henrich Schlier,[20] and John R. W. Stott.[21]

The list of names supporting this view is impressive, although the bases of the interpretation are few and feeble, namely, the claim that the *kai* (KJV, "and"; NASB, "and"; NIV, "even") before the term "the Israel of God" is an explicative or appositional *kai*; the fact that the members of the church may be called "the seed of Abraham" (cf. Gal. 3:29); and the claim that if one sees the term "the Israel of God" a believing ethnic Israel, they would be included in the preceding clause, "And those who will walk by this rule, peace and mercy be upon them."[22]

10. N. A. Dahl, "Der Name Israel: I. Zur Auslegung von Gal.6, 16," *Judaica* 6 (1950):161-70, a two-part article containing a debate with Gottlob Schrenk over the meaning of the term.
11. Donald Guthrie, ed., *Galatians,* The Century Bible (London: Thomas Nelson, 1969), pp. 161-62. Though relating the terms *peace* and *Israel* to Ps. 125:5, where the latter term refers to ethnic Israel, Guthrie says, "Israel seems to refer to the same people as 'all who walk by this rule,'" that is, the church.
12. Hendriksen, pp. 246-47.
13. Robert L. Johnson, *The Letter of Paul to the Galatians* (Austin: Sweet, 1969), pp. 179-80. He has confused the question of the proper punctuation of the text.
14. M. J. Lagrange, *Saint Paul Épître aux Galates* (Paris Libraire Lecoffre, 1950), p. 166. Lagrange, however, denies the explicative sense by which Lightfoot and others understand the *kai* before *epi ton Israel tou theou.* He understands it as simply copulative, "ouvrant un plus large horizon."
15. Hans K. LaRondelle, *The Israel of God in Prophecy: Principles of Prophetic Interpretation* (Berrien Springs, Mich.: Andrews U., 1983), pp. 108-14. LaRondelle's defense of his position, made ostensibly according to sound hermeneutics, is faulty hermeneutically and logically.
16. R. C. H. Lenski, *The Interpretation of Saint Paul's Epistles to the Galatians, to the Ephesians and to the Philippians* (Columbus: Wartburg, 1937), pp. 320-21. Lenski takes the *kai* to express "explicative apposition."
17. J. B. Lightfoot, *Saint Paul's Epistle to the Galatians* (London: Macmillan, 1896), pp. 224-25. Lightfoot takes the *kai* to be "epexegetic, i.e., it introduces the same thing under a new aspect" (p. 225). Cf. Heb. 11:17.
18. Martin Luther, *A Commentary on St. Paul's Epistle to the Galatians,* ed. Philip S. Watson (Westwood: Revell, n.d.), p. 565.
19. Herman N. Ridderbos, *The Epistle of Paul to the Churches of Galatia,* trans. Henry Zylstra (Grand Rapids: Eerdmans, 1953), p. 227; cf. also his *Paul: An Outline of His Theology,* trans. John Richard de Witt (Grand Rapids: Eerdmans, 1975), p. 336. In both works Ridderbos, for whose scholarship I have the greatest admiration, admits that Paul does not "generally," or "in general" *(Paul)* speak of *Israel* as inclusive of all believers. In fact, he states that Paul "in general" continues to reserve the names "Israel," "Jews," and "Hebrews" for the national Jewish people *(Paul,* p. 336). Ridderbos's use of "in general" and "generally" is a bit amusing, since he admits Gal. 6:16 is the only example of such usage (if it is).
20. Henrich Schlier, *Der Brief an die Galater* (Gottingen: Vandenhoeck & Ruprecht, 1951), p. 209. Schlier follows Lagrange in his understanding of *kai.*
21. John R. W. Stott, *Only One Way: The Message of Galatians* (London: InterVarsity, 1968, 1974), p. 180. Stott takes the *kai* as "even," but he also adds that it may be omitted, as the RSV does.
22. This is the contention of Anthony A. Hoekema in his well-argued *The Bible and the Future* (Grand Rapids: Eerdmans, 1979), p. 197. It is a clever observation but unconvincing, especially in the light of Mark 16:7 and its *kai tōi Petrōi* (KJV, "and Peter"). It is clear that the *kai* may single out for special attention someone or something from a larger body or element.

VIEW TWO: "THE ISRAEL OF GOD" IS THE REMNANT OF ISRAELITES IN THE CHURCH

The second of the important interpretations of Galatians 6:16 and "the Israel of God" is the view that the words refer simply to believing ethnic Israelites in the Christian church. Does not Paul speak of himself as an Israelite (cf. Rom. 11:1)? And does not the apostle also speak of "a remnant according to God's gracious choice" (cf. 11:5), words that plainly in the context refer to believing Israelites? What more fitting thing could Paul write, it is said, in a work so strongly attacking Jewish professing believers, the Judaizers, than to make it most plain that he was not attacking the true believing Jews? Judaizers are anathematized, but the remnant according to the election of grace are "the Israel of God." At the conclusion of the *Kampfepistel*[23] the battle ceases, an "olive branch"[24] is offered to the beloved saints who are brethren. The epistle after a couple of lines concludes appropriately on the note of grace, "The grace of our Lord Jesus Christ be with your spirit, brethren. Amen."

Perhaps this expression, "the Israel of God," is to be contrasted with his expression in 1 Corinthians 10:18, "Israel after the flesh" (KJV), as the true, believing Israel versus the unbelieving element, just as in Romans 9:6 the apostle distinguishes two Israels, one elect and believing, the other unbelieving, but both ethnic Israelites (cf. vv. 7-13).

The names in support of this second interpretation are not as numerous, but they are important for scholarly attainment. They include Hans Dieter Betz, the author of a very significant and original recent commentary on Galatians, one destined to be consulted by advanced students of the letter for years to come,[25] Charles J. Ellicott,[26] Walter Gutbrod,[27] Adolf Schlatter,[28] and Gottlob Schrenk.[29]

23. Schrenk's description of Galatians in his article, "Der Segenwunsch nach der Kampfepistel," *Judaica* 6 (1950):170.
24. Cf Cole, p. 183.
25. Hans Dieter Betz, *Galatians*, Hermeneia—A Critical and Historical Commentary on the Bible (Philadelphia: Fortress, 1979), pp. 320-23.
26. Charles J. Ellicott, *A Critical and Grammatical Commentary on St. Paul's Epistle to the Galatians with a Revised Translation* (Andover: Draper, 1880), p. 154. Valuable for grammatical analysis, his commentaries illustrate the fact that the old is not always to be overlooked.
27. *Theological Dictionary of the New Testament*, s.v. "*Ioydaios, Israēl, Ebraios* in the New Testament," by Walter Gutbrod, 3:387-88. Gutbrod's comments are quite significant. He points out that Paul "neither could nor would separate the term from those who belong to Israel by descent." Cf. Rom. 11:17-24.
28. Adolf Schlatter, *Die Briefe an die Galater, Epheser, Kolosser und Philemon* (Stuttgart: Calwer, 1963), pp. 150-51. He says Paul refers here in the blessing to the Israel that is a new creation in Christ, just as he is. Paul does not forget his genuine brethren (cf. Rom. 11:1; Phil. 3:5).
29. In two important articles Gottlob Schrenk argues persuasively for the second interpretation. His comments on the grammatical usage of *kai*, as well as the usage of *Israel* and *peace* (cf. Ps. 124:5, LXX; 127:6, LXX), are telling. Cf. Gottlob Schrenk, "Was bedeutet 'Israel Gottes'?" *Judaica* 5 (1949):81-95; "Der Segenwunsch nach der Kampfepistel," *Judaica* 6 (1950):170-90. The second article is a reply to Dahl's response to his first article. I find Schrenk much more convincing.

VIEW THREE: "THE ISRAEL OF GOD" IS THE FUTURE REDEEMED NATION

The third of the interpretations is the view that the expression "the Israel of God" is used eschatologically and refers to the Israel that shall turn to the Lord in the future in the events that surround the second advent of our Lord. Paul would then be thinking along the lines of his well-known prophecy of the salvation of "all Israel" in Romans 11:25-27. As F. F. Bruce comments, "For all his demoting of the law and the customs, Paul held good hope of the ultimate blessing of Israel."[30]

There are some variations in the expression of their views, but those who hold that *Israel* here either refers to or includes the nation as a whole that will turn to the Lord eschatologically, in line with Romans 11, include F. F. Bruce, Ernest De Witt Burton,[31] W. D. Davies,[32] Robert Govett,[33] Franz Mussner,[34] and Peter Richardson.[35]

30. F. F. Bruce, *The Epistle to the Galatians: A Commentary on the Greek Text,* The New International Greek Commentary (Grand Rapids: Eerdmans, 1982), p. 275.
31. Ernest De Witt Burton, *A Critical and Exegetical Commentary on the Epistle to the Galatians* (Edinburgh: T. & T. Clark, 1921), pp. 357-59. Burton argues for a change in the common punctuation of the verse, preferring to put a comma after *autous* (NASB, "them"), pointing out that if *eirēnē* (NASB, "peace") and *eleos* (NASB, "mercy") were taken together, the order is illogical, for the effect would be placed first and the cause afterwards. Further, in countering the claim that the fina clause of the verse is explicative of those who walk according to this rule and thus composed of both Jews and Gentiles in the church, he says, "there is, in fact, no instance of his [Paul's] using *Israel* except of the Jewish nation or a part thereof" (p.358). Burton takes the "and mercy" to be an afterthought and the final words, "and upon the Israel of God," to be a second afterthought. He contends that the *kai* (NASB, "and") following *eleos* (NASB, "mercy") is slightly ascensive, introducing the last clause, "and mercy upon the Israel of God" (Burton's rendering). This last clause refers to "those within Israel who even though as yet unenlightened are the true Israel of God" (ibid.). His view would be strengthened, it seems to me, if he had taken the first *kai* after "them" as copulative or continuative and the second one after "mercy" as adjunctive, rendering the verse, "And as many as shall walk by this rule, peace be upon them, and mercy also upon the Israel of God."
32. W. D. Davies, "Paul and the People of Israel," *New Testament Studies* 24:4-39. Davies specifically finds it difficult to see *Israel* here as the church of Jews and Gentiles, which would be contrary to Pauline usage elsewhere. He says, "If this proposal were correct one would have expected to find support for it in Rom. ix-xi where Paul extensively deals with 'Israel'" (p. 11, note). Davies's views are not very definite or clear, but he does admit that the desire for peace in verse 16, recalling the *Shemoneh Esreh,* may refer to the Jewish people as a whole (p. 10).
33. Robert Govett, *Govett on Galatians* (Miami Springs: Conley and Schoette, 1981 [orig. ed., 1872]), pp. 233-36. Govett, the well-known nineteenth century independent, scholar, and pastor, referred the clause "and upon the Israel of God" to "the renewed men of Israel, whom God will restore to Himself and to their land in millennial days" (p. 235). Cf. Ps. 135:5; 128:5-6; Isa. 54:7-8, 10; Mic. 7:20.
34. Franz Mussner, *Der Galaterbrief* (Frieburg: Herders, 1977), p. 417. He links the clause with Rom. 11:26. His final comments are, "So deutet der Apostel in Gal 6, 16 shon an, was er dann in Röm 9-11 explizieren wird. Paulus hat sein Volk nie vergessen" (p. 417). The "Israel of God" is identical with the "all Israel" of Rom. 11:26.
35. Peter Richardson, *Israel in the Apostolic Church* (Cambridge: Cambridge U., 1969), pp. 74-84. Richardson's discussion is one of the lengthiest of the treatments of the text.

It is perhaps appropriate at this point to note simply that the weight of contemporary scholarship is opposed to the prevailing interpretation of amillennial interpreters that "the Israel of God" refers to the church, composed of both Jewish and Gentile believers, although the subjective nature of this comment is recognized by the author. It is based upon the fact that those who hold to the second and third views unite in their opposition to the prevailing amillennial interpretation.

AN ANALYSIS OF THE COMPETING INTERPRETATIONS

VIEW ONE: "THE ISRAEL OF GOD" IS THE CHURCH

Grammatical and syntactical considerations. It is necessary to begin this part of the discussion with a reminder of a basic, but often neglected, hermeneutical principle. It is this: in the absence of compelling exegetical and theological considerations, we should avoid the rarer grammatical usages when the common ones make good sense.

We do not have the space to discuss the semantic range of the Greek conjunction *kai.* The standard grammars handle the matter acceptably. Suffice it to say, there are several well-recognized senses of *kai* in the New Testament. First and most commonly, *kai* has the continuative or copulative sense of *and.* Second, *kai* frequently has the adjunctive sense of *also.* Third, *kai* occasionally has the ascensive sense of *even,* which shades off into an explicative sense of *namely.*[36]

The ascensive sense, to my mind, is to be distinguished from an explicative, or epexegetic, sense. It expresses a further, a heightened, identification of a term. For example, I might say, "I visited Dallas, I even visited Dallas Theological Seminary." The *kai* would be an ascensive *kai.* But suppose I said, "I visited Dallas, even the home of the Dallas Cowboy football team." The *kai,* then, would be practically an appositional *kai.* It would be called explicative or epexegetical by some. The point I would like to make is that the English word *even* has multiple usage also. In fact, I tend to think that this may account for renderings such as the "even" of the NIV.

---

36. Schrenk lists as examples of the explicative usage 1 Cor. 8:12; 12:27f.; 14:27; 15:38; 2 Cor. 5:15. The usage is often found in conjunction with *kai touto,* as in 1 Cor. 2:2; 5:1; 6:6, 8, 10-11; Rom. 13:11; Eph. 2:8; cf. Heb. 11:12. A cursory study of these instances will cast doubt over the validity of some of the examples. Cf. F. Blass and A. Debrunner, *A Greek Grammar of the New Testament and Other Early Christian Literature,* trans. and rev. Robert W. Funk (Chicago: U. of Chicago, 1961), pp. 228-29; Maximilian Zerwick, *Biblical Greek Illustrated by Examples,* adapted from the 4th Latin ed. by Joseph Smith (Rome: Scripta Pontificii Instituti Biblici, 1963), pp. 152-54. Zerwick is undecided about Gal. 6:16 (p. 154).

The genuine and fairly common usage of *even* in the ascensive sense in Greek has been taken over in English and made an *even* in the rather rare explicative or appositional sense. Because the latter usage serves well the view that the term "the Israel of God" is the church, the dogmatic concern overcame grammatical usage. An extremely rare usage has been made to replace the common usage, even in spite of the fact that the common and frequent usage of *and* makes perfectly good sense in Galatians 6:16.

There are other uses of *kai,* such as an emphatic and an adversative use, but these uses are so rare that we may safely drop discussion of them.

Coming to the problem, the first interpretation referred to above, that in which the term "the Israel of God" is referred to the believing church, involves taking *kai* in an explicative sense[37] and the rendering of it as *even.* There are compelling objections to this view. In the first place, this usage in the light of *kai* in all phases of the literature is proportionately very infrequent, as both G. B. Winer[38] and Ellicott acknowledge. Ellicott contends that it is doubtful that Paul ever uses *kai* in "so marked an explicative sense."[39] There is not anything in recent grammatical study and research that indicates otherwise.

Finally, if it were Paul's intention to identify the "them" of the text as "the Israel of God," then why not simply eliminate the *kai* after "mercy?" The result would be far more to the point, if Paul were identifying the "them," that is, the church, with the term "Israel." The verse would be rendered then, "And as many as shall walk by this rule, peace be upon them and mercy, upon the Israel of God."[40] A case could be solidly made for the apposition of "the Israel of God" with "them," and the rendering of the NIV could stand. Paul, however, did not eliminate the *kai*.

These things make it highly unlikely that the first interpretation is to be preferred grammatically. Because both of the other suggested interpretations are not cumbered with these grammatical and syntactical difficulties, they are more likely views.

Exegetical considerations. Under this heading are covered matters of

---

37. Cf. Lenski, *Interpretation of Paul's Epistles,* pp. 320-21; Lightfoot, *Epistle to the Galatians,* p. 225; Hoekema, p. 197.
38. G. B. Winer, *A Treatise on the Grammar of New Testament Greek, Regarded as a Sure Basis for New Testament Exegesis,* trans. with additions by W. F. Moulton, 9th English ed. (Edinburgh: T. &. T. Clark, 1882), p. 546.
39. Ellicott, p. 154. He also discusses and questions other of the relatively few claimed instances of this usage.
40. Cf. Schrenk, "Der Segenwunsch," *Judaica* 6 (1950):177-78.

context, both general and special, and matters of usage, both Pauline and other.

We turn again to consider the first interpretation, namely, that the "them" refers to the present people of God, and the term "the Israel of God" is a further description of the "them." From the standpoint of biblical usage this view stands condemned. There is no instance in biblical literature of the term *Israel* being used in the sense of the church, or the people of God as composed of both believing ethnic Jews and Gentiles. Nor, on the other hand, as one might expect if there were such usage, does the phrase *ta ethnē* (KJV, "the Gentiles") ever mean the non-Christian world specifically, but only the non-Jewish peoples, although such are generally non-Christians.[41] Thus, the usage of the term *Israel* stands overwhelmingly opposed to the first view.[42]

The usage of the terms *Israel* and *the church* in the early chapters of the book of Acts is in complete harmony, for Israel exists there alongside the newly formed church, and the two entities are kept separate in terminology.

Occasionally Romans 9:6 has been advanced in support of the view that *Israel* may include Gentiles. Paul writes, "For they are not all Israel who are descended from Israel" (NASB). But that will not do, for Paul is here speaking only of a division within ethnic Israel. Some of them are believers and thus truly Israel, whereas others, though ethnically Israelites, are not truly Israel, since they are not elect and believing (cf. vv. 7-13). In the NASB rendering the words "who are descended from Israel" refer to the natural descendants of the patriarchs, from Abraham through Jacob, whereas the opening words, "they are not all Israel," limit the ideal sense of the term to the elect within the nation, the Isaacs and the Jacobs (cf. Rom. 4:12). No Gentiles are found in the statement at all.[43]

A book of recent vintage is that of Hans K. LaRondelle, entitled *The Israel of God in Prophecy: Principles of Prophetic Interpretation*. It launches a broad-scale attack on dispensational views and lectures dispensationalists

---

41. Cf. Jacob Jervell, *Luke and the People of God: A New Look at Luke-Acts* (Minneapolis: Augsburg, 1972), p. 49.

42. Cf. Davies, "Paul and the People of Israel," p. 11, who with others makes the point that if Israel here should include believing Gentiles, one would expect to find support for this in Rom. 9-11. But none is there.

43. Cf. Walter Gutbrod, "Israël," 3:387. He comments, "On the other hand, we are not told here that Gentile Christians are the true Israel. The distinction at R. 9:6 does not go beyond what is presupposed at Jn. 1:47, and it corresponds to the distinction between *Ioydaios en to krypto* and *Ioydaios en tō phanerō* at R. 2:28f., which does not imply that Paul is calling Gentiles the true Jews."

for their hermeneutical lapses. In his treatment of Galatians 6:16, Professor LaRondelle, a Seventh Day Adventist, takes a number of unsupportable positions, as well as largely avoiding obvious difficulties with his scheme of things. He misunderstands the general context of Galatians to begin with, contending that it is written by Paul to reject "any different status or claim of the Jewish Christians beside or above that of gentile Christians before God."[44] On the contrary, the apostle is concerned with correcting the gospel preached to the Galatians by the Judaizers, particularly their false contention that it was necessary to be circumcised to be saved and to observe as Christians certain requirements of the law of Moses in order to remain in divine favor (cf. Gal. 1:6-9; 2:1—3:29; 4:1-31; 5:1-4; 6:11-18). The apostle makes no attempt whatsoever to deny that there is a legitimate distinction of race between Gentile and Jewish believers in the church. His statement in Romans 11:5 should have warned Professor LaRondelle against this error. There is a remnant of Jewish believers in the church according to the election of grace. That the professor overlooked Paul's careful language is seen in his equation of terms that differ. He correctly cites Paul's statement that "'there is neither Jew nor Greek' in Christ"[45] (cf. Gal. 3:28) but then a couple of pages later modifies this to "'there is neither Jew nor Greek' *within the Church*"[46] (italics mine), as if the terms *Christ* and *church* are identical. This approach fails to see that Paul does not say there is neither Jew nor Greek *within the church*. He speaks of those who are "in Christ." For LaRondelle, however, inasmuch as there is neither Jew nor Greek within the church and in Christ, there can be no distinction between them in the church. But Paul also says there is neither male nor female, nor slave nor free man in Christ. Would he then deny sexual differences within the church? Or the social differences in Paul's day? Is it not plain that Paul is not speaking of national or ethnic difference in Christ, but of spiritual status? In that sense there is no difference in Christ.

Throughout LaRondelle's discussion of the text there is no acknowledgment, so far as I can find, of the fact that the term *Israel* is never found in the sense of the church. Is not that very relevant to the interpretation of Galatians 6:16?

Finally, to sum up his position, Professor LaRondelle affirms that since the church is the seed of Abraham and Israel is the seed of Abraham, the two entities, the church and Israel, are the same. The result is a textbook

44. LaRondelle, p. 108.
45. Ibid.
46. Ibid., p. 110.

example of the fallacy of the undistributed middle.[47]

Theological considerations. Peter Richardson has pointed out that there is no historical evidence that the term *Israel* was identified with the church before A.D. 160. Further, at that date there was no characterization of the church as "the Israel of God."[48] In other words, for more than a century after Paul there was no evidence of the identification.

To conclude the discussion of the first interpretation, it seems clear that there is little evidence—grammatical, exegetical, or theological—that supports it. On the other hand, there is sound historical evidence against the identification of *Israel* with believing or unbelieving Gentiles. The grammatical usage of *kai* is not favorable to the view, nor is the Pauline or New Testament usage of *Israel.* Finally, if D. W. B. Robinson's article is basically sound, the Pauline teaching in Galatians contains a recognition of national distinctions in the one people of God.[49]

VIEW TWO: "THE ISRAEL OF GOD" REFERS TO JEWISH BELIEVERS IN PAUL'S DAY

Perhaps it would be appropriate to confine attention to Hans Dieter Betz, due to the widespread recognition of his excellent commentary. He treats verse 16 as a conditional blessing upon those who walk according to the rule of the new creation mentioned in verse 15,[50] remarking also on its uniqueness in Pauline literature. After a discussion of the term "the Israel of God" Betz concludes amid some ambiguity that the sentence refers to a blessing on those who remain faithful Paulinists in the Galatian churches, including both those of Gentile extraction and believing ethnic Jews. His final comment is, "Thus, Paul extends the blessing beyond the Galatian Paulinists to those Jewish-Christians who approve of his *kanon* ('rule') in v 15."[51]

Grammatical and syntactical considerations. In order not to prolong the discussion, and also since the final interpretation has many similarities with the second, just a few comments are in order. So far as I can tell,

---

47. LaRondelle's comments on Gal. 6:16 indicate little, if any, interaction with Burton, *Critical and Exegetical Commentary,* the finest old technical commentary on Galatians; Betz, *Galatians,* the best new technical work in English; Bruce in his excellent work *Galatians: Commentary on the Greek Text;* or with the periodical articles of Dahl, Schrenk, and Robinson. The carefully thought through article by Robinson is particularly appropriate for questions concerning Gal. 6:16, as its title ("The Distinction between Jewish and Gentile Believers in Galatians") indicates.
48. Richardson, p. 83. Many amillennialists, including LaRondelle, overlook this.
49. Cf. especially pp. 47-48.
50. Betz, *Galatians,* pp. 320-21.
51. Ibid., p. 323.

there are no grammatical, or syntactical, considerations that would be contrary to Betz's view. The common sense of *kai* as continuative, or copulative, is followed.

Exegetical considerations. Exegetically the view is sound, since "Israel" has its uniform Pauline ethnic sense. And further, the apostle achieves a very striking climactic conclusion. Drawing near the end of his "battle-epistle" with its harsh and forceful attack on the Judaists[52] and its omission of the customary words of thanksgiving, Paul tempers his language with a special blessing for those faithful believing Israelites who, understanding the grace of God and its exclusion of any human works as the ground of redemption, had not succumbed to the subtle blandishments of the deceptive Judaizers. They, not the false men from Jerusalem, are "the Israel of God," or, as he calls them elsewhere, "the remnant according to the election of grace" (cf. Rom. 11:5).

Theological considerations. And theologically the view is sound in its maintenance of the two elements within the one people of God, Gentiles and ethnic Jews. Romans 11 spells out the details of the relationship between the two entities from Abraham's day to the present age and on to the fulfillment in the future of the great unconditional covenantal promises made to the patriarchs.

VIEW THREE: "THE ISRAEL OF GOD" REFERS TO THAT BODY OF ETHNIC ISRAEL WHO ARE SAVED AT THE MESSIAH'S RETURN

Exegetical considerations. The third view of "the Israel of God," namely, that the term is eschatological in force and refers to the "all Israel" of Romans 11:26, is an extension of the previous interpretation. It, too, takes the term "the Israel of God" to refer to ethnic Israel but locates their blessing in the future. Their salvation was a great concern of Paul, as his ministry attests (cf. Rom. 9:3-5; 10:1). An impressive array of contemporary interpreters hold this view, although with some minor variations.

Because Peter Richardson, largely following Burton, has discussed the matter at some length, his views will be emphasized. Seeking to overthrow the common misconception that "the Israel of God" refers to the church composed of both believing Gentiles and believing Jews, he makes the fol-

---

52. The force of 1:8-9 and its "let him be accursed" is very strong, since *anathema* referred ultimately to that under the divine curse. In Rom. 9:3 Paul says he could pray to be *anathema* from Christ, that is, consigned to Gehenna, if his people could be saved by his sacrifice. In other words, it is almost as if Paul were saying, "If any man should preach a contrary gospel, let him go to hell!" Galatians certainly is a "Kampfepistel!"

lowing points: First, the unique order of peace and mercy, probably suggested by Jewish benedictions, particularly Benediction XIX of the *Shemoneh Esreh* (Babylonian recension), may be significant. The prayer has the order of peace and then mercy in it, followed by a reference to "us and all Israel."[53] Other Old Testament passages, such as Psalm 124:5 (= 127:6), offer more general parallels. In such places "Israel" is used ethnically and, if there is Pauline dependence on them, he probably used the term ethnically.

Second, the strange order of peace and mercy suggests, as Burton contended, a repunctuation of the text as commonly edited. A comma should be placed after "them," and the comma after "mercy" found in many English versions[54] and in editions of the Greek text should be eliminated. The text may then be rendered, *And as many as shall walk by this rule, peace be upon them, and mercy also upon the Israel of God* (or *peace be upon them, and mercy, and upon the Israel of God*).

Third, Richardson suggests that the future tense in "shall walk" may carry, by analogy, its future idea over into the benediction regarding mercy. In other words, it may point to Israel's future belief. This seems questionable to me.

Fourth, "the Israel of God" is a part of the whole Israel (cf. Rom. 9:6).

Fifth, the *kai* is only slightly ascensive, forestalling any inference that Paul in Galatians is condemning everything about Israel.[55] Richardson thinks the presence of the *kai* is important and argues strongly against the view that the church is the Israel of God. If it were omitted, then that view would be strengthened, but its acknowledged presence is a major signpost pointing in another interpretive direction.

Sixth, just as Mussner, Bruce, and others, Richardson sees the expression as a reference to a hoped-for future conversion of ethnic Israel, a view that Paul expounds in detail in the great theodicy of Romans 9-11.

Mussner's identification of the phrase with Paul's "all Israel" of Romans 11:26 is in harmony with Richardson. Thus also Bruce, who concludes his discussion with, "The invocation of blessing on the Israel of God has probably an eschatological perspective."[56]

Evaluative summary. Grammatically and syntactically this last option is sound, whether we adopt Burton's repunctuation of the text or not. There

53. Cf. Richardson, pp. 78-80.
54. Contrast the NASB.
55. Cf. Burton, p. 358.
56. Bruce, p. 275.

may exist some question regarding the exegetical aptness of the eschatological perspective. That certainly has not been one of the major emphases
of the Galatian epistle as a whole, but in the immediate context it is very
appropriate psychologically, providing a note of hope and expectation after
a stern and severe admonition. And, further, the Abrahamic covenant and
its benefits have been constantly before the readers, and the whole of the
Old Testament as well as previous New Testament revelation testifies to its
glorious future consummation. Heirship of Abrahamic covenant blessing
and the kingdom of God, mentioned just a few lines previously (cf. 5:21),
fit in well with an eschatological note.[57]

Theologically the view harmonizes with the important Pauline teaching
that there are two kinds of Israelites, a believing one and an unbelieving
one. The teaching is plainly set out in such passages as Romans 2:28-29;
4:11-12; 9:6; and 11:1-36. Galatians 6:16 forms another link in the apostle's teaching.

CONCLUDING COMMENTS

REFLECTIONS ON CONTEMPORARY EXEGETICAL METHODOLOGY

It is not uncommon in our evangelical seminaries to hear exegetes criti-
cize the systematic theologians for the tendency to approach the biblical
text with dogmatic presuppositions that predetermine exegetical conclusions. Some of this criticism is justified, I will admit. Theologians do not
come to the text without their presuppositions. The measure of the good
theologian, such as a Calvin, an Owen, a Hodge, a Warfield, a Murray, and
a Berkower, is the skill with which one recognizes them, handles them,
and avoids their dominion over us.

What is not as common as it should be in our schools, however, is the
recognition of the fact that exegetes are exposed to the same perils and at
least as often succumb to them. Presuppositionless exegesis is an illusive
mirage, and exegesis is finest when it acknowledges the fact and seeks to
guard against it. Exegetes frequently are as guilty of false methodology as
that financial writer whose logic and unsound premises the *London Econ-*

---

57. Several linguistic matters lend further support to an eschatological perspective. In addition to the
    mention of the phrase "the kingdom of God," the frequent use of the concept of promise in the
    letter (cf. 3:14, 16, 17, 18 [twice], 19, 21, 22, 29; 4:23, 28) and the concept of inheritance (cf.
    3:14,18, 29; 4:1, 7, 30; 5:21), related as they are to the Abrahamic covenant, accent the future per-
    spective. And, finally, is there significance in the fact that the term *inheritance* in Romans 11 is
    related by Paul to God's saving work toward the nation Israel in the future? The concept is found in
    11:30, 31, and 32 in both noun and verb forms. And here in Gal. 6:16 the concept appears also.

omist once neatly impaled by commenting that he was "proceeding from an unwarranted assumption to a foregone conclusion."[58]

The present study illustrates this. If there is an interpretation that totters on a tenuous foundation, it is the view that Paul equates the term "the Israel of God" with the believing church of Jews and Gentiles. To support it, the general usage of the term *Israel* in Paul, in the New Testament, and in the Scriptures as a whole is ignored. The grammatical and syntactical usage of the conjunction *kai* is strained and distorted—and the rare and uncommon sense accepted when the usual sense is unsatisfactory—only because it does not harmonize with the presuppositions of the exegete. And to compound matters, in the special context of Galatians and the general context of the Pauline teaching, especially as highlighted in Romans 11, Paul's primary passages on God's dealings with Israel and the Gentiles, are downplayed. If, as LaRondelle asserts, "Paul's benediction in Galatians 6:16 becomes, then, the chief witness in the New Testament in declaring that the universal church of Christ is the Israel of God, the seed of Abraham, the heir to Israel's covenant promise (cf. Gal. 3:29; 6:16),"[59] then the doctrine that the church of Gentiles and Jews is *the* Israel of God rests on an illusion. It is a classic case of tendentious exegesis.

REFLECTIONS ON LOGICAL FAILURE

This is hardly the place to enlarge upon this theme. It has been done well elsewhere.[60] Nevertheless I think it is permissible to suggest that exegetes seem particularly prone today to logical fallacies. The case of the undistributed middle, mentioned earlier, underlines the importance of clear thinking in exegetical discussion.

REFLECTIONS ON CONTEMPORARY THEOLOGICAL POSITIONS

A certain rigidity in evangelical eschatological debate emerges again in the discussion of Galatians 6:16. For example, amillennialists seem to strongly desire to equate "the Israel of God" with the church. Some amillennialists, however, think an ethnic future for Israel is compatible with their system. An example of this is found in the fine work of Anthony A. Hoekema on eschatology. He grants that an ethnic future for Israel would

58. Stewart Chase, *Guides to Straight Thinking: With 13 Common Fallacies* (New York: Harper & Row, 1956), p. 122.
59. LaRondelle, pp. 110-11.
60. Cf. D. A. Carson, *Exegetical Fallacies* (Grand Rapids: Baker, 1984), pp. 91-126.

with certain strictures be compatible with his amillennial views, but he argues strongly against such an interpretation.[61]

Why, then, are amillennialists so opposed generally to an ethnic future for Israel? That is not an easy question to answer. It may be perfectly conceivable that an amillennialist would grant that an ethnic future for Israel at the Lord's return could be fitted into his system. But if such a normal interpretation of the language of the Old Testament is followed in this instance, it is difficult to see how one can then escape the seemingly plain teaching of the many Old Testament prophecies that the nation Israel shall enjoy a preeminence in certain respects over the Gentiles in the kingdom that follows our Lord's advent (cf. Isa. 60:1-4; 62:1-12; Mic. 4:1-5; Hag. 2:1-7; Zech. 14:16-21, etc.).

On the other hand, the case for premillennialism does not rest on the reference of the term "the Israel of God" to ethnic redeemed Israel here. Its case against the exegetical practice of the spiritualization of the Scriptures would be weakened a bit, but premillennialism's support in the history of the church's eschatological interpretation, in the use of the grammatico-historico-theological method of exegesis, and in the interpretation of Scripture by the prophets and the apostles would still stand firm.

Let the church, then, seek to avoid the practice of rigidly tendentiously defending its systems. Let us listen to the Holy Spirit speaking in the Scriptures, and then let us freely and forcibly proclaim what we are taught. After all, His system—and there is such—is the best one.

---

61. Hoekema, pp. 146-47. He also adds certain strictures to the common perception of a future for Israel. Referring to Romans 11:26 he says, "There is nothing in the passage which would rule out such a future conversion or such future conversions, as long as one does not insist that the passage points *only* to the future, or that it describes a conversion of Israel which occurs *after* the full number of Gentiles has been gathered in" (p. 147). That, of course, is just what Romans 11:25-27 does do. It points to the future, and the conversion of Israel is placed by the apostle after the gathering in of the Gentiles. It, therefore, really is difficult for Hoekema to include an ethnic future for Israel in his amillennial scheme.

ELLIOTT E. JOHNSON (B.S., Northwestern University; Th.M., Th.D., Dallas
Theological Seminary) is associate professor of Bible exposition at Dallas Theological Seminary.

Apocalyptic Genre in Literal Interpretation

Elliott E. Johnson

INTRODUCTION

Within the premillennial, literal school of biblical interpretation[1] a rich
body of materials focusing on the prophetic writings has appeared. Among
the eminent authors of that group is J. Dwight Pentecost, for whom this
collection of essays is being written. As one of his students I have underta-
ken this study with deep gratitude for the development and exposition of
the themes of apocalyptic literature in his writings.[2] Although Pentecost's
works have not focused on genre related issues, he did respect literary distinctions in the conclusions he reached. However, in view of his approach
an initial question must be considered: why do we need to examine the literary genre in literal interpretation? What contribution does a consideration of the style, form, and content of a biblical passage or document make
to a literal hermeneutic?

In the literal tradition there is this maxim: "The biblical text says what it
means and means what it says," uniting what the text *says* (focusing on
the verbal statements) to what the text *means* (focusing on the interpretation in communication). Accordingly, there is no division of textual statements and construed meaning. The maxim is a warning against interpreting biblical statements equivocally in the sense of a single text sponsoring
multiple, unrelated meanings. It also supports the conclusion that it is tex-

---

1. Literal interpretation means that the meaning is determined by the textual statements and includes corresponding historical references as determined in the text and as intended by the divine
   author expressed by the human writer.
2. J. Dwight Pentecost, *Things to Come* (Findlay, Ohio: Dunham, 1958).

tual statements that determine meaning. That is at the heart of literal interpretation.

However, when the interpreter seeks to discover "what a text means" by "what it says," questions do arise. The task is easier when the author speaks straightforwardly. For this reason literal interpreters have enjoyed the greatest agreement among themselves when the literary genre involves direct statements, such as in epistolary literature. But when an author says something indirectly (as in narrative literature) or metaphorically (as in parabolic literature), the interpreter has greater difficulty not only in recognizing what the author means but also in seeing all that he means. A consideration of literary genre helps with both of these issues. This is particularly true in the case of apocalyptic literature, for it often contains nondirect statements of meaning (e.g., in the description of a vision) and metaphorical communication (through symbolism). Thus a consideration of the interpretation of apocalyptic literature is important to those who employ the literal method.

Literal hermeneutics focuses on the propositional nature of biblical revelation, appropriately recognizing the cognitive components of an author's meaning. However, propositional statements often fail to capture the expressive, directive, and performative[3] components of verbal communication. Such components express the force and richness of a given passage. They are the meanings considered in literary genre and may themselves be included in a propositional statement, clarifying and specifying the way the proposition is expressed. This essay will attempt to construct such a statement in order to clarify the defining components of biblical apocalyptic as a type of literature.

The word *apocalypse* appears as the first word in the book of Revelation and means "disclosure," or "revelation." Thus apocalyptic literature involves an "uncovering of what is unknown." However, the term *apocalyptic* is used in modern discussions with a broad range of meanings,[4] which can be clarified if one distinguishes "between apocalyptic eschatology (the expectation of the end which structures religion's perspective), apocalypticism (a 'sociological ideology,' presumably that of the oppressed) and the literary genre apocalypse."[5] *Apocalyptic eschatology* would include a study of any biblical portion with common thematic content (cf. Isa. 24-27; 57-

---

3. John Austin, *Doing Things with Words* (Cambridge, Mass.: Harvard U., 1962).
4. Leon Morris, *Apocalyptic* (Grand Rapids: Eerdmans, 1972), p. 20.
5. E. P. Sanders, "The Genre of Palestinian Jewish Apocalypses," in *Apocalypticism in the Mediterranean World and the Near East,* ed. David Hellholm (Tubingen: Mohr, 1983), p. 450.

65; Joel 2-3; Matt. 24; 1 Thess. 5—although these passages all deal with the end of time, they bear few literary and formal characteristics of apocalyptic vision). *Apocalypticism* would be a study of the situations in life (*Sitz im Leben*) that help determine the meaning of the text. Sociologists find at the base of every apocalyptic movement a crisis: "The collapse of a well-ordered world view which defines values and orders the universe for a people, thrusting them into the uncharted chaos of anomie and meaninglessness."[6] In this perspective the setting in history is more than the occasion for the literary product; it becomes the context determining the literary meaning. This is a point of departure between form critical study and literal interpretation and has given rise to the conclusion that "one should distinguish between genre and *Sitz im Leben*."[7] Finally, *apocalyptic literature* not only involves a content of revelation of the end time but also a literary form in which it is expressed.

If content of revelation is a component that defines apocalyptic literature, consideration must be given to the difference between divine revelation as recognized in the canon and a human claim to revelation. Leon Morris dismisses this distinction on the basis of common scholarly practice, observing that "it is, however, much more usual to recognize that the name is applicable to a wide range of nonbiblical literature and to seek its essential characteristics there."[8] Such an approach would have support if there were evidence that the biblical author chose apocalyptic expression because it would communicate better to a historical audience. But unlike the study of Hittite treaties, there is little evidence that an apocalyptic literary form existed and was adopted because it was shared by the ancient world: "An extraordinary amount of the scholarly literature has been devoted to the quest for the 'origins of apocalyptic.' For much of this century opinion was divided . . . much of this quest must be considered misdirected and counterproductive. Any given apocalypse combines allusions to a wide range of sources."[9] The best conclusion is that literary form naturally arises out of the unique demands of the content to be expressed. That being the case, I hold to a view of special revelation that identifies biblical apocalyptic as distinct from other instances of apocalyptic literature referred to by Morris. Such an assumption limits the scope of the study. Only cases of canonical apocalyptic literature will be examined.

6. Paul D. Hanson, "Old Testament Apocalyptic Reexamined," *Interpretation* 25 (1971):455.
7. Sanders, p. 450.
8. Morris, p. 21.
9. John J. Collins, *The Apocalyptic Imagination* (New York: Crossroad, 1984), p. 16.

THE MEANING OF APOCALYPTIC LITERATURE

Having introduced the reason for studying genre and the use of the term *apocalyptic,* a definition of apocalyptic literature may be proposed. *Apocalyptic literature is prophetic revelation that challenges and encourages God's oppressed people by narrating contemporary historical issues and envisioning their outcome at the end of history in terms corresponding to what the prophet saw in the vision and heard from the divine interpreter.* This proposition attempts to clarify four components of biblical apocalyptic: (1) theological content, (2) literary function in historical communication, (3) literary structure in composition, and (4) the use of language. Before these components are examined, however, a word about the length of the textual unit called apocalyptic is required.

There is a growing consensus that the smaller segments of the text (forms) that form criticism studies are often unnaturally removed from their context.[10] The natural literary unit is the textual composition as a whole, which incorporates many features that contribute apocalyptic meaning in different ways to the message of the document. Thus the biblical books that could qualify as apocalyptic include Ezekiel, Daniel, Zechariah, and Revelation. Many other passages express apocalyptic eschatology, but these four books alone qualify in content and form as apocalyptic literature.

THEOLOGICAL CONTENT

This component of meaning is shared with all biblical and canonical literature regardless of genre. Apocalyptic genre, however, has a unique focus and content.

Critical scholars see a sharp disjuncture between prophetic and apocalyptic material. Paul Hanson, for example, concludes, "Prophetic eschatology is transformed into apocalyptic at the point where the task of translating the cosmic vision into the categories of mundane reality is abdicated."[11] According to these writers prophetic and apocalyptic literature contain two mutually exclusive kinds of eschatology in the Old Testament: prophetic eschatology expected God's kingdom to arise out of history and to be a kingdom within history; apocalyptic eschatology arose in the despair of history and expected the kingdom to come from outside of history. How-

10. Sanders, "The Genre of Palestinian Jewish Apocalyses," p. 450.
11. Hanson, "Old Testament Apocalyptic Reexamined," p. 454.

ever, evangelical interpreters argue "that the expectation of a cataclysmic irruption into history is intrinsic to the prophetic hope of the Old Testament. The kingdom of God will be established in this world, but with an entirely new quality of life."[12] So the differences in the eschatology of prophetic and apocalyptic literature are matters of degree, not of kind.

The broader and more basic revelation is prophetic. In content prophetic literature focuses on the *will of God,* and in form the will of God is expressed in the preaching of a prophet concerning God's dealing at a particular time in history but potentially extending to history's end. In content apocalyptic literature focuses on the *decreed events from God,* and in form these events, presenting the ultimate resolution of historical issues, are envisioned and described. Apocalyptic then provides an opportunity for men to see God's decree and in some detail the future resolution of conflicting issues.

There is a "determinism . . . characteristic of this class of literature. For the apocalyptists it was clear that the course of this world's history is preordained."[13] Envisioning God's decree, however, did not destroy human initiative toward evil, as evidenced by Daniel's responses in prayer, nor did it "engender an attitude of defeatism. The apocalyptists were not in the slightest dismayed, for they saw it as certain that this evil could not finally be triumphant."[14] The conviction created is "that God has already worked out His purposes in a heaven so that all that remained was for the same pattern to be repeated on earth."[15]

The content in apocalyptic revelation also involves what the divine interpreter says. The "essential feature of apocalyptic literature found in the Apocalypse is that a divine personage, usually an angel, guides John through the visions and interprets these portions which are not self-evident to John in the actions or speeches of the vision."[16]

One final aspect of theological content concerns the ultimate triumph of God. As early as the Exodus, when God established the Tabernacle and enthroned Himself above the ark, the nation was established as a theocracy with God as her ultimate King. The various prophetic and apocalyptic visions of Israel's climax in history saw the ultimate triumph of God in dif-

---

12. *International Standard Bible Encyclopedia,* 3d ed., s.v. "Apocalyptic Literature," by George E. Ladd (hereafter *ISBE*), 1:152.
13. Morris, p. 47.
14. Ibid.
15. Joyce G. Baldwin, *Haggai, Zechariah, Malachi* (Downers Grove, Ill.: InterVarsity, 1972), p. 72.
16. Ralph Alexander, *Hermeneutics of Old Testament Apocalyptic Literature* (Th.D. dissertation, Dallas Theological Seminary), p. 44.

ferent ways. "Sometimes God Himself was to reign upon earth; sometimes He was to reign, not in person, but through His viceroy, the Davidic King, His Anointed, or Messiah. There was not felt to be the slightest antagonism between these two ideals; they might well exist, and they did exist, side by side."[17]

LITERARY FUNCTION

Two primary elements are always present in communication: an author and an audience. Concerning authorship, a characteristic feature of noncanonical Jewish apocalypticism is pseudonymity. This is one of the most notable differences between biblical apocalypticism and other similar Jewish writings. "Daniel is not pseudonymous, for Daniel is not an Old Testament saint whose name could be used to lend authority to a book. . . . The Revelation was written by a living author who was well known to those to whom he wrote."[18] There is also strong support for the historicity of the prophets Ezekiel and Zechariah and for their authorship of the books that bear their names.[19]

Concerning audience, when each of the biblical apocalyptic works was penned both the authors and their intended audiences were being oppressed. Daniel, Ezekiel, John, and even Zechariah and the people of his day knew the oppression of Gentile hostility and government. The purpose of the apocalyptic works was to challenge and encourage these oppressed people. David Hellholm proposed that the literature is "intended for a group in crisis with the purpose of exhortation and/or consolation by means of divine authority."[20] John Collins adds the following summary:

> This apocalyptic technique does not, of course, have a publicly discernable effect on a historical crisis, but it provides a resolution in the imagination by instilling conviction in the revealed "knowledge" that it imparts. The function of apocalyptic literature is to shape one's imaginative perception of a situation and so lay the basis for whatever course of action it exhorts.[21]

17. Sanday, "The Apocalyptic Element in the Gospels," *The Gibbert Journal* 10 (1911-1912):97.
18. *ISBE*, 1:152.
19. Gleason L. Archer, Jr., *A Survey of Old Testament Introduction* (Chicago: Moody, 1974).
20. David Hellholm, "The Problem of Apocalyptic Genre and the Apocalypse of John," *SBL* 1982 Seminar Papers, ed. K. H. Richards, p. 168.
21. Collins, p. 32.

LITERATURE STRUCTURE IN COMPOSITION

Apocalyptic genre involves two primary literary structures: narrative and vision. On the one hand, "the form of the apocalypses involves a narrative framework that describes the manner of revelation."[22] Joyce Baldwin draws some important conclusions about the narrative framework of the biblical books. "In each of the books there is a clear arrangement of the material, so that it is not difficult to divide them into sections. Each begins at a given point in history."[23] Of even greater interest is the conclusion that "the periods referred to can be identified and described, and yet the content of the chapters has a universal application."[24] The narrative, in other words, concerns issues that take place during the time of the author but are treated in terms of God's dealings throughout history. So the experiences of a godly remnant under Babylonian and Persian kings are normative for all Jews subject to non-Jewish political leaders in the times of the Gentiles. Similarly the messages to the seven churches in Asia Minor are applied to all the churches (cf. Rev. 2:7, 11, 17, 29; 3:6, 13, 22). Although the messages are addressed to seven contemporary churches, the Word given to each is normative for all churches of that and every age.

Apocalyptic narrative begins in the day of the author and through the interplay of narrative and vision progresses to the end of history. The historical sequence, however, often includes a gap. In Daniel, for example, the reigns of the successive Gentile powers progress through the four metals in the statue that begins with Nebuchadnezzar, the head of gold. Yet there is a gap within the final kingdom from the iron phase to the iron-mixed-with-clay phase that is struck by the stone at the end. Again, in the book of Revelation a gap occurs between John's words to the seven churches (chaps. 2-3) and the thrones set for judgment in heaven (chaps. 4-5). Finally, Baldwin writes about Zechariah, "Chapters 1-8 are set in the prophet's own day, but there is eschatology. . . . In chapters 9 14 the starting-point is episodes in Israel's history, but the submission of the nations and the exaltation of God's people are conveyed. . . . Chapter 14 leaps to the day when the Lord will reign over all the earth, and so to the end of time (14:7)."[25]

On the other hand, the second primary literary structure is vision, in which God directs the attention of both the author and the reader to the

22. Ibid., p. 4
23. Baldwin, p. 70.
24. Ibid., pp. 70-71
25. Ibid., p. 71.

end of time and God's resolution of historical issues and tensions. The presence of visions alone in apocalyptic literature does not distinguish it from prophetic literature, which also contains visionary revelation. But whereas the prophets had visions of insight that provided them with a theological interpretation of the events of their day, apocalyptic visions are elaborate picture visions.[26] What is distinct is the imagery of the visions. "Amos and Jeremiah had also seen visions of a relatively simple impressionist type, pictures which conveyed their own message. The contrast between these and the involved imagery of Ezekiel marks one distinct step in the direction of apocalyptic."[27] This involved and sometimes grotesque imagery in apocalyptic vision has become the focal point in the discussion of interpretation. John Collins comments on it in his observation that it was Herman Gunkle who "by pointing to the mythological roots of much apocalyptic imagery . . . showed its symbolic and allusive character. Apocalyptic literature was not governed by the principles of Aristotelian logic but was closer to the poetic nature of myth."[28] Assessing the interpretation of these visions, Collins concludes:

> Biblical scholarship in general has suffered from a preoccupation with the referential aspects of language and with the factual information that can be extracted from a text. Such an attitude is especially detrimental to the study of poetic and mythological material, which is expressive language, articulating feelings and attitudes rather than describing reality in an objective way. The apocalyptic literature provides a rather clear example of language that is expressive rather than referential, symbolic rather than factual.[29]

THE USE OF LANGUAGE

Collins's conclusion must be strongly rejected, for though the language and imagery of the vision may only sketch the outline of the reality, it is not enigmatic;[30] though the language is expressive, it does not exclude specific reference; and though the genre includes symbolism, it does not negate actual and historical reference through the symbol. This may be defended by two lines of reasoning.

26. Willis J. Beecher, *The Prophets and the Promise* (Grand Rapids: Baker, 1963), p. 119.
27. Baldwin, p. 71-72.
28. Collins, p. 13.
29. Ibid., p. 14.
30. Leon Morris, p. 46. He quotes with approval E. Schurer, *A History of the Jewish People in the Time of Jesus Christ* (Edinburgh: T. & T. Clark, 1886).

(1) The concept of "prophetic revelation" necessarily includes the use of language that implies factual information (a reference to history) as well as expressions of attitude and feeling. George Ladd affirms, "A final characteristic of the apocalyptic genre is the use of symbolism in declaring the will of God to people and in predicting future events."[31] Although a vision might include symbolism, this does not eliminate reference to specific events involved in the outworking of God's will, nor does it dismiss predictions of future occurrences. When the future events are designated by a symbol, the designation is not direct but metaphorical. Still, the event designated may be historical and real. Numerous instances in the apocalyptic literature make this clear. Daniel interpreted the vision of the image of a statue and declared to Nebuchadnezzar, "You are that head of gold" (2:38), indicating that a symbol (head) has a real, historical reference (Nebuchadnezzar). The angelic interpreter in Daniel 7 identified the four beasts as "four kingdoms that will arise from the earth" (7:17).[32] The angel in Daniel 8 interpreted the ram as the "kings of Media and Persia" and the shaggy goat as the "king of Greece" and "four kingdoms that will emerge" (8:20, 21). In similar fashion Ezekiel was told that "these bones are the whole house of Israel" (37:11). John also was informed of the identity of the image he first encountered (1:12-16) when Christ said: "I am the First and the Last. I am the Living One; I was dead, and behold I am alive forever and ever" (1:17). Christ was not identified by name but through a series of descriptions of His role and experience in history, enhancing the relation between the image and its symbols and the historical reference. Thus in the case of biblical apocalyptic the use of images and language involve both referential and factual as well as expressive meanings.

(2) The concept of "literal interpretation" affirms that the meaning of a symbol is determined by textual and contextual considerations. It may appear that such a method would exclude figures and symbols altogether. Properly understood, however, literal interpretation does not claim that the interpretive approach or technique determines textual meaning; it is the literary genre that does that. Neither does the method disallow that other contextual uses of the image (biblical, historical, mythical) may inform the biblical usage, but it denies that those other uses determine the

---

31. *ISBE*, 1:152.
32. Collins, p. 82. "There is no doubt that Daniel 7 is describing the persecution of the Jews under Antiochus Epiphanes. The exaltation of the one like a son of man represents the triumph of the Jews. . . . The corporate interpretation holds that the one like a son of man is merely or purely a symbol, whose meaning is exhausted by the identification of its referent."

meaning. That determinative role, literal interpretation affirms, rests with the textual usage. This matter calls for closer examination.

THE ROLE OF CONTEXT IN INTERPRETING APOCALYPTIC LITERATURE

THE ROLE OF BIBLICAL CONTEXT

To what extent does apocalyptic draw on previous biblical images for its meaning? What is the role of previous biblical revelation in interpreting apocalyptic literature? Collins recognizes the importance of biblical allusions in this regard: "Like much of the Jewish and early Christian literature, the apocalypses constantly echo biblical phrases."[33] Henry Barclay Swete notes that of the 404 verses of the book of Revelation, 278 contain references to the Jewish Scriptures;[34] whereas the United Bible Society's second edition of the Greek New Testament cites more than five hundred Old Testament passages in connection with that book—a prominent context in the consideration of apocalyptic literature. However, an allusion must be carefully examined to determine whether the reference is to the sense of the earlier usage or only to the wording. When it is the former, as in the use of "sea" (Dan. 7:2-3) or the "four horns" (Zech. 1:18-19), one must be aware of the meaning defined in the earlier context and now used as a technical symbol. Great care must be exercised in the claim that a biblical symbol is only a rhetorical allusion, particularly if there are textual clues indicating that the author is employing the same meaning for the symbol.[35]

THE ROLE OF HISTORICAL, CULTURAL, AND MYTHOLOGICAL CONTEXT

Does apocalyptic literature draw on historical, cultural, or mythological images for its meaning? As a means of communication an apocalyptic vision frequently incorporates historical material, used and defined in the context of the vision. For example, Daniel saw the totality of Gentile government as a grand image of a ruler (Dan. 2) in accord with the many obelisks of Babylon (cf. Dan. 3). Zechariah saw the agents of God's will as horses and riders sent on patrol (Zech. 1:7-17) as was the practice of the Persian military. These images were readily evident to one living in the ancient world and are quickly recognized by the modern reader who takes

---

33. Ibid., p. 14.
34. Henry Barclay Swete, *The Apocalypse of St. John* (New York: Macmillan, 1906), p. cxxxv.
35. Collins, pp. 14-15.

the time to study the historical context. More difficult to interpret are those images that seem to draw on mythological sources, like the references to Leviathan and Rahab (Job 26:7-13; Isa. 51:9-10; 27:1). The recognition that such allusions do not depend on the facticity of the mythological source but only on its connotation eliminates the problems raised for inerrant Scripture. In these allusions the mythological sources connote the feelings of struggle with evil powers. In apocalyptic literature the allusions are defined in context as references to Satan, the evil one (cf. Rev. 12:9).

Difficulties arise in interpreting suggested mythological allusions where there is little if any shared meaning between the so-called allusion and its mythological source. For example, Collins tries to show that the phrase "son of man" is an allusion to the imagery of the theophanies of Baal. His argument is that

> Baal is repeatedly called 'rider of the clouds' in the Ugaritic texts. He is, of course, a divine figure, but in the Canaanite pantheon he is subordinate to El, the father of the gods and human beings. El is called *abu shanima* in a Ugaritic text, a phrase that is most plausibly interpreted as 'father of years' and suggests that El is indeed the prototype for the Ancient of Days.[36]

The question is whether there is any meaning (denotative or connotative) shared between "the son of man" and Baal. The points of analogy raise serious problems biblically. Does Baal's relation to the physical clouds and rain have any shared meaning with the Son of Man's "coming with the clouds of heaven?" Does the Bible anywhere suggest that the Canaanite pantheon is a model for God's being? By contrast, is not the tenor of the Old Testament revelation that God is One? Is deity in a pagan sense to be in any way compared to deity in the biblical sense? Collins's argument must be rejected. There is no shared or analogous meanings between Yahweh and El or between the "son of man" and Baal. Consequently, great care must also be exercised in searching for mythological allusions that are not apparent in the text.

THE ROLE OF THE VISION CONTEXT

The vision itself is the determining context in the quest for meaning. A

36. Ibid., p. 81.

framework for working with this context is the assumption that the author *recorded* the vision in words that correspond to what he saw. This approach is in distinction to the assumption that the author *interpreted* the vision in words that correspond to his world view. If that were the case, the revealed meaning of the original revelation would be lost to subsequent interpreters. Postulating the former alternative, however, eliminates the prerogative for the interpreter to seek equivalents because it assumes the author's words are an accurate record of his vision.[37]

Within the context of the vision the clearest guide to its meaning is the statement of the divine interpreter.[38] Because the original author needed and recorded the divine interpretation, the modern interpreter would be wise to use it to determine as much as possible the limits of the meaning involved. Nothing in the vision can be unrelated to or in contradiction of the divine interpretation.

However, the divine interpretation may still leave questions unanswered—the fundamental question, for example: is this a symbolic or actual representation of the future reference? (Although the vision often includes symbols, it may also present a straightforward portrayal of the future.) An answer to that question may be found by further probing of the vision context. Two inquiries can be helpful. First, does the text provide any clues to distinguish between a symbol and a future reality in the vision? For instance, in the case of the "son of man" referred to above, there are clues that it is the actual rather than a symbolic representation. One is that the name "son of man" may be an allusion to the expectation of a "seed of the woman" (Gen. 3:15); it at least implies a human, male descendant. The other is that the son of man's role in the vision implies an equal status and shared role with the Ancient of Days: He is led into the presence of the Ancient of Days (an experience shared by no other man in the Old Testament); He receives authority, glory, and sovereign power from Him; and finally, the son of man receives worship, as God alone does, from all peoples, nations, and men of every language. These textual indications clearly show that in spite of his being separate from the Ancient of Days, the son of man is not subordinate to Him.[39] At times interpreters are unwilling to settle for the limitations of meaning imposed by the immediate context. They search for additional material, hoping to advance beyond the boun-

37. Berkley Mickelsen, *Interpreting the Bible* (Grand Rapids: Eerdmans), pp. 295-96.
38. Alexander, p. 1190.
39. Collins, p. 81.

daries of the textual clues. But this practice is clearly unacceptable exegetical practice.

Second, it may also be asked, in what way does this textual element correspond to the future reality? Where the textual clues are not transparent, this may be the only method for specifying what is otherwise vague in the vision. For example, are the horses coming from heaven actual horses with different colors (cf. Zech. 1:8; Rev. 6:2-8) or simply symbols of divine agents with the colors symbolizing their function or identity? Again, will the battle of Gog and Magog be fought with shields, bows, arrows, clubs, and spears (Ezek. 39:9)? One danger in answering such questions is that the interpreter may judge the correctness of his answer from his own world rather than from the world of the vision; so grasshoppers become helicopters (Rev. 9:1-6). These kinds of interpretations lack textual support and thus are generally without value. A better course of action is simply to interpret in the terms given in the vision. When the world and events to which the vision refers appear, believing participants will be in a much better position to weigh the reference. Another danger in answering such questions is that the interpreter may explain the reference solely on the basis of a preconceived theological perspective. Such an approach can skew an interpretation away from the text, particularly if the theological construct is called on to produce unwarranted generalizations.[40]

A final difficulty in handling apocalyptic literature to be considered concerns the meaning of numbers in the visions. There is nothing in the conventions of the genre nor in the presence of other symbols in the visions that necessarily leads to the view that all numbers are to be interpreted symbolically. Rather, each number must be examined in context to determine its use, whether it refers to a vision of the actual future (New Jerusalem with dimensions, Rev. 21:15-21) or to a vision of a symbol (Lamb with seven horns and seven eyes, Rev. 5:6).

CONCLUSION

The preceding examination has attempted to specify and clarify some of the hermeneutical issues of apocalyptic literature by examining apocalyptic genre in relation to the method of literal interpretation. Careful attention to the four components of apocalyptic literature marked out in this essay can help the interpreter find support for the validity of his interpreta-

40. Mickelsen, pp. 295-99.

tion and recognize his limits as an interpreter. A study of the various contexts (biblical, historical, cultural, and mythological) can contribute to clarity of interpretation and to the specification of support for an interpretation in apocalyptic literature.

EUGENE H. MERRILL (A.B., M.A., Ph.D.,
Bob Jones University; M.A., New York
University; M.Phil., Ph.D., Columbia Un-
iversity) is associate professor of Semitics
and Old Testament studies at Dallas
Theological Seminary.

Daniel as a Contribution to Kingdom Theology

Eugene H. Merrill

The resurgence of the biblical theology movement of the past thirty years or so has given rise to a host of issues attendant to that discipline, including the search for a center, or organizing principle, around which the biblical data might be ordered.[1] It is impossible here to enter into the vigorous debate about what that center might be or indeed whether there is any one framework sufficient to incorporate the multifaceted aspects of divine revelation in Scripture. It is the thesis of this article that such a center does exist and that it lies in the concept of the kingdom of God, the only concept broad enough to encompass the diversity of biblical faith without becoming so broad as to be tautological.

The standard theological rubrics, God, man, and their relationship, though appearing to some to be categories of systematic theology foisted on the biblical texts,[2] are necessary if one is to think and speak meaningful-ly about theological truth at all. To suggest that God is the sum and sub-stance of the biblical message is to say nothing helpful, for God in such a case is the subject without a predicate. God plus an intransitive verb is of little more assistance, for surely theology is not concerned only with who God is or even with what He does. It is concerned to tell us also something about the objects of His intentions and actions. That is, theology must

1. For a complete and up-to-date discussion of this problem of a center see Gerhard Hasel, *Old Testa-ment Theology: Basic Issues in the Current Debate,* 3d ed. (Grand Rapids: Eerdmans, 1982), pp. 117-43.
2. Walther Eichrodt, *Theology of the Old Testament* (Philadelphia: Westminster, 1961), 1:33-35.

make a statement about God (the subject) who acts (the verb) to achieve a comprehensive purpose (the object).[3]

If this is the case, not only would one expect that statement to be the interlocking and integrating principle observable throughout the fabric of biblical revelation, but he would also expect it to be enunciated early on in the canonical witness in unmistakable terms. Hence, Genesis should most likely provide the seed-bed in which the anticipated proposition is to be found. And a careful reading of that book of beginnings reveals a statement of purpose that is so striking in its clarity and authority that there can be little question it is the very formula we seek to establish the Bible's own theological center: "Then God [the subject] said, 'Let Us make [the verb] man [object] in Our image, according to Our likeness; and let them rule [purpose] over the fish of the sea and over the birds of the sky. . . .' God blessed them; and God said to them, 'Be fruitful and multiply, and fill the earth, and subdue it; and rule over the fish of the sea and over the birds of the sky, and over every living thing that moves on the earth" (Gen. 1:26-28).

The theme that emerges here is that of the sovereignty of God over all His creation, mediated through man, His vice-regent and image. Thus Genesis, the book of beginnings, introduces the purposes of God, which remain intact throughout the Old and New Testaments despite the sin of man and the impairment of his ability to be and do all that God had intended. The failings of His creation—a major theme of human history and of the Bible itself—are unable to frustrate the ultimate purposes of God, for the language of eschatology is replete with the overtones of redemption and salvation that bring about a renewal of all that God desired to do in creation. There will be a new heaven and a new earth wherein dwells righteousness (Rev. 21:1; cf. Isa. 65:17; 66:22).

Nowhere is the notion of divine kingship more clearly articulated than in Daniel. Here, if anywhere, the mighty purposes of God are announced and the means of their achievement spelled out in brilliant clarity. We turn, therefore, to consider Daniel as a contribution to kingdom theology.

THE HISTORICAL AND THEOLOGICAL SETTING OF DANIEL

The last quarter of the seventh century before Christ witnessed earth-shaking historical events of such a magnitude as hardly to find parallel in

---

3. See already Gustave F. Oehler, *Theology of the Old Testament,* trans. George E. Day (Grand Rapids: Zondervan, n.d.; reprint of 1883 English translation), pp. 14-16.

the long recital of human affairs. For five hundred years Assyria had been the undisputed master of the Near Eastern world and then suddenly, under the hammer blows of the Medes and Babylonians, began to crumble almost overnight. Credit for the meteoric rise of the Babylonians must go to Nabopolassar, who almost single-handedly delivered his people from Assyrian suzerain and established what history would describe as the Neo-Babylonian, or Chaldean, Empire.[4]

The beginning of this liberation movement must be dated to Nabopolassar's first year, 626 B.C.,[5] a date also of significance to the history of Judah. Josiah had begun to reign in 650[6] and by his twelfth year (628) commenced his work of reformation in Jerusalem (2 Chron. 34:3). Then in 622 a copy of the Mosaic law was found in the Temple in the process of its restoration, and the reformation took on the character of a great spiritual revival. This in itself would account for Josiah's aversion to the idolatrous Assyrians, for he was eager now to sever any alliances with them that his royal predecessors had established.[7] Politically, however, the time was also opportune, for Josiah knew full well of the rise of Nabopolassar and the threat that that posed to the Assyrian domination of the Mediterranean world.[8] Thus he cast his lot with the Babylonians and even died in the process of thwarting an attack on them by the Egyptians, who in 609 were moving north to Haran to deliver the remnant of the Assyrians from Babylonian annihilation.

With Josiah's death both the Babylonian alliance and the renewed spiritual life of Judah began to disintegrate. His three sons and grandson who succeeded him were by and large disloyal to Nabopolassar and his son and successor Nebuchadnezzar, primarily because they believed their future was more secure with the neighboring Egyptians than with the distant Babylonians. This would prove to be a tactical error of enormous proportions. More serious, however, was the wholesale apostasy of the nation in its last twenty-three years under Josiah's descendants. Destruction by the Babylonians was not a foregone conclusion by virtue of Judah's political in-

4. A good survey of this period may be found in William H. Hallo, "From Qarqar to Carchemish: Assyria and Israel in the Light of New Discoveries," *Biblical Archaeologist* 23 (1960):33-61. For the texts see D. J. Wiseman, *Chronicles of Chaldean Kings (626-556 B.C.) in the British Museum* (London: British Museum, 1961), pp. 50-67.
5. Wiseman, pp. 5-7.
6. These dates follow Edwin R. Thiele, *The Mysterious Numbers of the Hebrew Kings* (Grand Rapids: Eerdmans, 1965), p. 163.
7. Thus Siegfried Herrmann, *A History of Israel in Old Testament Times* (Philadelphia: Fortress, 1975), pp. 265-71.
8. Abraham Malamat, "Josiah's Bid for Armageddon," *Journal of the Ancient Near Eastern Studies* 5 (1973):273.

discretions alone, for the Lord could have preserved her against any odds. What brought her to her knees, and to destruction and exile as well, was her persistent violation of her covenant commitment to her God, a violation attested by all the contemporary prophets.

It is no wonder, then, that Judah began to experience Babylon as a mighty rod of the Lord within four years of Josiah's death. Jehoiakim, the king of Judah, had become a vassal of Pharaoh Necho of Egypt since Josiah's death in 609. By 605 Egypt engaged the Babylonians at the decisive battle of Carchemish on the Euphrates River, an encounter that drove Egypt south of the river and out of Palestine.[9] Before Nebuchadnezzar could follow up his smashing victory by penetrating Egypt itself, he was forced to return to Babylon to secure the throne vacated by his father, who had died shortly after the Carchemish conflict had taken place.[10] He did not return empty handed, however, for en route he forced Jerusalem to submit and took prisoner certain of the Jewish royalty and nobility, including a youth named Daniel.[11]

Succeeding campaigns resulted in the deportation of Jehoiachin in 597 and the death of Zedekiah and the termination of the Jewish state as a viable and independent entity in 586. Most tragic of all, the Temple was destroyed; and with its destruction came an end to the religious life and immediate covenant hopes of the people. Only the promises of restoration and renewal sustained those in exile and the remnant at home who had faith in the eternal nature of the Lord's commitment to them.

Daniel thus found himself far from home in a strange land of strange customs. He, along with other choice young men, had been brought to the capital city of the empire, Babylon itself. There he was placed under Ashpenaz, a palace official, given a Babylonian name, and taught the arts and sciences for which the Babylonians were justly famous throughout the world. In spite of his refusal to compromise his devotion to Yahweh and adopt wholesale the life-style of his captors, Daniel rose to positions of

9. Wiseman, p. 25.
10. The battle occurred in May-June, 605. Nabopolassar died on the eighth of Ab (August 15/16, 605), and Nebuchadnezzar returned to Babylon and ascended the throne by the first of Elul (September 6/7, 605). See Wiseman, pp. 25-27.
11. According to Daniel 1:1 this deportation occurred in the third year of Jehoiakim, whereas Jeremiah 25:1 dates it in that king's fourth year. Both must refer to 605, the year of Nebuchadnezzar's first conquest of Jerusalem. As Thiele shows (*Mysterious Numbers*, p. 166), the apparent contradiction is easily resolved by recognizing that Daniel is employing the Babylonian system whereas Jeremiah uses the Palestinian system. See also A. R. Millard, "Daniel 1-6 and History," *Evangelical Quarterly* 49 (1977):67-73; Gehard F. Hasel, "The Book of Daniel: Evidences Relating to Persons and Chronology," *Andrews University Seminary Studies* 19 (1981):48-49.

great power and influence under Nebuchadnezzar, the king under whom he would serve until the king's death in 562 B.C. Even thereafter he rose from one position of authority to the next, outlasting the empire itself. When Cyrus the Persian overcame Nabonidus, the last of the Neo-Babylonians, in 539, Daniel survived and in recognition of his incomparable qualities of integrity and statesmanship was made a chief minister in the new Persian government. This post he held until at least the third year of Cyrus, the last datable reference to Daniel in the biblical record (Dan. 10:1). He therefore had spent nearly seventy years in exile,[12] becoming as intimately acquainted with the inner workings of human political institutions and power as it was possible to become.

All this has been discussed in some detail because it is necessary to know something of Daniel's vantage-point in determining his assessment of the kingdoms of the world and their relationship to kingdom theology. Surely his particular contribution has much to do with the geographical, historical, and even theological circumstances in which he found himself. On the human level the Jewish exiles, Daniel included, must have been profoundly impressed by all they saw in Babylon. Having come from a tiny, largely agricultural nation that for the most part had suffered decades of devastation and neglect, they arrived in Babylon at the zenith of that city's glory. It was the center of an empire that stretched from Iran to the Mediterranean, from the Persian Gulf to central Anatolia. To it flowed the wealth of conquered nations, wealth expended on the building of massive and strikingly beautiful temples and palaces. Broad boulevards paved with inscribed bricks traversed the city, and surrounding the whole were impregnable walls whose height and thickness were the amazement of the entire world.[13]

Even more impressive to the Jewish community than all this was the pomp and pageantry associated with the Babylonian cult. Centered in the worship of Marduk and his son Nabu, the religious processions and festivities were overwhelming in their display of wealth and power.[14] To the ob-

---

12. The third year of Cyrus, according to the Tishri-to-Tishri calendar used by Daniel, would fall in 535 B.C. He thus may have lived in Babylonian-Persian exile for exactly 70 years. See William H. Shea, "Wrestling with the Prince of Persia: A Study on Daniel 10," *Andrews University Seminary Studies* 21 (1983):225-28.
13. For an eyewitness account see Herodotus 1. 178, 182-83, Aubrey de Selincourt, trans., *Herodotus: The Histories* (Harmondsworth, England: Penguin, 1972). Archaeological support for this is abundant. See especially the excavators' report in R. Koldewey, *The Excavations at Babylon* (London: Macmillan, 1914).
14. James Muilenburg, "The Book of Isaiah, Chapters 40-66," in *The Interpreter's Bible*, 12 vols., ed. G. A. Buttrick et al. (New York: Abingdon, 1956), 5:397.

jective observer it must have seemed that the gods so revered were indeed the mightiest of gods, for the kingdom that sustained them was itself the ruler of the world. Conversely, how could it be that Yahweh, the God of Israel, retained any credibility at all, for at best He had been God of an insignificant nation and now with His people had been shamelessly defeated and exiled? In short, in what sense could there be a kingdom of God involving the people of the covenant in view of the stupendous kingdoms of the world to which these elect people were now enslaved?

A LITERARY-STRUCTURAL ANALYSIS OF DANIEL

Old Testament scholars are in general agreement that the book of Daniel should be divided into two main sections, chapters 1-6 consisting primarily of historical narration and 7-12 of visions concerning the future kingdoms of the world and that of the Lord.[15] The first half, then, consists of Daniel's firsthand[16] observation of the titanic power and influence of the kingdoms of Babylonia and Persia and the absorption into that structure of the exilic people of the Lord. He himself, though greatly elevated in both governments, was still the slave of a system that was anti-God and totally oblivious to Yahweh's creation and covenant claims on the earth. Israel, like Jonah, had been swallowed up by the great fish of international imperialism.

In chapters 7-12 the awesomeness of the coming kingdoms of the world is still a prominent theme, but increasingly there is the counter-theme of the kingdom of God, a kingdom that gradually achieves prominence in divine revelation but that radically and unexpectedly breaks into human history and replaces the kingdoms of men with His eternal sovereignty. Daniel therefore sees a day in which Israel, far from being trodden under the feet of men, will become a part of the sovereign plan of divine dominion in which all kingdoms and nations will yield in submission to the Lord.

These themes of universal dominion precipitated by direct divine inter-

---

15. David W. Gooding, "The Literary Structure of the Book of Daniel and Its Implications," *Tyndale Bulletin* 32 (1981):48-51.
16. It is impossible here to enter into the debate as to the authorship and dating of Daniel. A sixth-century composition by the traditional Daniel is defensible from every viewpoint; the alternative, a second-century work of pseudonymous origin, is usually maintained only on dogmatic grounds, that is, the impossibility of detailed predictive prophecy. For support of the early date see Gordon J. Wenham, "Daniel: The Basic Issues," *Themelios* 2 (1977):49-52; Edwin M. Yamauchi, "Daniel and Contacts Between the Aegean and the Near East Before Alexander," *Evangelical Quarterly* 53 (1981):37-47; Arthur J. Ferch, "The Book of Daniel and the 'Maccabean Thesis,' " *Andrews University Studies* 21 (1983):129-41.

vention in human affairs are characteristic of apocalyptic language and literature. Characteristic also is the notion that these are not events that one should expect to be fulfilled in the near future and in the normal course of events. Rather, they must await the "last days," the eschaton that God Himself will introduce.[17] In New Testament terms, these are events associated with the second advent of Jesus Christ in which the kingdoms of this world will become the kingdom of our God and of His Christ.

THE SIGNIFICANCE OF THE KINGDOM IN DANIEL

The major burden of the book of Daniel is the tension and conflict between the kingdom of God and the kingdoms of this world.[18] God had called His people to be a kingdom of priests (Ex. 19:1-6), He had prepared the way for them to establish a monarchial structure historically (Deut. 17:14-20), and He had brought this to pass in the Davidic dynasty. Beyond this, the promise throughout the Bible is in kingdom terms. The Lord will rule over all the earth forever in and through His elect and redeemed saints.

Attached to kingdom promises and blessings, however, are kingdom curses. The same covenant that brought Israel into existence as a nation and kingdom and that promised blessing for faithful obedience to the Lord as the Great King stipulated the results of disobedience and defection as well. This particularly would take the form of the destruction of the state and temple and the exile of the people. All the prophets from Moses through Jeremiah attested to this.[19]

Daniel, living after the fact, witnessed and in fact participated in the dissolution of the Davidic kingdom and its assimilation into Babylonia, the kingdom of men par excellence. That he was keenly aware that this was the judgment of God predicted by the prophets of old is clear from his observation that "the Lord gave Jehoiakim king of Judah into [Nebuchadnezzar's] hand" (Dan. 1:2). Moreover, Daniel himself was a member of Judah's

---

17. Important studies of the literary genre *apocalyptic* are by S. B. Frost, *Old Testament Apocalyptic: Its Origin and Growth* (London: Epworth, 1952); P. D. Hanson, *The Dawn of Apocalyptic* (Philadelphia: Fortress, 1975); H. H. Rowley, *The Revelation of Apocalyptic* (New York: Association, 1963); D. S. Russell, *The Method and Message of Jewish Apocalyptic, 200 B.C.-A.D. 100* (Philadelphia: Westminster, 1964).

18. Lourdino A. Yuzon, "The Kingdom of God in Daniel," *South East Asia Journal of Theology* 19 (1978):23-27.

19. Exodus 23:20-33; Leviticus 26; Deuteronomy 27-28; Joshua 24:19-28; Isaiah 63:18; Jeremiah 44:2; etc.

royalty and so represented the effective termination of the royal Davidic house (1:3).

Later on, under Belshazzar, that impious king ate and drank from the holy vessels of the Temple of Yahweh at the orgy on the night that Babylon fell to Cyrus (5:2-3). This desecration of the holy things of God pointedly reminded Daniel and his people that the religious life of Israel as well as the political had yielded to pagan sovereignty, at least for a while.

It is in Daniel's famous prayer of 9:4-19, however, that the theological meaning of the exile is best articulated. In language reminiscent of that describing the fall of Samaria more than 180 years earlier, Daniel confesses his sin and that of his people and recognizes that the exile is God's just punishment for their covenant infidelity (9:7-8, 10). In fact, he says, "the curse has been poured out on us, along with the oath which is written in the law of Moses, for we have sinned against Him" (9:11). Then, in a desperate appeal to God's mercy (9:18), he prays that Yahweh might effect redemption once again as He did long ago in the exodus from Egypt. The implication is crystal clear: Israel had once been redeemed and made the kingdom of God; now the prayer is that history might be repeated.

That Babylonia and Persia were mighty kingdoms Daniel does not deny. In Nebuchadnezzar's dream he is described as "that head of gold" (2:38). In another dream, that of the tree, the Babylonian monarch is identified by Daniel as that very tree, which has become great and strong. The prophet concedes that "your majesty has become great and reached to the sky and your dominion to the end of the earth" (4:22). Nebuchadnezzar also recognizes the might of his domain, and though he boasts of "Babylon the great" (4:30) and "the glory of my kingdom" (4:36), there seems little reason to discount his claims.

Daniel is not impressed with the boastings of men no matter how mighty and is careful to counterbalance their claims with the profound theological truth—and this is really at the heart of "kingdom theology"—that God is sovereign and that kings and nations exist as an extension of His grace. In fact, they exist to serve His overarching and ultimate purposes for all creation.

In his prayer for wisdom to interpret Nebuchadnezzar's dream of the image, Daniel confesses that God "changes the times and the epochs; He removes kings and establishes kings" (2:21). And then he boldly says to the king himself, "You, O king, are the king of kings, to whom the God of heaven has given the kingdom, the power, the strength, and the glory; and wherever the sons of men dwell, or the beasts of the field, or the birds of the sky, He has given them into your hand and has caused you to rule over them all" (2:37-38).

As he was about to interpret the second dream for Nebuchadnezzar, Daniel reminded the king that "this sentence is by the decree of the angelic watchers, and the decision is a command of the holy ones, in order that the living may know that the Most High is ruler over the realm of mankind, and bestows it on whom He wishes, and sets over it the lowliest of men" (4:17). The reduction of Nebuchadnezzar to a state of bestiality,[20] the content of that dream, was for the purpose of causing the king to "recognize that the Most High is ruler over the realm of mankind, and bestows it on whomever He wishes" (4:25-26; cf. vv. 31-32).

Belshazzar, the royal successor to Nebuchadnezzar, learned also that the mighty Babylonian had reigned only because "the Most High God granted sovereignty, grandeur, glory, and majesty to Nebuchadnezzar your father" (5:18) and it was only after he recognized that his kingship came from God that he was restored from his madness (5:21). As for Belshazzar, he was about to lose his kingdom and his life because, as Daniel put it, "the God in whose hand are your life-breath and your ways, you have not glorified" (5:23).

Though there is no indisputable evidence that Nebuchadnezzar, Belshazzar, or any of the Medo-Persian kings came to true faith in Yahweh as their God,[21] they did give verbal assent to the claims Daniel made for Yahweh and, in fact, must have at least elevated Him to their pantheon. Following the interpretation of his first dream, Nebuchadnezzar professed, "Surely your God is a God of gods and a Lord of kings and a revealer of mysteries, since you have been able to reveal this mystery" (2:47). Admittedly, the extravagant language may be a diplomatic way of commending Daniel himself rather than his God, but this does not seem to be the case following the miraculous deliverance of the three Jewish young men from the blazing furnace. When he saw that they were alive, Nebuchadnezzar was forced to admit that "there is no other god who is able to deliver in this way" (3:29).

---

20. Nebuchadnezzar's madness, a tale usually associated by the critics with the Qumranian text "The Prayer of Nabonidus," now finds apparent confirmation in a British Museum table published by A. K. Grayson in *Babylonian Historical-Literary Texts* (Toronto: U. of Toronto, 1975), pp. 87-92. For its content and meaning see Hasel, "The Book of Daniel: Evidences Relating to Persons and Chronology," pp. 38-42.

21. As Joyce Baldwin points out in *Daniel, An Introduction and Commentary* (Leicester: Inter-Varsity, 1978), p. 95., "the king is not committing himself to the notion of one true God, as Daniel no doubt realized. As a polytheist he can always add another to the deities he worships."

Even more significant is the royal public proclamation in which it is said of Yahweh: "How great are His signs, and how mighty are His wonders! His kingdom is an everlasting kingdom and His dominion is from generation to generation" (4:3). In the same proclamation, a testimony given following the king's restoration from madness, Nebuchadnezzar acknowledged that Yahweh "does according to His will in the host of heaven and among the inhabitants of earth. And no one can ward off his hand or say to Him: 'What hast Thou done?'" (4:35). From bitter experience he learned that "He is able to humble those who walk in pride" (4:37).

Darius, king of Medo-Persia,[22] also learned that lesson. After Daniel was delivered from the den of lions, that potentate was forced to concede that the God of Daniel "is the living God and enduring forever, and His kingdom is one which will not be destroyed, and His dominion will be forever. He delivers and rescues and performs signs and wonders in heaven and on earth" (6:26). There was thus a recognition by the kings with whom Daniel had contact that Yahweh, the God of Israel, was the God of the whole earth, the omnipotent One by virtue of whose permission even they occupied their thrones.

Although this truth may have been preached by Daniel and even occasionally confessed by the kings whom he served, there was nonetheless an uneasy sense of coexistence between the kingdoms of men and that of the Lord. Nebuchadnezzar and Darius knew full well that Yahweh was supreme above all, but they were not about to surrender their crowns to him and abdicate their kingdom to the kingdom of heaven. Judah, Yahweh's earthly kingdom, had after all suffered ignominious defeat at Babylonian hands and was clearly an inferior power in every way.

On the other hand, the very elevation of Daniel to a position of authority in both the Babylonian and Persian governments[23] appears to represent a tacit confession by their kings that Daniel the Jew, an ambassador of the kingdom of Judah (and of Yahweh), was entitled to special consideration. Hard upon his interpretation of Nebuchadnezzar's first dream, and cer-

---

22. John C. Whitcomb and others have argued vigorously to equate Darius the Mede with Gubaru, governor of Babylon. It seems best to accept this view rather than the position of D. J. Wiseman that Darius is none other than Cyrus himself. See respectively Whitcomb, *Darius the Mede* (Grand Rapids: Baker, 1959), pp. 64-67; Wiseman, "Some Historical Problems in the Book of Daniel," *Notes on Some Problems in the Book of Daniel*, ed. D. J. Wiseman, et al. (London: Tyndale, 1965), pp. 9-16; and now (in support of Whitcomb's Gubaru but with another Gubaru in mind) William H. Shea, "Darius the Mede: An Update," *Andrews University Seminary Studies* 20 (1982):229-47.

23. For the historical likelihood of this and its place in the Babylonian-Persian chronologies see William H. Shea, "A Further Note on Daniel 6: Daniel As 'Governor,'" *Andrews University Seminary Studies* 21 (1983):169-71.

tainly because he had been able to do so through the power of his God, Daniel was made "ruler over the whole province of Babylon" (2:48). The king's motives here are more than merely utilitarian. He is interested in merging the kingdom of God with his own, at least to the extent of allowing its ambassador to serve in his own administration.

Of far greater importance is Daniel's own understanding of the relationship of the kingdoms of this world to the kingdom of his God. Though previous revelation had made it clear that the Lord, creator of all things, was, is, and will be King of kings and Lord of lords, nowhere is this specified as clearly as in Daniel's dreams and visions. In fact, it is safe to say that it is in this very revelation that the theology of Daniel must be centered. In the language of apocalyptic the prophet foresees the course of world history that finds its commencement in his own times and its culmination in the eschatological kingdom of God.

Ironically, this theme finds expression first of all in the dream of the pagan king Nebuchadnezzar (2:31-35). He saw a great statue whose various sections in ascending order were made of iron mixed with clay, iron, bronze, silver, and gold. Daniel identified Nebuchadnezzar himself as the head of gold, that is, his kingdom was at the very top and appeared first in the unfolding of human history from that time forward. There can be no question that that kingdom is Babylonia.

Next in order and inferior to the kingdom of Nebuchadnezzar is the silver kingdom. Though many scholars, for reasons other than objective historical necessity, identify this as the kingdom of the Medes,[24] that is impossible on historical grounds, for the Median kingdom had ceased to function as an independent entity by 539 B.C., the date of the fall of Babylon. The silver kingdom can only be that of Persia, which prevailed from 539 to 331 B.C. The only possible interpretation of the third kingdom, the even more inferior bronze, is that it is Greece, for Persian domination of the Near Eastern world was wrested from her violently by Alexander of Macedon. The fourth kingdom, that of iron, is Rome, for only Rome can in any valid historical sense be the successor to Greece.[25] Though inferior to the other metals in intrinsic terms, iron is incomparably stronger and so, Daniel predicts, this fourth kingdom will "crush and break all these in pieces" (2:40).

The kingdom that follows, that made of iron mingled with clay, is differ-

24. So, e.g., Robert J. M.Gurney, "The Four Kingdoms of Daniel 2 and 7," *Themelois* 2 (1977):39-52.
25. Baldwin, p. 162.

ent from Rome and yet derived from her. As Daniel says, this will be a divided kingdom with both of its parts partly strong and partly brittle. History suggests that this finds fulfillment in the division of the Roman Empire into its eastern and western elements, the ten toes becoming extensions of those elements in the form of ten subsequent kingdoms.[26]

Finally, however, these kingdoms are brought to a decisive and dramatic end by the intervention of the kingdom of God. This cannot be the church because the church appeared in history contemporaneous with the rise of the Roman Empire and not after its fall and division into two and then ten parts. It is, to quote the prophet, "a stone . . . cut out of the mountain without hands" (2:45). That is, it is the kingdom that God Himself will establish and that will intercept and replace the stream of human sovereignties.

Daniel's own dream of the four great beasts (Daniel 7) confirms and clarifies that of Nebuchadnezzar. The first three fearsome animals, the lion, bear, and leopard, represent respectively the kingdoms of Babylonia, Persia, and Greece, all of which had arisen on the historical scene to such an extent that they lay within Daniel's sixth century purview. The fourth, however, was unlike anything he had ever seen before. Its iron teeth and ten horns removed it from the realm of contemporary identification and projected it to the distant (to Daniel) future. The iron and the number 10 are obviously to be compared to the same motifs of the fourth kingdom of Daniel 2, that is, the kingdom of Rome.[27]

This awesome kingdom, too, was crushed by the advent of the kingdom of God. This time, however, the king of one of the ten horns, that is, of one of the extensions of the Roman Empire, rose up with boasting words and waged war against the saints of God until it seemed they would be destroyed (7:8, 11, 21). Before this could happen the Ancient of Days[28] took His place on His throne and, immersed in His awful glory, undertook the judgment of the kingdoms, a judgment that resulted in the introduction of "One like a Son of Man"[29] (7:13) who "was given dominion, glory, and a

26. John F. Walvoord, *Daniel: The Key to Prophetic Revelation* (Chicago: Moody, 1971), pp. 71-75.
27. Baldwin, p. 140.
28. Clearly a reference to God. See, e.g., Louis F. Hartman and Alexander A. DiLella, *The Book of Daniel*, The Anchor Bible (Garden City: Doubleday, 1978), p. 217.
29. In terms of Old Testament theology alone one is hesitant to identify this figure as messianic. New Testament revelation, however, makes the identification certain. Robert D. Rowe, "Is Daniel's 'Son of Man' Messianic?" *Christ the Lord*, ed. Harold H. Rowdon (Leicester: Inter-Varsity, 1982), pp. 94-96, uses the helpful term *proto-incarnational* to describe this heavenly being, one with whom Jesus identified Himself (Mark 14:62). For a thorough discussion of the "son of man" concept in Daniel see Arthur J. Ferch, *The Apocalyptic "Son of Man" in Daniel 7* (Ph.D. dissertation, Andrews University, 1979), pp. 158-74.

kingdom" (7:14). His dominion will last forever and will be exercised through the saints of God,[30] the rulers of all nations of the earth (7:27). The kingdom of the Lord that, as expressed by Israel and Judah, had become the vassal people of pagan kingdoms will in turn become the sovereign extension of the rule of God and will hold sway over all men for all time.

Confirmation of the identification of the kingdoms listed in the sequences of the dreams of Daniel 2 and 7 is found in the vision of chapter 8. That revelation, given in Belshazzar's third year (8:1),[31] consists of a series of animals and horns representing the kingdoms of men yet to come. The first, the ram with a longer and shorter horn, is the Medo-Persian empire. There is no distinction between the two kingdoms except that one (the longer horn) grew out later than the other (the shorter horn). Thus, the Medo-Persian empire had begun with the Medes but was eventually superseded by the Persians.[32] From Daniel's standpoint the end of the Babylonian hegemony was already a foregone conclusion, so he begins this series with what was the second kingdom in the previous revelations, Medo-Persia.

This kingdom became great but was suddenly attacked by one symbolized by the goat with the horn between its eyes. Before long, however, the horn was itself broken and replaced with four others (8:8). Out of one of these horns grew yet another horn, which fomented rebellion against the holy people of the Lord and brought about an end of Temple worship. This kingdom and its offshoots, Daniel is informed, is Greece. The horn between its eyes is clearly Alexander, the four horns that take his place were the rulers of the partitioned Macedonian Empire, and the rebellious horn was none other than the Seleucid king Antiochus Epiphanes, who desecrated the second Temple in the days of the Maccabees.[33] This master of intrigue (8:23), who rises to prominence through the offices of another higher authority, will "even oppose the the Prince of princes" (8:25) but will himself be destroyed by divine judgment. Gabriel's word to Daniel that this vision concerns "the time of the end" (8:17) is sufficient to indicate that Antiochus alone cannot be its fulfillment, for the language is eschato-

30. Vern S. Poythress, "The Holy Ones of the Most High in Daniel VII," *Vetus Testamentum* 26 (1976):213, correctly identifies the "holy ones" of Daniel 7:18, 22, 25, and 27 as "eschatological faithful Israel."
31. This would be 548/547 B.C., or only two years after Cyrus claimed sovereignty over Medo-Persia. He had already begun his rapid conquests to which the vision of Daniel 8 testifies. For chronological detail see Hasel, "The Book of Daniel: Evidences Relating to Persons and Chronology," pp. 43-44.
32. A. T. Olmstead, *History of the Persian Empire* (Chicago: U. of Chicago, 1948), pp. 36-38.
33. Virtually all scholars accept this identification, though most do so only on the assumption that the author of the passage was contemporary with or posterior to Antiochus. So Raymond Hammer, *The Book of Daniel* (Cambridge: Cambridge U., 1976), pp. 4-5.

logical. There yet remains a rebellious horn that will seek to subvert the kingdom of God.

The clearest evidence for this is in Daniel's second vision, which came to him after Babylon's fall in the third year of Cyrus (10:1). In detail so remarkable that critical scholars must relegate it to *vaticinia ex eventu,* the Lord himself revealed to Daniel the progress of the kingdoms of Persia and Greece until their disintegration and division (11:2-4). Then, in even greater detail, the interrelationship between two parts of the erstwhile Macedonian Empire, the Seleucid and Ptolemaic dynasties, is recounted from the time of its fragmentation in 323 until the death of the infamous Seleucid Antiochus Epiphanes in 164 B.C. (11:5-35). There is no question that it is he who is described as the "despicable person" who rose to power without the benefit of royal ancestry (11:21-35).[34] Careful comparison of this person to the one described in Daniel 8:20-26 as the rebellious horn reveals that they are one and the same.

The second vision goes on, however, to speak of this despot in terms that exceed even his capacity for evil (11:36-45). He will launch a campaign of unparalleled rebellion against the Lord God and will even seek to elevate himself to deity. His success will be short-lived, however, for he will be set upon by other kings and hemmed in by them to the narrow confines of the Holy Land. At last he will come to his end, helpless and unaided.

That this evil ruler transcends Antiochus[35] is clear from the fact that he is placed by the vision "at the time of the end" (11:40), a phrase reserved for eschatological times. Moreover, his career is linked to the time of the unprecedented distress (12:1), a tribulation to be followed by resurrection (12:2-3), by the phrase "at that time" (12:1). Clearly, the eschatological dimensions of the tribulation and resurrection passage must apply to the reign of terror of the king described in Daniel 11:36-45. Without going into the full argument here, it is safe to conclude with many scholars that this king of blasphemies is none other than the Antichrist of subsequent revelation.[36] It is he who gives final expression to the effort of human kingship to contend with that of God. His destruction, followed by that of the arch-enemy Satan, sounds the death-knell of every kingdom that fails to recognize and submit to the sovereign lordship of the King of kings and Lord of lords.

---

34. Hartman and DiLella, p. 295.
35. Gooding, pp. 72-79; Wenham, p. 51.
36. J. Dwight Pentecost, *Things to Come* (Findlay, Ohio: Dunham, 1958), pp. 321-23; Eugene H. Merrill, "Antichrist in the Book of Daniel," *Henceforth* 3 (1974):13-21.

CONCLUSION

The sovereignty of God and its expression through the rule of men over all creation is the single theme most able to encompass and integrate the rich diversity of truth revealed in Holy Scripture. The task of biblical theology is both to demonstrate and apply this premise to the task of exegesis and hermeneutics. If the premise be granted, it follows that each part of the divine revelation was composed to contribute to this theme, which, conversely, must elucidate the meaning of each part.

It is not difficult to see that Daniel more than almost any other author is concerned with the kingdom theme. He was a Jewish exile who witnessed the beginning of the end of his own Jewish kingdom, who rose to the very highest eschelons of power and privilege in the kingdoms of Babylonia and Persia, and who nonetheless recognized the tensions between those kingdoms and the kingdom of God of which he was an ambassador first and foremost. Nowhere in all the Bible are the lines more clearly drawn and the issues more dramatically set forth: human kingdoms, though impressive and powerful, will rise and fall; such is the pattern of history past and history yet to come. Still, God is on His throne and in and through historical events demonstrates His sovereignty, even if in hidden ways. The day will come, however, when that sovereignty will not be exercised permissively and secretly. God Himself will destroy the kingdoms of men, will sit in glory and power upon the throne of the universe, and will rule over all creation through His saints whom He has elected and redeemed for that very purpose. This is Daniel's burden. It is his contribution to kingdom theology.

JOHN F. WALVOORD (A.B., Wheaton College; M.A., Texas Christian University; Th.M., Th.D., Dallas Theological Seminary; D.D., Wheaton College; Litt.D., Liberty Baptist College) is chancellor and professor of systematic theology at Dallas Theological Seminary.

The Theological Significance of Revelation 20:1-6

John F. Walvoord

Few verses in the Bible are more crucial to the interpretation of the Bible as a whole than the opening verses in Revelation 20. They are determinative in their support or contradiction of the three major millennial views: postmillennialism, amillennialism, and premillennialism. They are of vital importance to the doctrine of the righteousness of God and His ultimate triumph over evil. They relate pointedly to the question of the resurrection of both the righteous and the wicked. Further, they are essential to the doctrine of satanology, that is, the present power and program of Satan as well as his destiny.

In view of the importance of this passage of Scripture, it is unfortunate that scholars of almost all points of view have been needlessly dogmatic in attempting to settle what it teaches or does not teach. Even the best of scholars seem to come to a crucial point and settle the question by a dogmatic statement. Seldom is the passage allowed to be its own statement of truth. Anyone who attempts to explain this portion of Scripture should be cautious both in his explanation of what the passage does state as well as what it does not state.

THE CONTEXT

These verses lie in an important context that portrays the second coming of Jesus Christ. All major conservative theological views agree that chapter 19 is the graphic description of Christ coming from heaven to earth to judge the world and to bring righteousness to bear upon the human situation. Chapter 19 is clearly climactic to the great events that precede in the revelation given to John. Following all the evil course of the beast and the false prophet, the armies that are gathered by demons, acting as the emissaries of Satan in Revelation 16:13-16, are described as destroyed (Rev. 19:17-18, 21). At the time of their destruction the beast who is the world ruler and the false prophet who is associated with him are captured and thrown alive into the lake of fire (Rev. 19:20). The revelation of the entire chapter 19 is sequential in time and describes cause and effect in action. Most verses are connected by the simple conjunction *kai*, usually translated "and." The temporal sequence is not simply in the time of revelation but also in the action described. For these reasons it would be normal to assume that chapter 20, a human division that is not part of the original text, should continue the sequential and causal relationship of the events. In other words, what is described in chapter 20 is another result of the second coming of Christ, sequential in point of time and causal in the sense that Christ's power brings it to pass.

The sequential character of chapter 20 is denied by postmillenarians, who believe the second coming of Christ follows the Millennium, and by most amillenarians, who consider chapter 20 a recapitulation of the church's history beginning with the first coming of Christ. The matter is usually settled, however, dogmatically. Henry B. Swete, for instance, without any supporting data states, "It must not, therefore, be assumed that the events now to be described chronologically followed the destruction of the Beast and the False Prophet and their army."[1] Likewise, Leon Morris, after explaining the various approaches of different millennial views, states that John "does not mention the second advent in this chapter at all. . . . It appears that John is simply taking us behind the scenes as he has done so often before. . . . John says nothing to place this chapter in the time sequence."[2]

Even Robert H. Mounce, a premillenarian, states of this passage "that it contains no specific indication that their reign with Christ takes place on earth or that it necessarily follows the second advent."[3] The obvious purpose of denying connection between chapters 19 and 20 is to avoid settling

1. Henry B. Swete, *The Apocalypse of St. John* (Grand Rapids: Eerdmans, n.d.), p. 259.
2. Leon Morris, *The Revelation of St. John,* Tyndale New Testament Commentaries (Grand Rapids: Eerdmans, 1969), pp. 234-35.
3. Robert H. Mounce, *The Book of Revelation,* The New International Commentary on the New Testament (Grand Rapids: Eerdmans, 1977), p. 351.

the main question of whether this passage supports the premillennial or other millennial views. All these writers completely overlook the grammatical evidence in that the verses are connected by the simple conjunction *kai,* or "and," which would normally indicate sequence chronologically. Though it is clear that some chapters of Revelation are not in chronological sequence, there is a causal factor in this section in that all the events of chapters 19 and 20 result from the second coming of Christ and would be impossible without it. The sequential order of the events is also supported by the expression "I saw" that appears frequently in the narrative (Rev. 19:11, 17, 19; 20:1, 4, 11, 12). The events described are also a natural consequence of the power and presence of Christ at His second coming. Under these circumstances it would be proper to request proof that chapter 20 is not sequential chronologically to chapter 19.

An overview of the book of Revelation as a whole, however, would seem to point rather clearly to the sequential character of chapter 20. All of the preceding chapters up to Revelation 19:10 describe graphically the events leading up to the second coming. The second coming itself occupies Revelation 19 and is obviously the high point of the book. Having discussed in great detail the events leading up to it, it would be only natural for the revelation now to concern itself with the aftermath of the second coming. Chapter 19 identifies two major events: the destruction of the armies and the casting of the beast and the false prophet into the lake of fire. The next step would be to deal with Satan, who has been the power behind their government. It would take the strongest kind of evidence to interrupt this narrative and swing back to the first coming of Christ, which has not been the subject of the book as a whole and would in large measure be extraneous to the progress of thought in Revelation.

Most of the problem, however, is in the dogmatic statement that the passage means this or does not mean that when the text itself does not support it. This will be brought out in the exegesis of the passage itself.

THE BINDING OF SATAN

In Revelation 20:1-3 John has a vision of the binding of Satan. Scholars of all classifications tend to come to this passage with their minds made up that it must conform to their preceding conclusions. Seldom is the passage allowed to stand on its own statement.

In opening this section John simply declares, "And I saw an angel coming down from heaven, having the key to the abyss and a great chain in his hand" (Rev. 20:1). The abyss that is mentioned is referred to earlier in Revelation 9:1, 2, 11; 11:7; and 17:8. It is described as the home of the demon world and of Satan himself.

The angel is said to have the key to the abyss and a great chain in his hand. It should be obvious that it would take a great chain to control one as powerful as Satan. Paul refers to himself in Acts 28:20 as being bound with a chain and declares himself not to be ashamed of his chain in 2 Timothy 1:16. Numerous Hebrew and Greek words are used to describe chains or methods of confinement of a prisoner. Even if taken symbolically, reference to the chain in this passage indicates Satan is being bound. The abyss is in contrast, however, to the "lake of fire which burns with brimstone" (Rev. 19:20) into which the beast and the false prophet are cast. The abyss is a place of confinement rather than of punishment.

In verse 2 the angel "laid hold of the dragon, the serpent of old, who is the devil and Satan, and bound him for a thousand years." Verse 3 adds, he "threw him into the abyss, and shut it and sealed it over him, so that he should not deceive the nations any longer, until the thousand years were completed; after these things he must be released for a short time." Amillenarians, in anticipation of their denial that this occurs at the second coming of Christ, with one voice declare the passage symbolical. Morris states, for instance, "Both are clearly symbolical for there cannot be a key to the abyss, nor can a spirit be shackled with a chain."[4]

Obviously John is seeing a vision, but the vision is intended to have meaning. Even symbolically the key would necessarily indicate that the angel has authority to close the opening of the abyss, and the chain would also indicate that he has power to control and restrict the activity of Satan. Because a passage is symbolical does not mean that it does not have a real meaning. Accordingly it is futile to point out that a chain would not confine a spiritual being like Satan. The obvious intent of the passage is to indicate that Satan is bound and the chain, whether real or symbolic, portrays this situation.

The crux of the problem is that Satan is said to be bound for a thousand years. This introduces the whole question of the Millennium and its relation to the second coming of Christ as illustrated in the amillennial view, which denies a literal Millennium after the second coming; the postmillennial view, which places the second coming at the end of the Millennium; and the premillennial view, which places the second coming before the

4. Morris, *Revelation*, p. 235.

Millennium. Amillenarians in particular are immediate in their denial that the thousand years should be taken literally.

Typical of their view are the remarks of Abraham Kuyper, "In every other writing the construction of the first ten verses of chapter 20 would require a literal interpretation, but as in Revelation the idea 'thousand' is *never* taken literally, and also here merely expresses the exceeding fulness of the divine action, the precise, literal and historical understanding can not be imputed to God, and the exegete is duty bound to interpret what as Divine language comes to us according to the claim of the exegesis that is adaptable to it."[5]

What Kuyper overlooks is the fact that the word thousand is not used in the book of Revelation for a thousand-year period except in this chapter, and the dogmatic statement that numbers are never literal in the book of Revelation is itself subject to question. Dogmatism is used where facts are not supportive. Even Kuyper admits that normally a thousand years would be literally a thousand years in any other passage. I have found in my study of all numbers in the book of Revelation that all the numbers are literal.[6] Some postmillenarians also take the number literally as referring to the last thousand years of the interadvent period.

Before discussing this further it should be noted that verse 3 not only pictures the devil as being bound with a chain but as being thrown into the abyss with the door of the abyss shut and sealed as well. If a symbolic presentation of the binding of Satan were intended to teach that Satan was rendered completely inactive, what more dramatic picture could be provided than is here portrayed?

The denial that the thousand years is literal is sometimes supported by reference to Psalm 50:10 where cattle are represented to be on a thousand hills and 2 Peter 3:8 where one day and a thousand years are equated. However, it first must be demonstrated that there is a connection between these passages and Revelation 20. Further, the reference in 2 Peter 3 depends on the literal meaning of a thousand years, for the statement is that a thousand years with men is as one day with God, indicating God's eternal point of view. At the same time it presents the microscopic view that the complex interwoven activities of one day of the entire earth is as complicated as a thousand years of human history. In both cases the thousand years are literal, not symbolic.

5. Abraham Kuyper, *The Revelation of St. John* (Grand Rapids: Eerdmans, 1935), p. 277.
6. John F. Walvoord, *The Revelation of Jesus Christ* (Chicago: Moody, 1960), pp. 28-30.

In the record of the revelation given to John concerning the binding of Satan, distinction should be observed between what John saw and what was revealed to him by direct revelation. According to the record, John saw the angel with the key and the great chain seize Satan, bind him, cast him into the abyss, and lock and seal the entrance to the abyss. What John could not see was the purpose and duration of this confinement. That had to be revealed. According to John the purpose was that Satan could not deceive the nations any more and the duration was to be one thousand years. Although the symbolic is obviously subject to interpretation, when God directs a prophet to record the meaning of what he saw, what is recorded is not symbolic but literal. Accordingly there is no just ground to deny the purpose of God in binding Satan, that is, that he could not deceive the nations anymore for the duration of his confinement. The duration was not part of the symbolic revelation but a direct communication from God to John. Strange to say, commentators rarely note this very important distinction.

The concept often advanced that Satan was bound at the first coming of Christ does not find support in the Scriptures themselves. That Satan is as active in the present age as he was before the first coming of Christ is indicated in Luke 22:3; Acts 5:3; 2 Corinthians 4:3-4; 11:14; Ephesians 2:2; 1 Thessalonians 2:18; 2 Timothy 2:26; and 1 Peter 5:8.

The final reference in 1 Peter 5:8 is especially dramatic. Christians are exhorted, "Be of sober spirit, be on the alert. Your adversary, the devil, prowls about like a roaring lion, seeking someone to devour." The New Testament does not teach that Satan is now bound and rendered inactive and not deceiving the nations. The spread of every false religion in the world and the obvious commitment of many nations to godless philosophies should be sufficient proof in the twentieth century that Satan is alive and well and very active. History does not support the concept of Satan's present inactivity as described in Revelation 20.

Some weight to the concept that the binding of Satan is a result of the second coming, not the first coming of Christ, is found in the very fact that an angel can bind Satan. Prior to the second coming the Scriptures recognize the tremendous power of Satan. When Michael the archangel contended with Satan about the body of Moses, all he could do was ask the Lord to rebuke him (Jude 9). The preceding events in Revelation 4-18 clearly picture a dominance of Satan in the world, plunging it into unprecedented blasphemy and rebellion against God.

Donald Grey Barnhouse noted the change in Satan's authority: "But now, where once the angel Michael trod softly, a simple angel comes forth in the power of the God of the universe and lays hold of the rebel to bind him. . . . A few days before this moment, Satan may have thought that all power was in his grasp and that he was about to have complete victory. All the hosts of the fallen angels, the hosts of demons, the Antichrist, and the False Prophet, together with all the world of unregenerate men, were under his complete domination. . . . Yet a few short months and he has lost all."[7]

One should also take note of the change that took place in Revelation 12 where Satan is cast out of heaven (Rev. 12:7-9) As this event is placed in the midst of end-time events and is followed by the Great Tribulation, the attempt of amillenarians to remove this casting down of Satan to the first coming of Christ indicates how dogmatic and unsupportable is their contention that Satan is now bound.

The whole concept that Satan's loosing at the end of the thousand years is still future further confirms that the thousand years is still ahead. As George Ladd expresses it, "This idea of the deception of the nations reappears after Satan is loosed (20:8); he gathers the nations again in a further revolt against the Messiah, like the revolt that already occurred under Antichrist (13:14; 16:14). This suggests that this binding is different from the binding of Satan accomplished by our Lord in His earthly ministry; the latter had special reference to demon exorcism by which individuals were delivered from satanic bondage (Matt. 12:28-29)."[8]

Ladd, however, spoils his argument by saying that this does not mean that Satan ceases all his activity. It is far more consistent with the passage and with the facts of prophecy that Satan is completely inactive during the Millennium.

Ladd also unnecessarily considers it a problem that the nations are mentioned here. It is obvious that Satan deceived all nations in the period preceding the second coming. When Satan is loosed at the end of the Millennium only a portion of the nations follow him. These come from those who have been born in the millennial kingdom but have superficially followed Christ. Their true colors are shown when Satan reappears.

As Ladd points out, however, the loosing of Satan after the thousand years is most difficult to understand if the binding of Satan occurred at the first coming of Christ. Ladd states, "These words are difficult to under-

7. Donald Grey Barnhouse, *Revelation* (Grand Rapids: Zondervan, 1971), pp. 376-77.
8. George E. Ladd, *A Commentary on the Revelation of John* (Grand Rapids: Eerdmans, 1972), p. 262.

stand if they are applied to our Lord's binding of Satan in His earthly ministry. The victory He won over Satan was won once and for all. Satan was never loosed from bondage to Christ, won by His death and resurrection."[9]

If one comes to this passage without predetermination of eschatological views, it teaches quite obviously that subsequent to the second coming of Christ Satan is rendered inoperative for a thousand years but that he will be loosed again for a short period at the end of the thousand years. The fulfillment of this passage in the present age is totally unjustified. The passage itself points to the prospect of future fulfillment.

THE RESURRECTION OF THE MARTYRS (Rev. 20:4-6)

If the earlier verses of Revelation 20 have suffered from commentators, the verses here considered have likewise been twisted to mean almost precisely what they do not teach. Again the passage makes sense if taken in its plain ordinary meaning. When used to justify some preconceived idea, the passage often contradicts what has formerly been held. The passage begins with a familiar quote, "I saw," indicating a vision subsequent to the previous one. There is chronological sequence to the revelation, but there is also chronological sequence to the events described. In chapter 19 the armies are destroyed and the beast and false prophet cast into the lake of fire. In chapter 20 Satan the rebel is bound and rendered inactive. Now the narrative naturally turns to how the saints of God are related to this. John first has a vision of a scene of judgment. "And I saw thrones, and they sat upon them, and judgment was given to them" (Rev. 20:4). The passage to some extent is enigmatic because we are not told who the judges are or the location and situation of the thrones. Inasmuch as all the preceding revelations from chapter 19 on have dealt with the earth and divine dealing with it, it would seem that this judgment, whether on earth or in heaven, would also relate to the earthly scene.

The concept of many judges is not uncommon in Scripture. Though the question of who the occupants of the thrones are is not answered in the text, the apostles were promised in Matthew 19:28 that they would sit on twelve thrones judging the twelve tribes of Israel. According to 1 Corinthians 6:2-3 saints also are said to judge the world as well as angels. Some believe these saints are represented by the twenty-four elders seated on thrones in Revelation 4-5. Though some have placed the martyrs on the thrones mentioned later in the verse, there is no real evidence that this is

9. Ibid., p. 263.

the case. It is rather that what John is beholding is in a judgmental situation where the martyrs are being judged and rewarded.

Revelation 20:4 continues, "And I saw the souls of those who had been beheaded because of the testimony of Jesus and because of the word of God, and those who had not worshiped the beast or his image, and had not received the mark upon their forehead and upon their hand; and they came to life and reigned with Christ for a thousand years."

One of the amazing facts about the common exegesis of this verse is that commentators frequently make no effort to determine the meaning of the principal terms. Most common is the concept of trying to make this refer to all martyrs or to all saints. Even more divergent from the meaning of the text is the normal amillennial interpretation that this refers to the new birth.

As Ladd[10] and Mounce[11] both indicate, the central problem is what is meant by the Greek verb *ezēsan,* translated "came to life." The argument that other verbs are used for resurrection is faulty because there is no single word used for bodily resurrection. The same verb is used in Revelation 2:8 of Christ and in Revelation 13:14 of the beast. In Matthew 9:18 it is used of the daughter who was restored to life. In Revelation 20:6 the resurrection of the martyrs is contrasted to those who are not resurrected, and the contrast becomes meaningless unless both refer to bodily resurrection.

In spite of these evidences, however, the common amillennial point of view is that this refers to the new birth of the believer. Luther Poellot states, for instance, "We take the words 'they lived' (or 'came to life'), as referring to the beginning of spiritual life at the moment when the elect come to faith here on earth (John 5:24-25; Eph. 2:5, 6). That is the real beginning of life in the fullest sense. . . . the expression 'the rest of the dead' (Rev. 20:5), refers to those who remain dead in trespasses and sins, as opposed to those who were thus dead, but were made alive (Eph. 2:1, 5, 6; Col. 2:13)."[12]

The interpretation that this refers to the new birth pays no attention whatever to the exact statement of the text. People who receive the new birth are not those who have been beheaded. Those described in the passage are said to reign with Christ a thousand years, a reference that is without meaning if it refers to spiritual new birth. Also, does the resurrection at the end of the Millennium refer also to new birth? Amillenarians are

10. Ibid., p. 265.
11. Mounce, p. 356.
12. Luther Poellot, *Revelation* (St. Louis: Concordia, 1962), p. 263.

strangely silent on that point. What does the text actually state?

Those who are pictured in this passage refer to a particular generation who are described as not worshiping the beast or his image. This refers back to the situation in Revelation 13:15-17 where those in the last generation before the second coming of Christ are faced with the alternative of either worshiping the beast, the world ruler whom Christ casts alive into the lake of fire at His second coming, or being killed. The reference, therefore, is not to all the saints, nor even to all martyrs, but to those who specifically follow this description. Why is this special resurrection described here?

Although it is too much to impose on this passage the burden of proving the rapture of the church as occurring before or after the end-time events of the Tribulation, those who are pretribulationists, that is, those who believe that the saints are raised before the end-time tribulation, find in it supporting evidence for the special resurrection of those who at the time of the rapture were not saved but came to Christ later. They were martyred in the final conflict with the beast. A specific picture of that is given in Revelation 7:9-17 where a large multitude is seen in heaven as having come out of the Great Tribulation, and the implication is that they are martyred. This is in contrast to the 144,000 in Revelation 7:1-8 who are sealed and preserved through the tribulation without dying. The special resurrection of these martyred dead is to make possible their inclusion in the millennial kingdom that follows and their exaltation to a place of sharing the rule of Christ.

In contrast to those who are here resurrected, those who are unsaved are not resurrected at this time, but their resurrection follows a thousand years later. This is stated in Revelation 20:5-6, "The rest of the dead did not come to life until the thousand years were completed. This is the first resurrection. Blessed and holy is the one who has a part in the first resurrection; over these the second death has no power, but they will be priests of God and of Christ and will reign with Him for a thousand years." The sharp contrast in the passage is between those who are raised at the beginning of the thousand years and those who are raised at the end. Both are physical resurrections, but those who are raised at the beginning of the Millennium, designated as the "first resurrection," are contrasted to those who "come to life" at the end of the Millennium, who face judgment according to Revelation 20:11-15.

The question has sometimes been raised as to whether the expression "first resurrection" means that there have been no previous resurrections. Obviously there were previous resurrections, the first being that of Jesus

Christ when He was raised from the dead following His crucifixion. A token resurrection is also mentioned in Matthew 27:51-53 where some were raised from the dead on the occasion of the resurrection of Christ and appeared on the streets of Jerusalem. This token resurrection signified that there would be many others who later would be resurrected on the basis of the fact that Christ Himself was raised from the dead.

Pretribulationists, of course, also hold that the entire church is raised from the dead or translated at the time of the rapture, an event that predates the second coming by more than seven years. Even though posttribulationists are accustomed to challenge this on the basis of the term "first," it should be obvious that the implication of the passage is not that there were no preceding resurrections. It is rather that there are two resurrections in chapter 20. The resurrection of the martyred dead is first, and the resurrection of those who are cast into the lake of fire is second. It is not first in the sense of something that had never occurred before but first in the sense of being before the later resurrection.

Those raised at this time are declared to have a special blessing and to share in the reign of Christ on earth for a thousand years as priests of God. A similar promise is given to the twenty-four elders in Revelation 5:10.

If the passage is allowed to speak for itself, it reveals that there will be judgment in connection with the second coming of Christ and reward of the saints. Those who were martyred in that last generation will be the subjects of special resurrection and blessing. They will share with other saints who have participated in the first resurrection. The resurrection is contrasted to the resurrection of the wicked at the end of the thousand years. During the thousand years they will enjoy the privilege of reigning with Christ as priests of God.

Although the revelation given through John in Revelation 20:1-6 obviously has symbolic elements, nevertheless it is intended to teach factual information. Satan will be rendered inactive for a thousand years, after which he will be let loose for a short period, later expanded in Revelation 20:7. The martyred saints who were the object of Satan's wrath in the Great Tribulation are given a special resurrection and share with other saints in the millennial reign of Christ. The wicked dead, on the other hand, are said not to be raised from the dead until after the thousand years. All attempts to explain this passage in harmony with the amillennial or postmillennial view requires a denial of the literal teaching of the passage and the arbitrary spiritualization of the facts that are presented here. As such, the passage remains a bulwark of the premillennial interpretation of Scripture in keeping with the general tenor of the book of Revelation and the many passages of the Old Testament that speak of Christ's kingdom on earth.

Moody Press, a ministry of the Moody Bible Institute, is designed for education, evangelization, and edification. If we may assist you in knowing more about Christ and the Christian life, please write us without obligation: Moody Press, c/o MLM, Chicago, Illinois 60610.